Stoke Bishop

Bristol's leafy suburb

Keith Sheather

Published in 2024 by Stoke Bishop Local History Group

© Keith Sheather 2024

Keith Sheather asserts his right under the Copyright, Designs and Patents Act 1988 to be identified as the author of this work.

ISBN 978-1-3999-9468-2

Book design by Andrew Buchanan (buchanan-communications.co.uk)
Printed by Doveton Press, Bristol (dovetonpress.co.uk)

Further copies may be obtained from Stoke Bishop Local History Group
(sblocalhistory@gmail.com | tinyurl.com/stokevillagehistory)

Front cover picture:
Painting by William Tippett of a Victorian house in Hollymead Lane 1900

Back cover pictures (clockwise from top left):
Watercolour of Roman quay at Sea Mills (Abona) by Christine Molan
Ena Clarke and friend on Druid Hill looking towards Sunnyside c 1925
Stoke Bishop Village from Druid Hill c 1933

Contents

Introduction

In 1998, Penny Jetzer and members of what was then the Stoke Bishop and Sneyd Park Local History Group published A Pictorial History of Stoke Bishop and Sneyd Park. It was the first book to attempt a comprehensive history of the area and was the result of years of research by Penny and the gathering of a unique collection of photographs and documents that now form the basis of today's Stoke Bishop Local History Group's archives. Sadly Penny has since died but her pioneering work has been carried on by her successors. Much new material has been discovered and the Group felt the time was right to commission a new history. I have been honoured with the task of writing this.

Hitherto histories of the area have been largely picture books, often in the form

An 18th century view from Clifton Down looking across Durdham Down towards Stoke Bishop. Cook's Folly and Old Sneed Park can be seen in the distance

of walks around north west Bristol. In this work I have attempted a chronological narrative that tells the story of Stoke Bishop from prehistory to pandemic, while at the same weaving Stoke Bishop into the national story. We are blessed with an identifiable geographical area, defined on three sides by natural features, most spectacularly by the Avon Gorge, by the wild sweep of the Downs and by the River Trym. Only in the east does the land merge with that of Westbury-on-Trym. It is this geographical phenomenon that has determined Stoke Bishop's history.

And what a history it has been. Stone Age peoples have left their mark, the Romans tramped across the ground, the Anglo-Saxons settled and established the village of Stoce, the Normans registered the place in the Domesday Book and the Bishops of Worcester carved out a deer park for themselves which they called Snaed (land outside). And all this before the Tudor servant of Thomas Cromwell, Sir Ralph Sadleir, was given the lands of Stoke Bishop for his services to the Crown and so began the process of creating large estates that became the envy of travellers far and wide. The estates' owners were wealthy Bristol merchants who sought to escape from the city, with its mercantile overtones of slavery and privateering, and pursue the life of a country squire. By the nineteenth century more came and built grandiloquent mansions with the same desire to grab a slice of the countryside.

Cows graze on the slopes above what is now Glen Drive

It, of course, became a vicious circle. The more people wanted a part of this utopian landscape, the more its existence was threatened. Yet when the soldiers returned after the end of the First World War, Stoke Bishop was still largely rural, with farms being the dominant feature. But the push by Bristol to expand its boundaries sounded the death knell for the old world. Throughout the nineteen thirties farms were sold for housing and Stoke Bishop moved from being a rural retreat to becoming a suburb of Bristol.

Despite further encroachments from Bristol after the Second World War and the wholesale demolition of the fine

View today over Stoke Bishop looking towards Abbots Leigh

Victorian villas and the usurping of their grounds for large scale flat building, the fight back to preserve something of what made Stoke Bishop *sublime* in the first place became the overriding theme of the last few decades. Among the memories that have that have been shared with us, as a result of our appeal, many recall the quiet sense of leafiness that they have experienced.

Perhaps nothing sums this up more than the discovery of John and Sue Holliman of Druid Hill. Doing research into their family history they found that John had family forebears in Abbots Leigh churchyard. *'From our attic window we can see right across the Avon and we see the trees and we see the fields and we can see the church tower of Abbots Leigh church. By the entrance porch there is a gravestone that says John and Susanna Holliman.'* Thanks to this uninterrupted view over the countryside they feel connected to their past family in a tangible way.

Throughout this book I shall be tracing the theme of country versus town as it has played out over the decades, a theme that still resonates today.

Chapter One

From the Stone Age to the Romans

On Friday 13 July 1928, the Western Daily Press reported the visit to a garden in Stoke Bishop of a group of residents from the Merchant Venturers' and St Nicholas' Almshouses in Bristol.

They were guests of Alderman and Mrs Featherstone Witty, whose house lay at the top of Druid Hill. The day was hot and all that most of the guests wanted to do was seek a *'shady nook'* to gossip or sip *'cooling drinks'*. But tea must have refreshed the assembly as *'one or two gathered their fellows around a certain stone and with much assurance explained that it was the altar stone of the ancient Druids.'* This was, of course, romantic nonsense which had long been in currency, a notion perpetuated by naming the roads in the area – Druid Stoke Avenue, Druid Road and Druid Hill – after the ancient sect. But if the Druids ever came to Stoke Bishop, it was long after the stones had been erected.

Guests at the annual tea party hosted by Alderman and Mrs Featherstone Witty gather around the Cromlech

However, the presence of these stones is evidence of human footfall in Stoke Bishop from earliest times. At the end of the last ice age, 20,000 years ago, the land was a sparsely vegetated tundra and the Gorge much shallower than it is today. It was still attached to Europe and had become the home of migrating animals, including the woolly mammoth, rhinoceros, reindeer, wolf and bear, a fact confirmed in the 19th century when the bones of these animals were uncovered in a rock fissure on Durdham Down. As the earth warmed up, hunters, armed with bows and flint axes, followed the game. At first they were only transient, but by the Neolithic (or Stone Age) period (3,500-1,700 BC) people had started to settle. Two significant events brought this about, the cultivation of cereals and the domestication of animals and once settled a community needed to develop ways of burying its dead. It is to this subject that we must look to understanding the Stoke Bishop stones.

The site was first identified by the Revd. John Skinner in 1811. He was the rector of Camerton in Somerset, who, when not delivering sermons, was an inveterate traveller, painstakingly noting everything he saw in his diaries. He was also, like many clergymen of his day, a keen archaeologist. He sketched the stones which he found lying in a field on the estate of what became Druid Stoke House. They were described in more detail a few years later by another clergyman, the Revd.

The field in which Skinner and Seyer would have seen the Cromlech. The stones are more upright than today

Samuel Seyer, whose Memoirs Historical and Topographical of Bristol, published in 1821, was an important history of the city. He precisely located the stones as lying *'about three miles from Bristol on the road to Shirehampton on the top of the hill, after you have passed the watering place, in a field close to the roadside on the left hand'*. He noted a very large slab resting on a slim upright with two other stones close by. *'For what purpose they were erected... is a difficulty in our history not yet resolved.'*

The first archaeological survey, conducted by Francis Were in 1913, was equally inconclusive. This was carried out under the auspices of the Bristol and Gloucestershire Archaeological Society and its task was made more difficult as the stones now lay in

2

a private garden. In 1899 the owner of Druid Stoke House had sold a two acre plot that included the megalith. In 1907 a house called The Cromlech was built close to it and excavating the site now meant digging up the garden.

It wasn't until 1983 that a more extensive survey was undertaken by George Smith for English Heritage. Four trenches were dug. They confirmed what had already been suggested by archaeologist Leslie Grinsell that the site was a Neolithic chambered long barrow. All traces of a mound had disappeared, probably flattened by later ploughing in the Roman period, but *'cobble-like rubble... mixed with loam'* was uncovered in sufficient quantity to suggest it followed the contours of the burial mound. This lay on an east-west trajectory with the stones that are now visible forming the entrance. A human toe bone was dug up and was carbon dated to between 2880 and 2450 BC, a date thought to relate to a later secondary burial.

Smith concluded that the Stoke Bishop monument, *'on the high point of a ridge on the edge of a valley'*, bore a close resemblance to other neolithic tombs in the Severn-Cotswold area and therefore, he wrote intriguingly, *'we should expect to find*

Cromlech

The Revd. John Skinner's view that he sketched in 1812 makes it very easy to see that the end of Druid Stoke Hill could have had a settlement on it. He describes it as a *'stronghold'* with *'the demolished cromlech'* a pin prick at the far end of the ridge

The stones today. In the foreground is the upright which would have supported the large roof stone (rear) to form the entrance to a long barrow

a neolithic enclosure in the vicinity of Druid Stoke.' No work has been done but a stone-age settlement could have existed at the end of Druid Stoke Avenue.

But what of the Druids? It was Seyer who first mentioned the association, describing the monument as a *'Druidical remnant'*. But the idea stuck and was continued through the Victorian period. It appeared on the 1878 Ordnance Survey map as *'Druidical Stones'*. Druids certainly came later, but of a more modern incarnation. When Druidism was revived in the 18th century, groups naturally gravitated to prehistoric megaliths to conduct their rituals. This included Stoke Bishop. The daughter of William Munro, who owned Druid Stoke House, remembered their presence:

> *'In my recollection, once a year a body of men, calling themselves Druids, with a priest dressed in wonderful garments, used to hold a service at the Druid's Stone... I'm almost sure that the Druids' ceremony took place in the spring before the grass was put up for mowing. I have a dim recollection that the Druids wished to have the ceremony later but were told that they could not be allowed to tread down the growing grass as they came in considerable numbers.'*

The Iron Age

A thousand years later, with the advent of what is known as the Iron Age (500 BC-43 AD), much had changed. The population had grown. Bronze and iron manufacturing had been developed, workshops set up and trade established. Individual communities formed larger groupings and England became a patchwork

4

The Roman road across the Downs in the low light of winter. The ditch beside it can be seen to the right

of loosely aligned tribal kingdoms.

The land around the Severn and Avon was inhabited by the Dubonni, a people who had migrated from the continent, inhabitants of northern Gaul (now France) originally called the Belgae. Their most visible impact is the string of hilltop encampments along the Avon, among them Kings Weston Down, Blaise Castle, Clifton Down, Burwalls and Abbot's Leigh. Recent excavations have also uncovered evidence of a village for summer grazing on the salt marshes close to the M48 and a burial site in the grounds of Henbury School, where 21 bodies were found, male, female and child, all in a crouched position, a sufficient number to suggest that a farming settlement was nearby. Britain may now have been cut off from the continent, but it was far from isolated. Rich in minerals such as lead and tin, it traded extensively with the mainland and it was an attractive target for the rapacious ambitions of an expanding Roman Empire.

The Roman Invasion

Two attempts to occupy Britain were made by Julius Caesar in 55 and 54 BC. Neither was successful. A hundred years later, in 43 AD, the Emperor Claudius launched a further invasion. The Romans landed in Kent and with the help of the southern tribes who had already established friendly relations with Rome, they achieved a foothold, which allowed them to attack the north and west. One of their top commanders, Vespasian (later to become emperor), was given the task of subjugating the west. He established a base at Exeter where the Durotriges (Dorset) and the Dumnonii (Devon and Cornwall) were resisting Roman rule. To the north around the Avon, the Dubonni were more friendly towards the invaders.

Portus Abonae (Sea Mills)

We now come to consider Stoke Bishop's second ancient monument, the Roman settlement of Portus Abonae in Sea Mills. Most of it is under the earth with post-war prefabs built on top. Spasmodic excavations have occurred over the years and from what has been found an imperfect picture can be drawn of what happened here. The first we know of Portus Abonae (or Abona as it is more often called) is from an entry in a road map of the time. The Antonine Itinerary was an atlas of Roman Roads throughout the Empire and included Britain. It has been attributed to the Emperor Antoninus although not necessarily produced by him. In route No XIV of the Antonine Itinerary, Abona is listed as a way station on the road from Caerleon to Bath:

Isca Silurum (Caerleon) – Venta Silurum	9 miles
Venta Silurum (Caerwent) – Abona	9 miles
Abona – Trajectus (Bitton)	9 miles
Trajectus – Aquae Sulis (Bath)	6 miles

We do not know exactly when the Romans came to Sea Mills, but because of the friendliness of the native Dubonni it was probably a few years after the invasion. In the first instance they might have built a small defensive fort at the confluence of the river Avon and the river Trym. It was an ideal strategic position with easy access to the sea and defended by the notorious Horseshoe Bend. Any marauding ship would take so long negotiating the bend it would be easily spotted. Those conducting excavations have expected to find evidence of a fort but so far nothing has come to light.

Abona, like the Avon, took its name from the Celtic word meaning river and it was a Celtic tribe that was to change its fortunes. Across the Severn the Silures were putting up stout resistance to Roman rule. The army needed to get its troops into South Wales as quickly as possible and Abona was the ideal embarkation point. It changed from being a small fort to becoming a vital staging post for ferrying troops and supplies across the Severn. The fight against the Silures was long and bitter and it is not difficult to imagine the thousands of men from the Second Augusta Legion, who had been charged with the assault on Wales, standing on the banks of the river waiting for the tide to refloat their ships, anxious to know what was ahead of them. Traces of a quayside have been uncovered near the Signal Station on the River Avon, along with two tiles and a brick stamped 'Leg II Aug'.

By 78 AD the Silures had been pacified and a fort built at Caerleon in South Wales to keep them in check. Abona lost its military function and became a commercial port for the surrounding countryside, a small but bustling centre with good river and road connections. The Via Julia ran from Bath to the port and part of it can still be seen on Durdham Down (on the

Fragments of Samian ware found at Abona

section of ground between Ladies Mile and Stoke Road). From the Downs the road passed the Old Halt and followed the line of Pitch and Pay Lane and Mariners Path. Quite how it reached Abona is uncertain as no connection has been excavated.

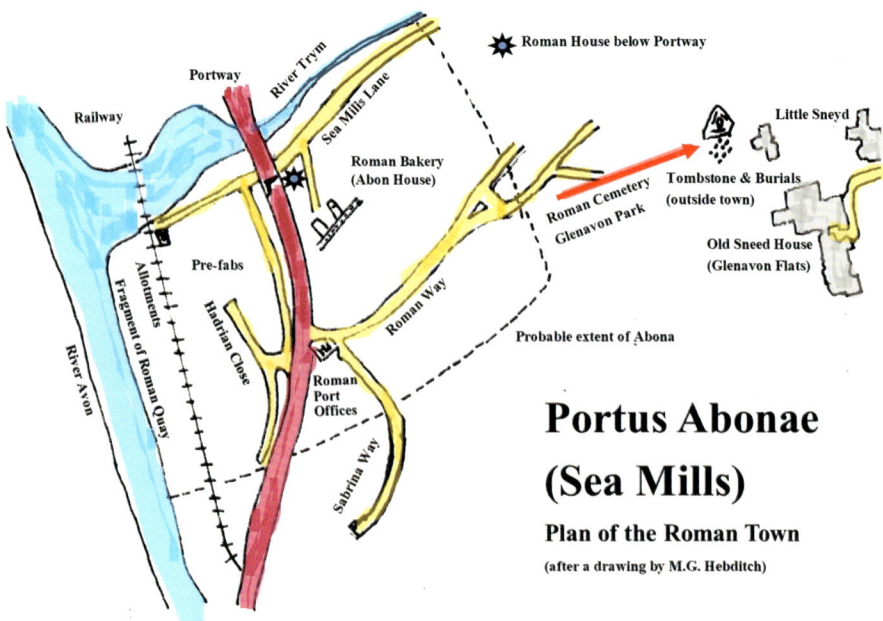

Portus Abonae (Sea Mills)

Plan of the Roman Town

(after a drawing by M.G. Hebditch)

Christine Molan's reconstruction shows the quayside at Abona (Sea Mills) as being on the River Avon. In 2011 the Sea Mills Archaeological Research Team found traces of this quay and a 1st century Roman cobbled surface close to the Old Signal Station (below), on which flat-bottomed barges could rest for unloading at low tide.

Christine Molan's reconstruction of the bakery based on the Abon House discovery

Town Life

When the soldiers left, a small population of shopkeepers, traders and quayside workers remained. Women who arrived as camp followers might also have stayed. The port exported local produce and imported luxury goods such as wine, olive oil and fine earthenware. Everywhere fragments have been unearthed of the highly prized dishes made in Gaul known as Samian ware. One collection was discovered in the Sea Mills allotment gardens by George Widgery in the late 1950s. The surviving shards are in great evidence from the early years of occupation but grow fewer in the later years, a reflection perhaps of subsequent decline.

However the town never really grew like Gloucester or Cirencester. Its extent is roughly the area occupied by the allotments and prefabs. In the 1960s a major excavation took place at Abon House (the flats between Sea Mills Lane and Roman Way) and showed the town had extended beyond the Portway. One building revealed an oven and opened out onto a metalled road (which might have gone to Gloucester) suggesting that it was a bakery.

In the first instance buildings were wooden, but excavations have shown that there was a serious fire around 98 AD and subsequent rebuilding was a mix of stone and wood or stone and tiles. As this was a working town, there has been little evidence of any grand Roman houses with hypocausts and mosaic floors, although tesserae have been found on two occasions giving hope that a mosaic floor may one day surface.

The Discoveries

Until recently digs at Abona have been opportunist, intermittent and the preserve of the enthusiast. The port was first identified by the Revd. Samuel Seyer in 1821. Using The Antonine Itinerary, he noted *'we have sure evidence that there was on this river several miles below Bath, a Roman or romanised town, called Abona'*.

Not much happened until 1923 when the Portway was being constructed. E.K. Tratman, a professor of dentistry but with a lifelong interest in caving and prehistoric archaeology, was told of a skull found by the workmen. He was able to do some digging and uncovered the walls of a simple house, the first real evidence of Roman occupation. The site now lies beneath the Portway, but a few years later in 1934 when Roman Way was being laid out, Arthur Selly, an amateur archaeologist and collector of antiquities, undertook to excavate close to where Tratman had worked. He revealed a multi roomed building that is now thought to be port offices and is most likely connected to Tratman's discovery. Selly persuaded the City Engineers to reroute the end of Roman Way to keep the site on view.

Tratman's wall. Note the rail track in the background built to move materials during the construction of the Portway

George Boon working at Long Cross villa in 1948

But the most intriguing story of amateur endeavour came at the end of the Second World War. Prefabs were being built in Hadrian Close and a young schoolboy, George Boon, persuaded the City Museum to let him dig on the site before the concrete floors of the prefabs were laid. He was helped in his task by school friends and German prisoners of war who had been seconded to prepare the foundations of the prefabs. The Director of the Museum gave him money and cigarettes so that he could persuade the POWs to hand over any artifacts they found. Boon discovered a beautiful Samian ware vase and a male body, which must have been unnerving for a boy still at school. But he went on to discover greater things. Using the same pestering approach he persuaded the authorities to let him excavate while they were surveying Long Cross in Lawrence Weston and he uncovered an impressive Roman villa with a fine mosaic.

The Abon House excavations between 1965 and 1968 were undertaken by the City Museum and the Ministry of Works. They produced a wealth of artifacts including an altar and an exquisite figurine of Jupiter, both dated from when Abona was an established Roman settlement.

Even if official excavations have been infrequent, people living in the locality are continually unearthing coins, jewellery and pieces of pottery. A young girl in Roman Way found a copper alloy brooch while helping her father dig their fish pond. It was used for fastening clothes and was likely to have been imported, an indication that while not a place of fashion, the citizens of Abona could still dress fashionably.

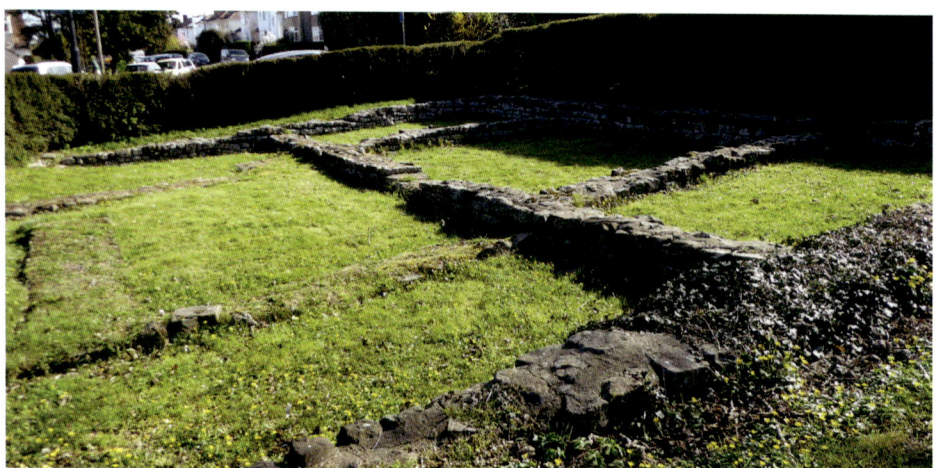

The port offices in Roman Way

Roman altar also on display at
M Shed

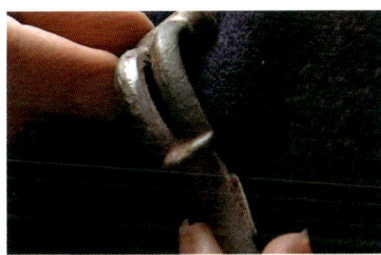

The surviving portion of a Roman tombstone
on display at M Shed. The smaller symbols,
including a star (top) and cockerel (right),
suggest it might have a Christian connection

A fine Roman brooch
unearthed in Roman Way

But perhaps the most spectacular find has been the discovery of a Roman
tombstone in 1873 in an orchard at Little Sneyd in Sneed Park. A workman
digging below the turf inadvertently broke the stone before he realised what it was.
But enough of it was saved to make it a star exhibit in Bristol Museum's M Shed.
A woman's face, adorned with earrings, surmounts an inscription 'Spes C Senti'
(The Hope of Gaius Sentius). It was erected by Gaius Sentius in memory of his
wife or daughter.

When the site for what is now Glenavon Park was being developed in 1972,
excavations were carried out in the vicinity of the 1873 find to determine whether
it was the location of a Roman cemetery. Nine burials were found and, as it was
Roman law that bodies were buried outside the precincts of a town, this confirmed
that the site was a cemetery and marked the extent of Abona.

Over the years a lot has been discovered about Abona's history, but its full story will never be known until more is excavated. One day this may come about as the land where prefabs once stood has now been designated a scheduled monument.

Decline

Most of the quality finds discovered in the excavations have come from the second and third centuries AD suggesting that, once Caerleon and Caerwent in South Wales had been established around 80 AD, Abona had become something of a backwater. Trading doubtlessly continued and was given a boost when villa-farms, like Lawrence Weston, started to need shipping facilities for their produce. But the town never recovered from the loss of army patronage and by the fourth century it started to go into decline. The biggest blow came around 410 AD when the Roman Empire found itself reeling from powerful barbarian attacks on its frontiers. The legions were recalled to go to the aid of the besieged Emperor Honorius and Britain was left to fend for itself. The effect on small settlements like Abona was catastrophic, although the town, unlike a number of villas in the Bristol area, was never burned.

Chapter Two

From the Anglo-Saxons to the Middle Ages

What happened to the people of Portus Abonae, in a period when there was little or no written material to draw on, is uncertain.

If there was a Roman garrison still stationed there, by 410 AD it would certainly have been recalled leaving the town defenceless and at the mercy of the Scotti from Ireland who raided in boats along the Severn estuary in search of slaves. Roman law had forbidden the carrying of weapons and after 400 years of peace the populace had no experience of warfare. With the threat of attack from the sea, their wisest course of action was to flee inland or emigrate to the continent of Europe. The odd coin of a later date than 410 has been found, so occupation of sorts may have carried on for a few years, but when the Saxons arrived over a hundred years later they showed no inclination to inhabit the crumbling ruins on the banks of the Trym.

The Saxons

A feature of the Abona excavations is the lack of any presence found of the indigenous Britons (or Romano-British as they became known). It is most likely they continued to live in their own settlements outside the town and came into the town to work. There is a suggestion that after the recall of the army they reoccupied the hill forts in the area. There is certainly evidence of post Roman settlement inland. In 2005 a cemetery was uncovered at Hewlett Packard in north Bristol which was in use well into the sixth century.

But the indigenous Britons were soon to face a new threat, greater than attacks from marauding pirates. In the last years of Roman occupation, Britain underwent a series of probing assaults from the continent. They came from peoples known collectively as Saxons, who occupied the lands of northern Europe and southern Scandinavia. They were composed of many tribes from Schleswig-Holstein and Lower Saxony (Germany), Frisia (Netherlands) and the Jutland peninsula (Denmark) and why they came is one of history's great mysteries. Until recently,

14

Reconstruction of life in an Anglo-Saxon Village

based on the few written sources of the period (The Anglo-Saxon Chronicle and Bede's Ecclesiastical History of the English People), the story has been one of invasion and conquest, with the Romano-British population being replaced by German speaking invaders. This is no longer the perceived view. Population growth, crop failure and the steady encroachment of sea in the lowlands was putting pressure on the Germanic peoples of Europe and the current view is that they migrated to Britain in search of new land to scttle. A recent study of the gene pool of hundreds of burials across the east of the country has highlighted a mass migration, settlement and, to a varying extent, integration with the local population.

In the west the situation was different. The Romano-British were prepared to resist the new migrants. They rallied under a single leader, Vortigern (possibly the legendary King Arthur), and stopped the advance at a place called Mount Badon, described by Gildas, a monk and first historian of the age, as *'the siege of Bath-hill* (and) *the slaughter of our cruel foes... and also the time of my own nativity'* (c 500 AD). The victory gave the British 50 years respite, but the Saxons returned and by the end of the sixth century they had settled across the region. To what extent they integrated with the locals we do not know, but on the evidence of what was happening in the rest of the country it is possible that some integration went on. And it is equally possible that they established or took over a settlement where today's village is located.

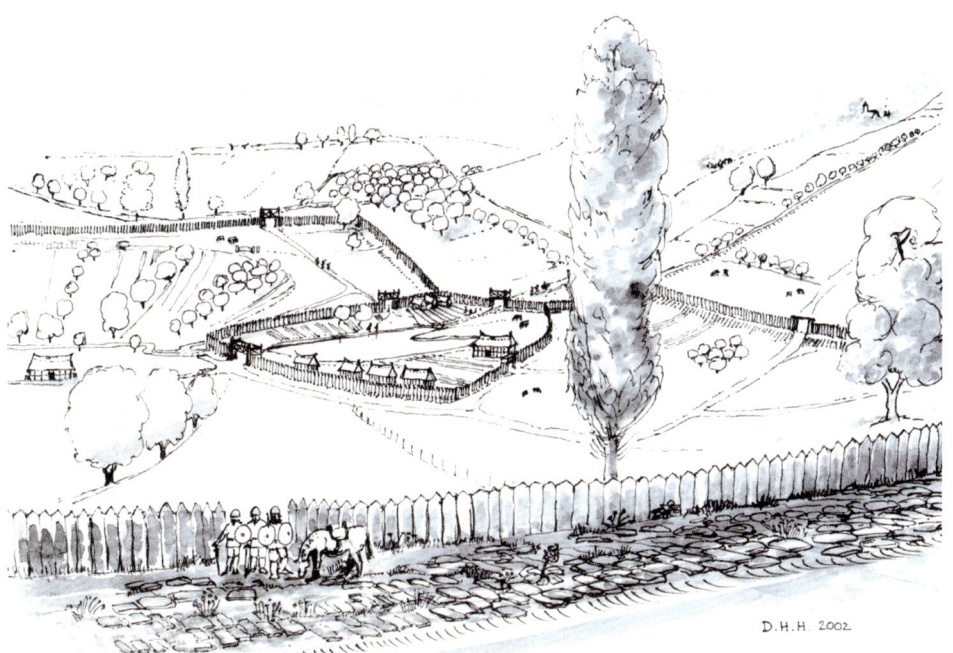

The Saxon Village as imagined by David Higgins. Hollybush Lane is in the foreground overlooking the village

Hollybush Lane following the line of a defensive Anglo-Saxon ditch

Saxon Village

David Higgins, a local historian, who researched the period extensively, has drawn a reconstruction of what that Saxon village might have looked like in the ninth century. It shows the advantages of the site, in a deep valley, surrounded by hills. At its heart was the great hall, where public gatherings would take place and around it, an inner stockade and a more extensive defensive outer stockade. The line of the latter, he suggests, is still visible in the sunken path and earthwork that runs between Ormerod Road and Kewstoke Road down Hollybush Lane. The Anglo-Saxons routinely located their settlements

(Clockwise from above) In an 1860s map an extensive fish pond is shown stretching back from the village between the Tunstall Close flats and Hollybush Lane; the water was substantial in the 1930s; until recently a small pond was visible at the back of the old School House. The ground is still soggy

near ancient burial sites and the long barrow at the top of the hill would have been an added attraction in choosing the site. The village also had a good source of water with streams and a spring feeding in to the lower part of the village where even today much of the ground is soggy. Seyer mentioned a watering place at the bottom of the hill.

Mercia and the See of Worcester

Small settlements did not remain so for long. By force of arms or by coercion and bullying, villages with a strong leader forced themselves on their neighbours and, as happened among the Britons, larger groupings emerged. By the middle of the eighth century seven kingdoms had been established, each with its own ruler or king. In the south the largest of these was Mercia, stretching from the Romano-British (Welsh) border to London and in 757 AD a man called Offa seized the throne and made Mercia the most powerful kingdom in Anglo-Saxon England. He is known locally for the dyke that bears his name, a massive earthwork which hugs the border of Wales from sea to sea. Historians are not sure why it was built. Most likely it acted as a deterrent to free movement across the border, but for Offa it was also a statement of Mercia's might and prestige.

Another way in which he could show his authority and demonstrate his largess was by issuing charters. These were legal documents which recorded the grant of land made by the king to one or more of his subjects. They made the title to the land legally binding.

Often a charter was issued to provide land for a church or monastery. By the seventh century, all of England had been converted to Christianity and the country divided into dioceses headed by bishops.

Offa's Dyke is still walkable today

These prelates wielded considerable influence, none more so than the Bishops of Worcester, whose diocese fell within the kingdom of Mercia. It is now that Stoke Bishop enters the written records for the first time.

The Stoke Bishop Charters

A series of early charters, collectively known as The Stoke Bishop Charters, highlighted a serious land dispute between the diocese of Worcester and Berkeley in Gloucestershire. Between 793 and 796 AD, Offa took substantial lands from the area of what was to become Westbury-on-Trym and gave it to the church of Worcester and his thegn, Ethelmund (a nobleman). The latter's son, Ethelric, willed his portion to his mother, Ceolburga, abbess of Berkeley, with the proviso that it reverted to the church of Worcester on her death. Berkeley naturally was keen to retain the land given it and, when Ceolburga died, contested the instruction to return it to Worcester. A synod held at Clovesho (somewhere in Mercia), was called to adjudicate between Worcester and Berkeley. It found against Berkeley, with the exception of 12 hides of land (a hide being the amount of land that supported one household). These stayed with Berkeley and included Stoke Bishop.

However, the decision was reversed a few years later in a charter of 883 AD. In it Ethelred, a Mercian earl, with the consent of his son-in-law, King Alfred of Wessex, instructed Berkeley Abbey to give up the self-same hides to Cynulf, son of Ceolute (possibly the grandson of Ceolburga) and the whole to revert to the bishopric of Worcester after *'three lives'*. The charter described the land as being in a place called *'stoce'* (its literal meaning being a house or dwelling place).

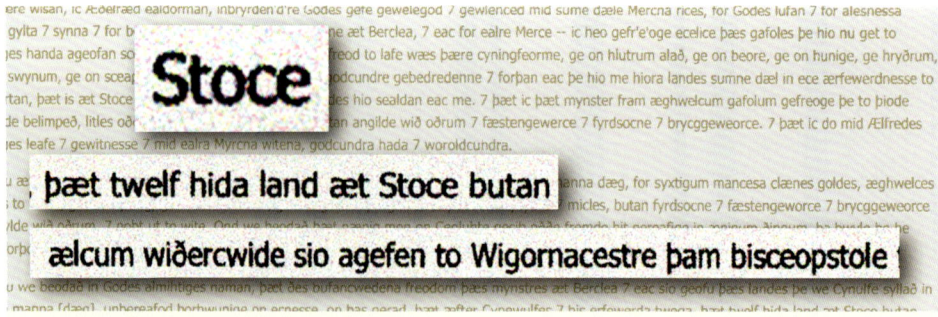

A line from the 883 AD Charter mentioning Stoce (Stoke Bishop) by name:
'þæt twelf hide land æt Stoce butan ælcum wiðercwide sio agefen to Wigornacestre pam bisceopstole' ('then twelve hides of land in Stoke with reversion to the episcopal see of Worcester')

The reversion to Worcester had clearly happened by 969 AD as in that year a later Saxon king, Edgar, granted to his minister, Ethelward, some land in *'Stoce'*, confirmed by a further charter of 984 AD that referred to the area as *'Bisceopes Stoc'*, showing indisputably that it belonged to the Bishop of Worcester.

The 883 AD Charter

For the first time Stoke Bishop had been identified by name. Furthermore, David Higgins believes that the boundaries outlined in the charter coincided with much of today's parish. He describes them thus:

Ærest on thæs byrnan be westan Stoce...

> First to the corner of the fence (stockade?) on the west side of Stoke *(centre of the village)*
> From there to the old earthwork, then northwards to the old boundary *(Hollybush Lane)*
> From the old boundary into the north part of the open field *(Stoke Lodge playing fields)*
> From the north part of the open brook to the sunken brook *(junction of Coombe Bridge Avenue and Bell Barn Road)*
> From the sunken brook to the River Sweoperl *(River Trym)*
> From the River Sweoperl to the beginning of Dinning's Grove *(Sea Mills Wood)*
> From the beginning of Dinning's grove to the rampart and the military

watch-tower in the meadow *(ruins of Abona)*

From the meadow to where the old rivulet conjoins the old military road *(Mariners Path)*

From the old military road to where the stockade comes out by Stoke Hill

Westward back to the corner of the stockade *(Church Road/Stoke Park Road)*

.... westan efton thæs beges byrnan

Often attached to these charters was a *feorm*, a rent in kind levied on the produce of the land that was payable to the king. The details are a snapshot of what was being produced in these small communities. The 793 charter of Offa granting 60

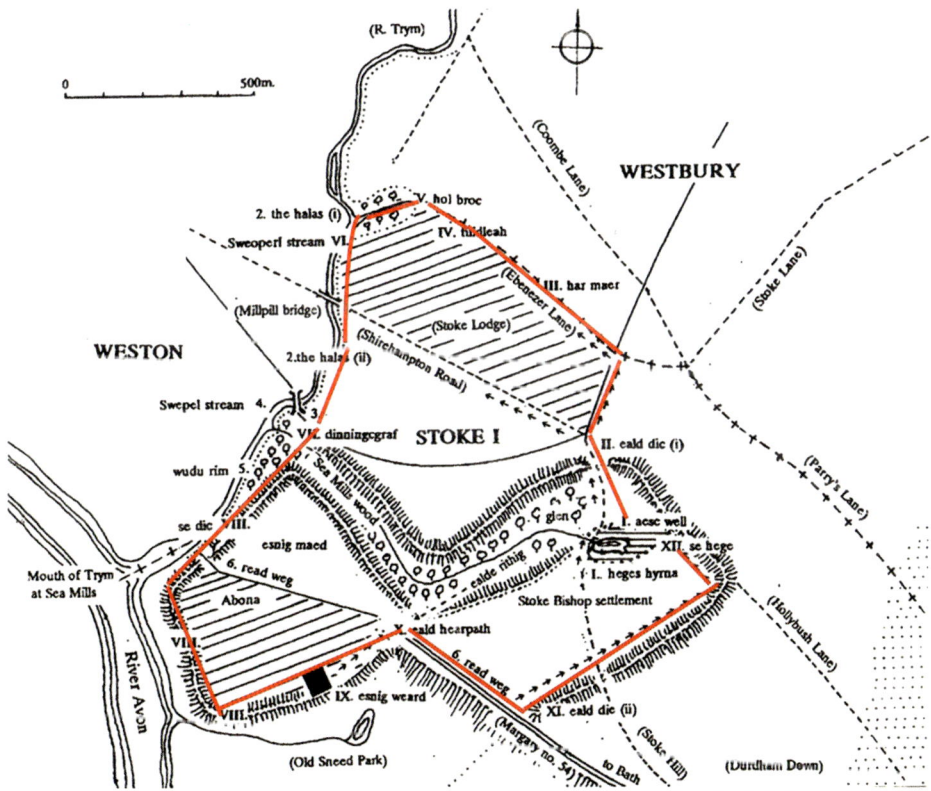

David Higgins' projection of the Charter boundaries on a modern map. The red line shows how closely the Charter's directions follow today's parish boundaries

hides of Westbury land to the church of Worcester stipulated what was to be given in rent:

> Two *tuns* of full clear ale
> One *cumb* of mild ale
> Seven oxen
> Six wethers (castrated rams)
> Forty cheeses
> Thirty ambers of rye corn (1 amber = 4 bushels)
> Four ambers of meal

That these taxes were not light is illustrated by the fact that Berkeley, when it held the Stoce lands, successfully petitioned to have the *feorm* rescinded.

Another feature of the charters was the spotlight they shone on the physical character of the landscape. It was no longer as wooded as earlier eras. In the 894 charter there is only one woodland mentioned, Dinning's Grove (Sea Mills Wood), traces of which are still visible today in the valley from Glen Drive to Druid Woods. Furthermore, landmarks were often only individual trees. From the moment the hunter gatherers arrived, woodland came under threat and by the 10th century wood for buildings, weapons and ships was in great demand.

The charters show that Anglo-Saxon society had become highly organised and Stoke Bishop had become tied to the community at Westbury and dependent on the bishopric of Worcester. Individual households carried on working their land and providing themselves with a living but they now had obligations outside their settlement.

The Normans

The charters suggested a settled society, but the stability of the Saxon kingdoms was suddenly threatened by a series of Viking raids on the north. United under the leadership of Wessex and its king, Alfred, these attacks were halted at the battle of Edington, near Chippenham, in 878 AD. A treaty drawn up by Alfred and the Viking leader, Guthrum, divided the country in half with the east being settled by the Vikings, in an area from Northumberland to East Anglia known as Danelaw. The other half was ruled by Alfred, who now styled himself King of the Anglo-Saxons. An uneasy peace existed between the two regions, until, in 1066, the Anglo-Saxon king, Edward the Confessor, died childless. The first to claim the throne was a powerful nobleman, Harold Godwineson, the king's brother-in-law, but he was

A scene from the Bayeux Tapestry: the Norman knights cut the Saxon army to pieces

soon challenged by a close cousin of Edward, the ruthless and ambitious, William, Duke of Normandy. The two fought at Hastings, where Harold was killed and his army defeated. William was acclaimed king of England on 25 December 1066.

Conquest

Like the Romans, the Normans saw Britain in terms of conquest, not assimilation. They were a Viking tribe who had been given land in northern France. They were called the Norsemen (hence Normans), but quickly acquired the culture and language of their French hosts, while seeking to expand their territory by warfare. England was a rich prize.

The knights who accompanied William and gave him victory expected to be rewarded. This was accomplished by a seamless transfer of land. The English estates were not broken up and redistributed, but merely changed ownership. Norman replaced Anglo-Saxon and life carried on. But in Stoke Bishop there was a difference. It never changed ownership. Wulfstan, Bishop of Worcester, kept his pre-conquest lands, one of the few Anglo-Saxons to do so.

Worcester had been throughout the Saxon period one of the most powerful dioceses in the country, second only to York and Canterbury. Among its bishops were important and influential churchmen like Dunstan, Oswald and Wulfstan, who had the king's ear and were often signatories to important charters. This pre-eminent position in the political hierarchy ensured the bishopric held onto its lands.

Bishop of Coutances

A long held belief locally has been the notion that with the Conquest Stoke Bishop came under the lordship of Geoffri de Mowbray, the Bishop of Coutances, a

The coat-of-arms of Geoffri de Mowbray carved over the entrance to what is now called the James chapel on the south side of St Mary Magdalene church

powerful Norman who arrived with William in 1066. Certainly this warrior bishop, who in the words of a contemporary, *'knew more about training soldiers than teaching the niceties of singing psalms'*, was given manors in the Worcester diocese, a reward for his valour in fighting alongside William at Hastings. But these did not include Stoke Bishop. The error seems to have come from a misreading of The Domesday Book, which confused Stoke Bishop with Harry Stoke, a tything that did indeed belong to the Bishop of Coutances. But the confusion has led to de Mowbray being commemorated on the outside of Stoke Bishop church. The Revd. David Wright, the first vicar, noted in his memoirs, *'upon the strength of this interesting fact of our connection with the Norman Bishop, search was made for his coat-of-arms, which was carved over the entrance to the chancel, now the south chapel door'*.

The Domesday Survey

Stoke Bishop did not escape being listed in The Domesday Book, the great land survey that William the Conqueror commissioned at Gloucester in 1085. At the time there had been a breakdown of law and order with lords squabbling over their territorial gains. William needed to know who owned what and the value of every holding in the country. His enquiries were thorough and intrusive. As the Anglo-Saxon Chronicle put it:

'there was not one single hide, nor a yard of land, nay, moreover (it is shameful to tell, though he thought it no shame to do it), not even an ox, nor a cow, nor a swine was there left, that was not set down in his writ.' (The writer of the Chronicle was no friend of William!)

Whatever its purpose, Domesday has given us today a series of snapshots of life in rural England at the time. Stoke Bishop or *'Stoche'* featured in the entry for the diocese of Worcester described as the *'Land of the Church of Worcester'*. It went on to emphasise the continuity of Worcester's holdings, and stated that *'St Mary's* (the Cathedral church) *of Worcester had held before the conquest and still held the manor of Westbury'*. Westbury included the parishes of Henbury, Redwick, Redland, Stoke Bishop and Yate.

At the time of the survey Westbury held nine ploughs (in Domesday a plough was a measure of land and was reckoned to be the area a plough with eight oxen could turn in a day). The entry listed 27 villagers and 22 smallholders with between them 26 ploughs. There were 20 male and two female slaves and 20 freedmen with 10 ploughs (a freedman was a class above a slave with the right to own land). There was a mill, probably a corn mill, but there is no indication as to where it was located. Because the figures refer to an area much larger than Stoke Bishop, it is impossible to know the numbers for the individual parishes, but it is a fair assumption that the population of Stoke Bishop would have been very small, more hamlet than village.

A curious entry stated *'to this manor belong six riding men who have eight hides and eight ploughs. They could not be separated from the manor'*. A riding man or *'radman'* provided an escort for the lord of the manor whenever he chose to visit.

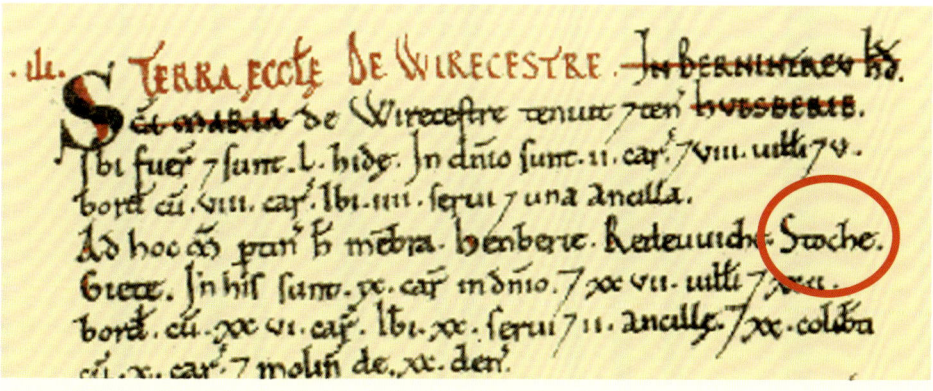

The Domesday entry for the church of Worcester

Slavery

It will be noted that the inventory included a substantial number of slaves. The Anglo Saxons took slavery for granted and acquired slaves in many ways, through conquest, purchase or kidnapping. If there were slaves in Stoke Bishop, it is possible they came from nearby Bristol. Brycgstow, or *the place of the bridge'*, was starting to establish itself as an important trading town and one of its most lucrative enterprises was its slave market. Bishop Wulstan of Worcester was foremost in a campaign to eradicate the hateful trade. He visited Bristol several times and fulminated against it. His biographer, William of Malmesbury, has given us a graphic description of the conditions in the Bristol market.

> *'They dragged people from all over England to sell to Ireland in hope of a great profit. They displayed slave women for sale, including those they had wantonly taken to bed and who were now pregnant. You would have observed and bemoaned rows of wretched people bound together with ropes, and youth of both sexes, who with dignified beauty, with healthy age, are prostituted and are put up for sale daily.'*

Wulfstan's assault had its effect and, when the Normans abolished slavery in England, the trade in Bristol ended. But in the villages it did not go away entirely. Many in rural areas found themselves in a form of servitude known as serfdom. Unlike slavery they could not be bought or sold, but they were tied to the land and had no freedom of movement.

The Middle Ages 1066-1486

Sadly, for the next three hundred years Stoke Bishop vanished from the historical record. We can only make assumptions of what life was like based on evidence from other sources. Part of this invisibility must be attributed to the later loss of local manuscripts in a catastrophic fire at Westbury College in Westbury-on-Trym and to the continuity of land ownership of the Bishops of Worcester. The area seemed to have escaped the baronial upheavals that beset the country, from the conflict between Stephen and Matilda (1135-1154) to the Wars of the Roses (1455-1486). How the Black Death (1348) affected the community we have no way of knowing, but most likely it kept the population down. One tussle that was closer to home was an ongoing struggle at Westbury-on-Trym over whether the ecclesiastical establishment there should be monastic or become a house of secular canons. The latter won and a college was set up for their instruction.

But none of this would have meant much to the peasant toiling in the fields. His life was nasty, brutish and short, an unending cycle of hard labour, locked into the rigid stratification we call feudalism. Rural society was ordered in a strict hierarchy of king, lord, knight, freedman, villein (peasant), serf, each obliged to pay to the one above taxes in money or kind. The lord of an estate was obligated to the king to provide men for 40 days military service a year, while freedman, villein and serf had to hand over to their lord a substantial portion of whatever they grew.

Medieval husbandry was subsistence agriculture. The returns in Domesday shed light on what was grown. There would be permanent pasture with grasses and clover, fields of wheat and other cereals, root vegetables, cabbage and rape. Orchards would be planted and land set aside for woodland. The bulk of the land, unlike later farming, would be given over to arable crops.

One echo of this time still survived until very recently. It was the Domesday Oak that grew in the grounds of the Holmes, now the University of Bristol Botanic Garden. It is doubtful as to whether it was as old as Domesday, but its gnarled, hollowed trunk and great mass gave it an ancient and venerable air.

'The tree died in 2004 and collapsed after extensive decay made it unstable.
Its remains are lying on the ground where it once stood as a specialised habitat
for insects' (Nicholas Wray, Curator).

'Land set apart'
During this period we get first mention of an area of Stoke Bishop that was to become a distinctive part of its history. Alfred Ellis in his book Of the Landholders in Gloucestershire named in Domesday Book (1879) writes:

'a small park, a residence for the bishop, was ... separated from the manor (of Stoke Bishop) *and called for that reason Sneyd or Snaed* (land set apart)'.

The Domesday Oak from an old newspaper cutting

It seemed to have happened in 1272 in the final year of Henry III's reign. Godfrey Gifford, the then Bishop of Worcester, enclosed the area with ditches and hedgerows and furnished it with deer. At the time meat was not easily available and venison was highly prized.

But the tenure of Worcester was not to last for ever and its buildings and landholdings were to fall victim to the cataclysmic religious movement that swept across Europe in the early part of the 16th century. The Reformation was to change Stoke Bishop forever.

Chapter Three

The Sadleir Legacy

Part 1 1544-1691

Stoke Bishop was still a hamlet at the beginning of the Tudor Age.

Not surprisingly it has no Tudor buildings surviving, but the end wall of of a house in Sunnyside has within it red Tudor bricks, suggesting that an earlier building may once have stood on the site. It probably dates from the end of the 17th century, making it the oldest structure in Stoke Bishop.

But change was to come about through what was happening in nearby Westbury-on-Trym. Westbury College, the striking ecclesiastical building that stands in the centre of the village, had been rebuilt with crenelated walls and guard towers by John Carpenter, Bishop of Worcester, in 1444. Carpenter had been born in Westbury and chose to elevate the College to a position of influence and wealth within the diocese. When Henry VIII launched his policy of dissolving monastic and other religious institutions in order to seize their assets, Westbury fell within his sights.

Traces of red brick in the walls of a house in Sunnyside suggest Tudor origins

The College was surrendered to the king's commissioners on 8 February 1544 and later granted to one of his principal agents, Sir Ralph Sadleir, who turned the College buildings into a private mansion. This in the first instance was of little importance to Stoke Bishop as the grant only applied to the College and its immediate lands. The estates beyond were still in the ownership of the Bishop of Worcester, but not for long.

Westbury College's fortified structure dominates College Road

Such was Sadleir's service to the Crown that Henry promised him a number of Gloucestershire manors that belonged to the diocese of Worcester but died before the land could be legally transferred. However, shortly into the reign of his son, Edward VI, Sadleir was granted the manors promised to him, which included Stoke Bishop. The Letters Patent confirming the title are in the Bristol Record Office. The document states: *'Letters Patent granting to Ralph Sadleyr ... Stoke Bishop ... parks called snede park*

The beautiful illuminated title on the Letters Patent shows Sir Ralph Sadleir kneeling before the teenage king, Edward VI. Sadleir can be recognised by his ginger hair

A portrait of a gentleman by Hans Holbein, the Younger, thought to be Sir Ralph Sadleir

and penpark ... and all appurtenances in Stoke Bishop, Hembury Saltmarshe, Westbury, Auste and Shirehampton in Glos ... manor of Olveston, Glos.' The lands of South Gloucestershire that had for so long been in the ownership of the Bishop of Worcester now fell into the hands of one of the country's most powerful men, a man who survived four Tudor monarchs and died in his bed.

Sir Ralph Sadleir

Ralph Sadleir was born in 1507, in Warwickshire, into a humble trading family. His father, Henry, was steward in the house of Sir Edward Belknap, a powerful court official, who in 1520 was charged with planning the Field of the Cloth of Gold, a spectacular tournament near Calais to celebrate the meeting between the king of France and Henry VIII. Henry Sadleir was responsible for supplying the buckram and canvas needed for the pavilions. He made enough money to buy himself a house in Hackney and to get his son introduced to the household of Thomas Cromwell, Henry's powerful advisor and architect of the monastic revolution. The young Ralph learnt quickly and he soon became one of Cromwell's principal secretaries, helping to draft, write and deliver his master's voluminous correspondence. He would have played a part in the downfall of Anne Boleyn, conspiring to engineer the charges of infidelity and treason that brought her to the scaffold. His natural sense of diplomacy ensured he survived the many upheavals of a tumultuous era, but the one incident that nearly ruined him was a domestic one.

While he was in Cromwell's household, he met and married Ellen Barre who was serving as a laundry maid. She had been married before but her husband was presumed dead, drowned at sea. Alas, this was not the case and, when Sadleir had become an important court official, Matthew Barre reappeared. This was serious. It made Ellen a bigamist – a capital offence in Tudor times – and threatened to ruin Sadleir. But his influence was such he was able to pay Barre off.

For much of his career he acted as Ambassador to Scotland both for Henry and later Elizabeth and in the course of his duties he became involved with Mary, Queen of Scots. On one occasion he was asked to ascertain the health of the newly born Mary as Henry was anxious one day to wed her to his son Edward. It had been rumoured she was a sickly child. Sadleir observed that her mother

'caused me to go with her to the chamber where the child was, and shewed her unto me, and also caused the nurse to unwrap her out of her clothes that I might see her naked. I assure your Majesty it is as goodly a child as I have seen of her age.'

Later Sadleir was appointed Mary's custodian, when she was incarcerated in various houses around England. It was a difficult undertaking as he was often caught between the wiles of the two monarchs. Whatever Mary's faults, Sadleir found himself drawn to the Scottish Queen and it must have been with a heavy heart that he sat on the commission that tried her for treason. She was found guilty and executed. A month later Sir Ralph Sadleir himself died. At the time of his death, he owned 23 manors and was said to be *'the richest commoner in England'*.

Sadleir's effigy lies on his tomb in St Mary's church, Standon, Hertfordshire, where he had his country seat

Stoke Bishop: the Sadleir Years

We have no evidence that Sadleir ever visited his properties in South Gloucestershire. It is unlikely given his heavy state duties. We have a record of his accounts for 1564. They were scrupulously kept by his bailiff, Stephen Bales, and suggested that his affairs were organised from London or Standon, his country estate in Hertfordshire.

He would have worked through agents based at his various properties. They would be responsible for collecting the money owed to him. They would then organise a courier to transport the monies back to Standon. The accounts give us a number of examples. In April of 1564, Thomas Loveridge, John Hiatt and Richard Clarke transported £227 and were paid 30s in expenses. In October it was the turn of Richard Pack who carried £200 and the following April a lesser sum of £40 was taken by *'Will Godson my smith'*, no doubt a safe courier! It wasn't only money that was sent but also goods that had been purchased, for example, *five tones of gascon wyne'* at £53 15s 0d and 24 oxen purchased for £56 by Roger Bacher at Coventry Fair. Roger Clarke was paid 7s 10d *for the frayht of three Barrells of sammon'*.

The account book is testament to the wealth Ralph Sadleir was accruing. Total income from the properties for 1564 was £800, equating in current value to £186,648 (using the National Archives historical currency converter). In the book, 18 manors were listed, one of them being Stoke Bishop. Income drawn from the estate was £71 0s 7p (£16,338). This was a sizeable sum when compared with

Bristol (£30) and Westbury (£42), perhaps an early indication of the value of Stoke Bishop real estate!

But it is important to remember that grants of land handed down by the monarch were not giveaways. The King expected the recipient to pay for them. The grant that included Stoke Bishop cost Ralph Sadleir £1837 1s 8p (£428,592), a hefty fee which had to be paid before he could start earning a profit. But a profit he did achieve that provided his children with a substantial legacy and one that was to have profound implications for Stoke Bishop.

Sadleir's Inheritance

Ralph Sadleir had three sons and three daughters. The Westbury estates passed to his eldest son, Thomas, who seemed to have set up home in the refurbished buildings of Westbury College. He also began the process of letting out parts of his demesne. In 1590, he separately leased two pieces of land in Sneed Park to Bartholomew Cook, one time Sheriff of Bristol. One of these leases passed through several hands. A document exists that secured a transfer in 1616 from William Slade to John Moore, both Bristol merchants. It contained a summary of the original tenancy clauses which has given us a graphic picture of what Sneed Park looked like at the beginning of the 17th century.

The enclosed land, once a deer park, was now in part given over to agricultural use, although as we shall see much parkland remained. I am grateful to Ian Beattie for letting me reproduce his translation of the transfer deed. The lessee was given the right *'to have and to hold all and singular the said park or enclosed ground called Sneed Park* (note the spelling has segued over time from Snaed to Sneed to Sneyd) *... and the ... messuage* (dwelling house with outbuildings), *tenement or lodge aforesaid together with all ... the lands, tenements, meadows, leasows* (grazing), *pastures, feedings, woods, underwoods, fishings, waters and millponds ... and also all those water mills builded under one roof commonly known by the name of Sea Mills'*. The area of the park was greater than today including as it did mills along the River Trym. Some of the meadows are individually named, *'Woodcombe, Somerlease, Cademead and Poleburies'*.

But in the matter of the all important woodland the landlord wasn't going to relinquish his ability to source timber. He retained the right to access *'all manner of great timber trees of the age of thirty years and upwards growing, standing or being in or upon any part or parcel of the said ... premises with the free ingress, egress and regress ... to fell, sell and carry away the same timber trees of such age or upwards and every time leaving sufficient timber trees upon the premises for the necessary reparations of the houses and buildings'*. In an age when wood was all important this was gain for the landlord and loss for the tenant. Nor was there any mention of sustainable replanting!

Thomas Sadleir died in 1608 and his estates passed to his son Ralph, who probably continued to live in Westbury. But that ended with the catastrophic events of the Civil War which began in 1642. Bristol, which had started out in the war supporting Oliver Cromwell and the Parliamentarians, had by 1645 become a Royalist city under Prince Rupert. But the hostilities were not going well for the king, Charles I. Bristol found itself threatened by a large Parliamentarian army. To stave off the attack, Rupert adopted a scorched earth policy and burnt Westbury and some surrounding villages (although we don't know whether this included Stoke Bishop). The college and all its valuable papers went up in flames and Ralph Sadleir rather than rebuild it cut his losses and returned to the family home at Standon. At the same time he began to dispose of his west country estates.

In 1652, Joseph Jackson, a wealthy Bristol merchant bought the greater part of Sneed Park for a mere £83,000. About the same time most of the remaining part of the Sadleir estate (Stoke Bishop) was bought by another Bristol merchant, William Cann. Soon after, in 1660, Charles II was restored to the throne, heralding a period of optimism and with it the confidence to invest in building grand houses. Interestingly neither Joseph Jackson Snr. nor William Cann took advantage of this, but their sons did. Joseph Jackson Jnr. and Robert Cann both erected magnificent edifices on the land they had inherited.

Stoke House

The house that Robert Cann built still exists. It stands at the top of Stoke Hill and is now a theological college. The 1669 date above its entrance was probably the year it was completed. It was built in the Jacobean tradition with distinctive Dutch gabling. In style it looked to the past, as the newly fashionable classicism of the period had not yet reached Bristol. Nevertheless it was sufficiently grand to be pictured by Johannes Kip, a noted engraver (see page 38). Kip came to England from his native Holland when William of Orange and his wife Mary became joint rulers in 1688 in what has been called the Glorious Revolution. Such was Kip's talent and business acumen he quickly built a thriving trade in selling to the gentry engravings of their country houses. His images were highly flattering, with a birds-eye view that showed off the extent and sumptuousness of the owner's property. He filled them with kinetic activity, scurrying figures, horsemen, carriages, ships. His creation would have pleased the first owner of Stoke House.

The Dutch-style façade of Stoke House with 1669 elaborately carved over the door

Robert Cann

Robert Cann was a colourful character, whose activities often sailed close to the wind. His family home was the manor of Compton Greenfield (near Cribbs Causeway). Like his father, a merchant and civic elder, he pursued both careers with vigour. He was appointed Master of the Merchant Venturers in 1658, mayor of Bristol in 1662, alderman a year later and in 1662 he was knighted by Charles II. Made Baron of Compton Greenfield in the same year, he capped his meteoric

Despite his eminent position, no portrait of Robert Cann has come to light. But the fine Jacobean staircase in Stoke House has two faces carved on it thought to be Sir Robert and his third wife Anne

rise by becoming MP for Bristol on three occasions.

His naturally combative character got him into trouble on several occasions, most notably when he denied the Popish Plot, an alleged Catholic conspiracy to assassinate Charles II, fabricated by a scoundrel called Titus Oates. Cann, in reaction perhaps to the hysteria that raged in the country as a result of Oates' accusations, argued controversially that there *was no Popish Plot*. He was brought before Parliament to explain himself and only made matters worse by muttering under his breath as he sat down, *God damn me, 'tis true*. He was expelled from the House and committed to the Tower, a sentence that proved short as days later he recanted and was released. On another occasion as mayor of Bristol, he had a furious dispute with Lord Chief Justice, George Jeffreys, whose 'Bloody' Assize against the Somerset rebels who had taken part in the Monmouth Rebellion had made him infamous. Jeffreys had come to Bristol with the express purpose of *cleaning out the corporation* and *humbling that proud body*. In a diatribe against Cann and his perceived corruptions, he called him a *stinking, whining, presbyterian that could be smelled forty miles off*.

The Canns and the Bristol Slave Trade

Jeffreys had more of a case against Cann when it came to his mercantile activities. Like many Bristol merchants of the time, his wealth derived from his investments in shipping and the purchase of land in the colonies. Sugar was bringing wealth to Bristol. John Evelyn the diarist visited the city in 1654 and observed sugar refining for the first time. Naval records show that on one tide 30 merchantmen sailed into the city laden with sugar from the West Indies.

Robert Cann took full advantage of this trade. He had plantations in Barbados and along the coast of North America. But there was a problem. Sugar was a labour intensive product. The sugar plantations suffered from an acute shortage of workers. Bristol found a way of solving this. After Cromwell's victory against the Royalist Scots in 1648, *the gentlemen of Bristol applied to have liberty to transport 500 of the prisoners to the plantations*. Cann and fellow Bristol merchants saw a lucrative trade opening up. In 1652, the Governor of Waterford in Ireland was ordered *to deliver to Robert Cann, Robert Yate and Thomas Speed as many Irish rebel prisoners as they might choose to embark in their ship bound for the West Indies*. But when the Civil War ended, the supply of convicts dried up and Cann resorted to kidnapping to fill his ships. It was against these *spirits* that supplied the West Indian plantations with labour that Judge Jeffries fulminated on his visit to Bristol. He summoned Cann to the bar and ranted at length about his kidnapping activities and fined him

£1,000. *'Had it not been in respect of the city,'* he swore later, *'I would have arraigned him and would have hanged him… A kidnapping knave!'*

What are we to make of these activities? I am indebted to Dr. Jamie Davies of Trinity College for letting me have access to his research on the Cann family's involvement in the slave trade. The victims of Robert Cann's kidnapping were white and in the first instance would have been sold to the plantations as indentured servants. They would serve their masters for five to seven years, during which time they could not leave the plantations. They were treated as a commodity and could be sold on, but at the end of their contract they were released to something like a normal life and would be given money or land. Soon, however, owners found that kidnapped Africans were better value, as the plantations could keep them for life and didn't have to pay them.

During Cann's lifetime, Bristol had no access to the African trade. The Royal African Company (of which Edward Colston was a deputy governor) had been established by Charles II in 1660 which gave a monopoly to London in the buying and selling of slaves from Africa. This threatened Bristol's trading position and, through the City's powerful Society of Merchant Venturers, it sought *'a proper peticion to the Parliament for letting in the merchants of this Citty to share in the African trade.'* In 1698 Bristol was successful and in the words of the Merchant Venturers' website *'the monopoly of the London based Royal African Company ended and all subjects of the Crown were allowed to trade with Africa. Bristol, which had already been the second city and port in England for the past three hundred years, would now profit greatly from the slave trade and grow wealthier still.'* Did this include the Canns?

Robert's father, William, had married Margaret Yeamans and Robert himself was married to Cicely Hooke. Both the Hookes and the Yeamans later became major investors in the triangular trade, with Robert's son, William, profiting from the will of Abraham Hooke, a prolific slaver. Robert died before the London monopoly ended, but as John Latimer in his History of the Society of Merchant Venturers of the City of Bristol has noted, the Merchant Venturers *'carried on a surreptitious trade between the west coast of Africa and the English plantations in America while the monopoly was in existence'.* With the need to provide labour for their overseas plantations and given their family connections it is difficult to see how, even if Robert himself was not involved, his sons, who carried on their father's business, would not have profited from the transatlantic trade.

The Burrell Collection in Glasgow has a grand chair that once belonged to the Cann family. It is dated 1699 and bears the family crest. It has been tagged by the museum as an exhibit associated with the slave trade and as an example of the

The Kip engraving of Stoke House looking towards the Avon and the Severn Estuary. The tower to the left overlooking the Avon is Cook's Folly and the path to the right carved through the trees is Hollybush Lane. Stoke Bishop is beyond the trees

wealth amassed by the family from their Caribbean trade.

Robert Cann: The Last Years

Retrobate in many respects though he was, Robert Cann also had his admirers. Samuel Pepys, the diarist, found him *'a sober merchant, very good company and so like one of our sober wealthy London merchants as pleased me mightily.'* Certainly *'the morose old merchant'* could be curmudgeonly one minute, genial the next, as Sir Dudley North, Sheriff of London, found out when he sought to marry Cann's daughter, Anne. He couldn't afford the settlement Cann requested and offered a lower one. To which Cann replied: *'Sir, my answer to your first letter, is my answer to your second.'* North responded by pressing Anne to marry him without her father's consent. She agreed. In time the

Cann chair in Glasgow's Burrell Collection

old knight came round and would say to his son-in-law: *'Come son, let us go out and shine'* (that is walk about the streets with six footmen in liveries attending.) Yet as Pepys noted Cann had been jolted by his life's *'journeys, troubles and perplexities'*. Unwisely he switched *'from Bristol milk* (cream sherry), *morning, noon and night, to small beer, but nature would not long bear so great a change'*. He died in November 1685, age 64.

The Jacksons of Sneed Park

While Robert Cann was enjoying the life of a country gentleman, the Jackson family was emulating his lifestyle less than a mile away. The Jacksons were also wealthy merchants. Miles, the founder of the business, apprenticed his son, Joseph, on 26 October 1620. It was a turbulent time to be trading. Dutch men o' war, French privateers, Irish and Barbary pirates prowled the seas ready to pounce on laden merchant ships. The Jacksons were both members of the Society of Merchant Venturers and their names were attached to a number of pleas to the government for greater protection. In 1620 Miles was a signatory to a letter to the Mayor of Bristol asking to be let off part of what the Society owed the city as a result of *'the manifold losses, which we have lately susteyned both by shipwracke and depredacion of Pirates'*. But his business nevertheless flourished and he was able to pass his fortune onto his son, Joseph, and it was Joseph who purchased the lands of Sneed Park in 1652.

Like his father and his neighbour Robert Cann, Joseph Jackson climbed the ranks of Bristol society, becoming an Alderman, Mayor, Sheriff and Master of the Merchant Venturers, an office he held four times. He was also elected MP for Bristol during the Third Protectorate under Oliver Cromwell. He must have made an impact on the Merchant Venturers as his portrait, attributed to Antony van Dyke, dominated the Hall where they met. Its impact was such that in 1701 it was resolved that future pictures should be *'made of equal length with Alderman Jackson's'.* Alas the portrait was lost in the Blitz.

Joseph, Snr., died in 1661. In his will he bequeathed to his son, Joseph Jackson Jnr., *'my land purchased of Mr. Sadler called Sneed Park'* along with £2,000. This allowed Joseph Jnr., in 1691, to build a fine mansion on an elevated position overlooking the Avon. Sadly it has been demolished and the Glenavon block of flats built on the site. But not all has disappeared. Like Stoke House, Sneed Park was engraved by Johannes Kipp in 1712 and from it we can spot one significant feature that is still there. Separating the house and the grounds from Sea Mills is a long and very tall wall that runs down to the river. About half way along is a lookout tower designed to spy the owner's ships arriving at the mouth of the Avon (a common feature of houses at this time). The tower has gone but parts of the wall survive and they are

Sneed Park on its eminence overlooking the parkland. The rampart, which is still there today, can be seen on the left

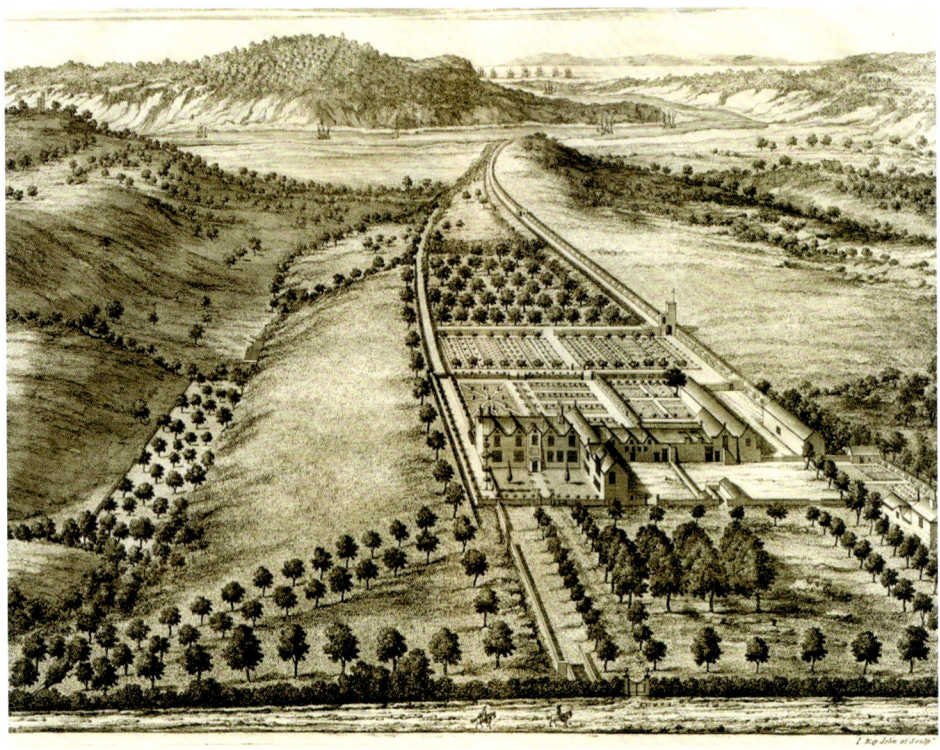

Kipp's bird's eye view of Sneed Park. To the left is the deep gully that has survived as the Sneed Park Nature Reserve

still very impressive. The walled buttresses that supported the terracing have also survived. The gardens in their day must have been spectacular. Celia Fiennes in her journal in 1698 described apricots growing.

They may have lived on separate estates, but the Jacksons and the Canns were bound together through their mercantile enterprises and their membership of the Merchant Venturers. On 4 May 1654, the ship, Goulden Lyon, arrived from Lisbon. In the record of *'monies collected for Wharfage'*, Robert Cann landed *'16 pipes of oyle and eight chests of sugar'* while on the same ship Joseph Jackson received *'12 pipes 18 hhds (hogsheads) of oyle and three chests of sugar'*. On another occasion Cann and Jackson were together on a small committee *'appoynted and authorized to write to the Commissioners of the High Courte of Admiraltye, to procure a Convoy for the Porte and Channell of Bristol to guard all ships belonging to this Porte'*.

Although Joseph Jackson would have known about the slave trade, no evidence has come to light to suggest that he was involved in the trade himself. But Sneed

Above, Glenavon flats built on the site of Sneed Park; parts of the terrace towers and walls have survived. Right, best viewed where it crosses Glenavon Park, Sneed Park's colossal boundary wall still survives in part

Park did have a later association with slavery. Madge Dresser in her book Slavery Obscured has noted *'that in 1823 the West Indian magnate and slave owner, Thomas Daniel Jnr, resided there'*. Daniel was known to his contemporaries as the *'King of Bristol'*. He had extensive holdings not only in the West Indies but in and around the city and Sneed Park appeared to be one of them. He is described in a sale document in the City Archives as *'Thomas Daniel the younger of Sneed Park'*. Although he never engaged in shipping slaves to the Caribbean he was a substantial slave owner and, when slavery was abolished in 1834, the compensation he received for his 4,967 slaves was among the largest in the country.

Chapter Four

The Sadleir Legacy

Part 2 1700-1800

Although Jackson and Cann owned the bulk of the Sadleir estate, small parcels resided in other hands.

A section, which bordered the Gorge near Sea Walls, was part of the land originally leased to Benjamin Cooke and was purchased outright by his son in 1693. John Cooke, like his neighbours, was a merchant and rose to enjoy high office. He was civic Chamberlain of Bristol Corporation, Sheriff of Bristol and Master of the Merchant Venturers. Like Cann, he got himself into trouble and was dismissed from his position as Chamberlain for *injustice, negligence and incapacity in fulfilling the duties of his office*. But it was what he did in Sneed Park that got him noticed. Latimer in his Annals of Bristol in the Seventeenth Century suggested there was already a house on the estate but, if there was, it was nothing to the spectacular tower that Cooke erected. It stood on the edge of the Gorge and was a landmark that could be seen for miles around and was much commented upon by travellers. It was a substantial structure with three habitable rooms and there is a suggestion that it was built on an existing medieval base, so thick were the walls. Quite what its purpose was is uncertain, but most likely it was designed as a lookout tower to allow Cooke to spy his incoming ships. But this modest purpose was overshadowed by the legend that sent shivers down the spine of any visitor.

The story goes that one day the owner was visited by a gypsy who foretold that his son would meet a terrible calamity after his twentieth birthday. He presented him with a scroll on which was written:

> *'That period past, another sun*
> *Shall not his annual journey run*
> *Before a silent secret foe*
> *Shall strike the boy a deadly blow...'*

Fearful for his son's life, the father built a tower in which he immured the boy until he reached his 21st birthday. For a whole year his son lived alone fed from baskets hoisted up to him. One day he complained of being cold and asked for firewood. A bundle of faggots came up in a basket and his father was happy to see flames lighting up the windows. What he didn't see was a viper silently uncoiling itself from the wood and delivering his son a mortal bite.

It is hard to believe that the officious John Cooke was the father of the legend, but whatever the reality, it stuck and Cook's Folly (as it became known) began to attract swarms of visitors, eventually leading to full blown entertainment. In 1852 an advertisement appeared in a local newspaper which announced that *'during the Easter holidays a Band will be in attendance and will continue twice a week during the season. Refreshment may be obtained at 'Bristol Prices'. Picnic and Tea parties accommodated on the shortest notice. India and Pale Ales, Bottled and Draught Beer can be had if required'*. It is easy to imagine what the seclusion loving residents of Sneyd Park would think of this today!

Writers, painters and poets all celebrated the mysterious tower sitting in its splendid isolation on the cliff top. J.M.W. Turner, Samuel Jackson, Francis Danby, William Müller, among others, delighted in the romantic prospect the tower gave them. In 1886 the Clifton writer, Emma Marshall, used the tower as a subject for her romance The Tower on The Cliff, a Story founded on a Gloucestershire Legend. But all this changed in 1858 when a new Victorian house incorporated the tower within its structure.

Above, 1825 view of the Gorge by the Bristol artist Samuel Jackson looking towards Sea Walls and Cook's Folly beyond. Right, visitors to the Folly in the 18th century

Pitch and Pay House and Lane

Tucked between the Cann and Jackson estates was another parcel of land that seemed to have originated as a farm. Little is known about it except that it consisted of 54 acres and a house dating from 1561. It was probably on lease from the Canns. It was later replaced by a Victorian mansion which kept its former name of Pitch and Pay, an odd name that has led to much speculation as to its origin.

Pitch and Pay Lane in the 1950s. Note the gate that once stood at the entrance

During the first half of the 16th century bubonic plague swept Bristol (eg in 1603 and 1646) and would have been an ever present fear for those living in the city. It was said that a stile existed at the top of what is today called Pitch and Pay Lane at the junction with Julian Road. Here during plague years people from the country would bring produce in baskets which they would *'pitch'* over the barrier to waiting Bristolians who in return *'paid'* for the goods by tossing coins into a bucket of disinfectant. It is a much loved story and one that makes historical sense of the name. John Latimer published his version of the story in 1884 in the Bristol Times. He wrote:

> *'When Mary attempted to get to the stile, some others crowded before her and pushed her back... A youth... who from his dress appeared to be a better class of farmer... asked her what she wanted. A little fruit, a brown loaf and chicken, the luxuries required for her sick father were all she asked. He held up the articles and several rushed towards that part of the bar behind which he stood, but he waved them back and said they were for the young maid with the red hood. Mary asked the price... but he would take nothing... But Mary persisted in paying, threw the money over the bar and returned with her welcome stock.'*

Sadly it seems, the origin of the story started much later than the plague years. It first appeared in Felix Farley's Journal in the middle of the 19th century. First to question its validity was local historian and vicar of Westbury-on-Trym, the Revd. Dr H. J. Wilkins. He argued that *'this spot is too remote from the town for it to be true'*. Therefore as the house adjacent to the lane was called Pitch and Pay, he suggested that the lane most likely took its name from the house. Certainly by the end of the 17th century, the house name had been fixed. In the Westbury-on-Trym Poor Book for 1675 there was a payment *for haling* (evicting) *of William Cary from pitch and pay*' and in 1698 one for the '*child which was left neare pitch and pay*'. A deed dated 1719 in the Cann-Lippincott papers concerned '*Pitch and Pay and other houses*' and the '*tenement called Pitch and Pay in the parish of Westbury*'.

But if the name is not related to the plague, what does its name mean? There have been many theories, that '*pitch*' indicates a place where pitch is to be found or is a reference to caulking ships with pitch, and '*pay*' a corruption of paving. Certainly pitch production for ships was carried on in Westbury-on-Trym. The Oxford English Dictionary defines one meaning of pitch as '*pave* (road) *with set stones*'. Thus the name could have derived from the Roman road, the line of which the lane follows. Alternatively '*pitch and pay*' was a phrase used in the 17th century to mean '*pay cash at the time of purchase*' (similar to '*pay on the nails*'). It is doubtful if anyone will really know for certain the origin of the name, but what is certain is that it is unlikely that the beloved story attached to it will ever fade.

Druid Stoke House

The origins of the house at the end of Druid Stoke Avenue are shadowy. The first owner was possibly an Edward Lloyd. On the 1712 map his estate is marked as '*Land of Edward Lloyd*'. The house was built on a promontory overlooking the Avon around 1700. The history before this is unknown. Possibly it was unclaimed Sadleir land. Or, as it lay on the boundary of the sprawling Kings Weston estate, it may have been bought from the owner Edward Southwell. At first it was a simple house in brick, but by 1817 it had been painted a light beige as a print by the Revd. John Skinner shows. A Mr Skidmore lived there in 1783, then in 1801 it was bought by Edward Webb, a servant of the East India Company and later MP for Gloucester. Webb purchased the house on his return from India.

Strangely, a year after acquiring the property, Webb seems to have put it back on the market. He was unsuccessful at auction and withdrew the sale. The auction prospectus has survived and gives us a valuable picture of a small country estate at the time,

> '*consisting of an exceeding good Brick fronted dwelling house with double coach house and stabling for 10 horses, barns, cow houses, sheds and other attached and detached offices; large walled in pleasure garden, fruit and kitchen gardens; and orcharding covered with fruit trees of every description,*

Druid Stoke House sketched by the Revd. John Skinner on his visit to Stoke Bishop in 1817

and now in full bearing; together with 51 acres of arable, meadow and pasture land, and about three acres of coppice wood, 30 acres of which are let to Mr Jacob Large for the term of 12 years 10 of which have expired and ten acres to Mr Miles as tenant at will, the rest is in hand.'

Edward Webb lived at Druid Stoke House until his death in 1829. It was bought the following year by William Munro, a Scot with an eye to land speculation. He had two daughters born out of wedlock while he was in Jamaica. Both became dressmakers, but his legitimate son, William, had a celebrated career, both as a soldier and as a botanist.

William Munro Jnr. was born in 1818 and brought up in Druid Stoke House. He joined the army in 1834 and saw service with the 39th (Dorsetshire) Regiment of Foot in India, Quebec, the West Indies and the Crimea. On 24 December 1843, he was badly wounded during the Battle of Maharajpore in India. But he remained in the army and rose to the rank of general. He married Sarah Tothill from a neighbouring house, The Grove, on 14 September 1854. Another example of the

From left, General William Munro of Druid Stoke House, Sarah his wife, and in civilian clothes

families of the big houses marrying into each other.

While in the army, he developed an interest in botany and being posted to the many far-flung corners of the British Empire allowed him considerable opportunity to observe plants in their varied habitats. He put his knowledge to practical use by establishing botanic gardens at some of the military stations where he served. He also encouraged his soldiers to grow their own vegetables. His advancing reputation enabled him to conduct plant collecting expeditions to India, Kashmir and Barbados. In 1840 he became a fellow of the prestigious Linnean Society. We have two letters from him written from Druid Stoke House to Sir William Joseph Hooker, the first director of Kew Gardens, acknowledging receipt of specimens that arrived by hamper from Kew. One letter reveals the hazards of plant collecting. *'I'm glad to hear Thompson is safe; I know no great harm could happen to him if taken prisoner, but I was afraid his collections might be taken from him.'* He

Jason Smith

Munroa squarrosa, a native grass of North America, named after Munro goes on *'there is no good map of the whole of the area your son will traverse, but the best is published by the East India Company. Still, much of the country is unsurveyed.'* His main research field was tropical grasses and he has a species named after him called Munroa.

More on Stoke House

In his will, Sir Robert Cann disinherited William, his eldest son by his first wife, in favour of Thomas, the son by his second wife. The will was bitterly disputed but judgement was finally found in favour of Thomas and Stoke House passed to him. He was succeeded successively by his sons, Robert and William.

It would not be fitting for a house as old as Stoke House not to have a ghost and it seemed that William provided one by refusing to allow his daughter to marry her lover. He shot her by mistake while she was hiding in an ilex tree into which she had climbed from her window with the intention of eloping. Her ghost thereafter has haunted the house. Many years later, she appeared at a dinner party to welcome the first vicar of Stoke Bishop, David Wright, and his wife. The guests fled in terror.

In 1765 William's son, Robert, died without heirs and the estate passed to his nephew, Richard Cann Jeffries, who was probably responsible for the house's new

Stoke House at the end of the 18th century after renovation in a more Gothic style with pointed windows

Turner sits painting with his friend Cann-Lippincott beside him. In his sketchbook he refers to the trees in the foreground as an 'olive' and a 'yew'

Gothic look. Jeffries died suddenly in 1773 and his sister, Catherine, became the most eligible spinster in Bristol. The man she married was Henry Lippincott, a member of an old Devon family, who became MP for Bristol in 1780. He also received the baronetcy of Stoke Bishop (a title that died out within two generations). He greatly enlarged the gardens at Stoke House and secured the diversion, at his own expense, of the turnpike road down Stoke Hill, so that he could create a lawn in front of the house. Sadly, he died in the same year he became MP and was succeeded by his son, Henry, who called himself Cann-Lippincott, bringing the Cann name back into the family.

J.M.W. Turner painted the house in 1791. He was 16 and was on a sketching tour of Bristol. He was staying with John Narraway who later became his patron. Narraway was a friend of Cann-Lippincott who introduced him to Stoke House. The resulting picture is one of Turner's finest early watercolours.

But would he have been so familiar with Cann-Lippincott had he known of the scandal in which his host was to be embroiled a few years later? In December 1809, Sir Henry and a fellow officer from the Bristol Militia accosted two girls on College Green, who were said to prowl *'in pairs after dark'*, and took them back to their nearby lodgings. One of the girls was probably only 15. Whether, with or without their consent, the girls were seduced, Sir Henry was certainly accused later of rape. He was arraigned before the Bristol Assizes in April 1810, but was acquitted on the grounds that there may have been blackmail involved.

Sir Henry died, unmarried, in 1829. The house was sold and came into the hands of the Harfords, the influential Bristol banking family, who were to be responsible for a major change in Stoke House's fortunes.

In 1810 Sneed Park had an uninterrupted view towards Cook's Folly, the Avon Gorge and the Severn Estuary beyond, as seen in this painting by William West

Sneed Park: An Earthly Paradise

In 1725 Joseph Jackson's son, Nicholas, married Anne, eldest daughter of Sir Thomas Cann, bringing the two families together. By 1783 the Jacksons had absorbed Cook's Folly into their domain. Nicholas's daughter, Mary, was described as owner of *'a pleasure house where there were three rooms fitted up, and the tower is made use of as a Belvedere to Sneed Park house'*. Although as we have seen, it continued to be a visitor attraction.

Writers of the time wrote lyrically about the area calling it *'a beautiful passage of scenery'*, which *'in summer may be justly stiled a terrestrial Paradise'*. A sale prospectus of 1802 described a house as

> *'most delightfully situated, commanding picturesque prospects of the river and of Blaise Castle, Cooks Folly, and all the beautiful surrounding country; which*

Sketching Cook's Folly from Sea Walls by James Baker Pyne, 1833

added to its proximity to Bristol, and a number of gentlemen's seats in the neighbourhood must render it truly desirable to anyone wishing to purchase a beautiful country residence.'

Sailing up the River Avon a traveller wrote:

'Nothing, especially to one coming in from the sea, can equal the variety of the country seats on each side of the River Avon. As you come up here, the trees, houses and agreeable villas of the merchants of Bristol, all contribute to make it delicious to the eye.'

Chapter Five

A New Dock

1732

Visitors to Sea Mills often mistake the ruined walls across the mouth of the River Trym for Roman remains.

They are not. They are what is left of a great enterprise in the 18th century to create a floating or wet dock where the Trym runs into the Avon.

Bristol is an ancient port with a long and flourishing history. But it has two considerable impediments to a smooth passage up river. Firstly, the Avon has one of the largest rises and falls of the tide in the world, second only to Fundy Bay in Canada. This means ships can only enter the port twice a day. Secondly, the river has treacherous bends, particularly the notorious Horseshoe Bend at Shirehampton. As ships got bigger in the 18th century the risk of running aground increased. When they got to their moorings, as the tide went out they would settle on the mud, putting a damaging strain on their hulls. Liverpool had begun a wet dock in 1709, which when complete would have threatened Bristol's trade.

At low tide the walls that held the lock gates of the 18th century dock are clearly visible

The Dock Scheme

In response to this, a group of Bristol merchants got together in 1710 to construct a wet dock on the River Avon. They chose the pill or inlet at Sea Mills at the mouth of the River Trym as being the ideal place, half way between the city and the mouth of the Avon, embracing the most navigable part of the river and being the site of the earlier Roman harbour. The consortium was led by Joshua Franklyn and 32 of his friends, who each invested £300. The land on either side of the River Trym belonged to Edward Southwell, the owner of Kings Weston Estate, and it was from him that the consortium secured, by Act of Parliament, a lease of one hundred acres for an optimistic 999 years. They were to pay an annual rent of £81. Building the dock was put in the hands of John Padmore, Bristol's leading engineer. His appointment was confirmation that the scheme had serious credentials.

Construction

Maps of the time show the dock extending from the mouth of the Trym back to where today's Trym Cross Road joins Avon Way. Construction consisted of a brick-lined outer dock with massive stone walls built across the river. At the entrance huge lock gates controlled the flow of water. It is the stone wall that is visible today. To one side of the back wall further lock gates led into a long

An 18th century map showing the dock layout at the mouth of the River Trym

basin, the foundations of which can still be seen at low water (beneath the Portway viaduct). The Trym was diverted into channels or leats that were laid around each side of the dock. A slipway for ship repairs and three substantial stone buildings were constructed on the eastern side. One, marked on a contemporary map as a public house, still survives and what on plans is described as a rope walk has become Sea Mills Lane.

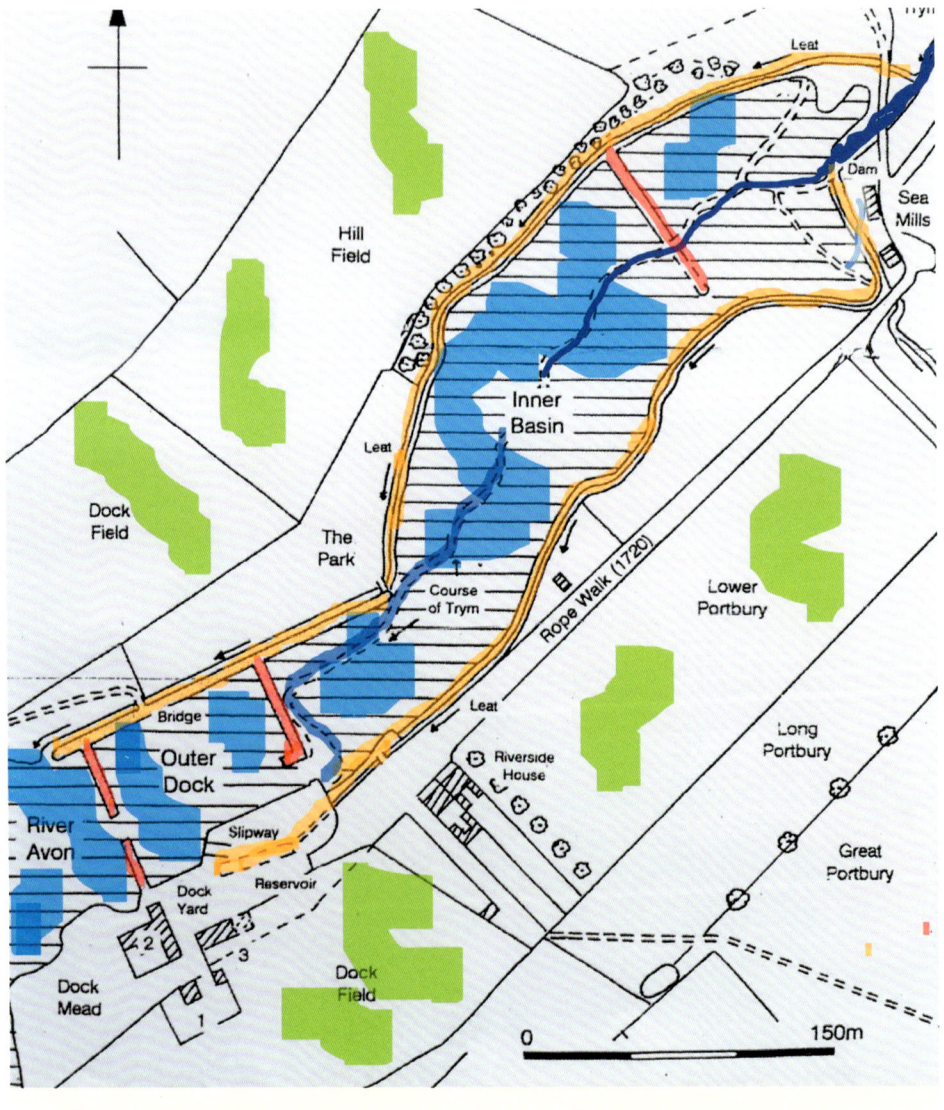

A detailed plan of the dock based on a reconstruction by James Russell

A late Victorian photograph of the crumbling outer dock wall with a surviving dock building in the background which is still there today (right)

Activity

Contemporary accounts have suggested that the dock had space for mooring as many as 150 vessels. This seems difficult to believe and certainly there is no evidence that it was used to capacity. Further, it is likely that its main function was less to unload cargoes than to berth empty ships and thereby take the pressure off the congested city docks.

Getting ships into the dock proved a complicated and costly business, heavy on time and manpower. A surviving account dated 1 December 1733 documented how the ship Queen Mary was brought into Sea Mills Dock under the care of the pilot, James Charles. Among the costs itemised were:

> *For unmooring her in Hungroad* (opp Pill) *two boats 31 hands (£1 14s 0p)*
> *From Hungroad to Sea Mills five boats 50 hands (£2 17s 6p)*
> *For piloting from Hungroad to Sea Mills (£0 12s 0p)*

The total bill would have been valued at £609 58s today, a hefty sum. Little wonder there was a note in the document that requested *'the Pilott to render reasons why so many men imployed in unmooring'.*

Privateers and Slave Traders

More profitable for the Dock, and which became its main business, was the repairing and fitting out of ships and particularly privateers, ships privately owned but commissioned by the government to engage enemy craft in times of war. Often the activities of privateers shaded into piracy. The Mariner's Mirror listed six vessels fitted out or sold as privateers at Sea Mills. Perhaps the most intriguing were two Spanish ships captured by the privateer Tyger and brought to Sea Mills. One was a noted privateer, the Nuestra Senora Vegonia, the other a new ship, the Vainqueur. Both were sold by auction. The capture must have happened during the War of Jenkins' Ear, a conflict between Britain and Spain over the lucrative slave trade in the Spanish Americas (1739-1748). Jenkins was a British captain, who allegedly had his ear severed by a Spanish coastguard.

The Southwell by Nicholas Pocock. The ship is shown engaged in slave trading. On the left slaves are loaded aboard the ship and on the right goods are brought ashore to pay the slavers.

Several of the privateers participated in the triangular trade taking goods to Africa to buy slaves for the Americas. One of these, the Southwell, (likely named after Edward Southwell, owner of Kings Weston) was fitted out in Sea Mills in September 1744. An advert was circulated to recruit crew:

'Any Gentlemen Sailors that are willing to serve on board the said Ship, let them apply to the Captain at the Custom House Coffee House in (Queen's) *Square.'*

The *Southwell* made two voyages to Africa in 1746 and 1748 with the express purpose of buying slaves. The ship was owned by Michael Beecher & Co. from Bristol. The

Riverside House, William Tregoe's house today on Sea Mills Lane

captain on both voyages was John Brackenridge. On the first voyage he delivered 629 Africans to Jamaica. But losses were often high and on his second voyage he limped into Antigua with 301 slaves, having lost 150 at sea.

Great Expectations

In 1732 a small group leased a plot of land from the consortium, in the optimistic hope the dock would prove profitable. One of their number, William Tregoe, a Bristol shipwright, built a house, no doubt expecting to make good money from ship repairs.

The house still stands on Sea Mills Lane and is known as Riverside House. But it all might have come to an early end. In his Annals of Bristol Latimer recounted how a bizarre protection racket broke out in Bristol.

Shipyards and other premises were being told that they would be burnt down unless protection money was paid. One yard did go up in flames and another fire-bombed. The ships at Sea Mills were threatened, but fortunately the extortionists failed to act. Latimer was vague about the outcome as it appeared the perpetrators were never caught.

Whaling

For 20 years business was constant, but profits were modest. In 1750, to boost their income, the consortium opened the dock up to whaling vessels from the Arctic. In that year two whales were unloaded and cut up on the quayside and their blubber boiled down. Two years later, according to Felix Farley's Journal for July 18 1752:

> *'a whale fishery company of local merchants had two ships, the Bristol and Adventure, fitted out for whaling and which returned from the Arctic having had the good fortune to catch five whales and 'tis said they are valued at £2000, which with the bounty money of 40s per ton, makes their voyage a very successful one.'*

A third ship, the St Andrew was sent out in 1755 and 1756. But cracks in the operation were starting to appear. Recruiting crews proved difficult. Whaling was a dangerous activity and less lucrative than privateering. Adverts sought to allay sailors' fears by stating *'a Greenland voyage is found by experience to be the healthiest in the world'*. But such assurances had no effect. In 1761 the Bristol Journal

Joseph Walter's painting of 1844 shows an abandoned harbour. Note the three-masted ship being towed by a steam tug along the Avon and a Severn trow slipping into the remains of the harbour. To the left is what survives of the warehouses and William Tregoe's house

announced that the Whale Fishery Company had been dissolved. Could there have been another reason? John Latimer refered to *'the oderiferous cargoes'*. The stench apparently was appalling and the Dock's influential neighbours must have had something to say about it, even in an age when unpleasant odours were more tolerated than today!

Decline of the Dock

Samuel Rudder in his New History of Gloucestershire observed in 1779 that *'the dock has been utterly abandoned for several years'*. Matthew's Guide and Directory of 1794 confirmed that *'it has been long disused and is now in ruins'*. The enterprise failed on a number of counts. Firstly, the consortium underestimated the problems of getting cargoes from Sea Mills to the city centre. Stoke Bishop's narrow roads were not suitable for heavy carts and the operators had to resort to loading goods onto barges for the final leg of the journey. Secondly, improvements to the course of the Avon made it easier for larger ships to navigate through the Gorge. Thirdly, keeping the dock mud free proved very costly.

After the whaling business was wound up, the dock never recovered. In January 1798 it was advertised to be let. We don't read of any takers. What happened to Joshua Franklyn, who, as Rudder wrote, had *'sunk the greater part of his fortune in this undertaking'*, we don't know, but as the harbour became a crumbling ruin it emerged as a picturesque magnet for artists.

The ruins, c1900, still attracting artists

Chapter Six

A Farming Revolution

1700-1801

During the two hundred years after the sale of the Sadleir land the population of Stoke Bishop barely grew.

But getting precise numbers is difficult as Stoke Bishop at this time was part of a larger Westbury Parish, which also included Redland, and therefore population figures that were produced were always higher than for Stoke Bishop itself. In the whole of Westbury Parish in 1712 there were only 140 houses and 650 inhabitants. Stoke Bishop village as such did not exist. This is confirmed by maps and paintings which show a very sparse spread of houses.

If there was a centre of population it would have been the New Dock. Even as a ruin, the warehouses still dominated the horizon. In an 1823 painting by Samuel Jackson, the eye is drawn to the buildings suggesting a place once bustling with life. Clustered around the warehouses and offices were shops and a public house, a more convenient hostelry for the dock workers than the Sea Mills Tavern at the end of the basin. The presence of Riverside House would have added to the social scene. William Tregoe's daughter married William Jackson, linking the docks to the Jacksons of Sneed Park.

Other clusters of population would centre around the two big houses, Stoke House and Sneed Park, where there would be annexes, cottages and gatehouses for those serving the estates.

Early Farms

The overwhelming source of livelihood in the 17th and 18th centuries was in agriculture. John Moore in his introduction to Clifton and Westbury Probate Inventories, 1609-1761 notes that the majority of entries were of yeoman and husbandmen (individual farmers) and the labourers working for them. In 1608, 95 out of a male population of 120 worked in agriculture. Samuel Rudder, the 18th

View of the River Trym at the junction of today's Trym Cross Road and Avon Way. The building on the left may once have been a mill, became Sea Mills Tavern and finally Hermitage farm before being demolished in the last century. In the distance can be seen Riverside House and the ruins of the dock buildings. Painted by Samuel Jackson in 1823

century historian, said in 1799 that Sneed Park *'has long turned into farms'*.

But agriculture was changing. The strip farming of the Middle Ages had largely vanished. Farmers were consolidating acreage and moving from arable to pasture. They found that the soil of the area was more suitable to producing a *'rich meadow and pastureland'* than growing crops. Only one field in the Sneed Park tithe map of 1836 was marked as *arable*, the rest was *pasture*. Allowing cattle to have free range spread disease and inhibited the introduction of new ideas of selective stock breeding. To prevent this, farmers began to enclose their land to allow their cattle to graze safely. The Druid Stoke House sale prospectus noted that *'the whole is within a ring fence'*. While a local surveyor of tithes in the 1830s wrote,

> *'all the* (enclosed) *farms... are dairy farms and in farms of this kind there are a great many pigs fattened and a great many potatoes grown for that purpose, to be used in the autumn, winter and early spring when whey from the dairy is scarce'.*

The landscape was much more open than today. Trees were sparse from years of felling and were not planted in mass until the next century. The main area of woodland in Stoke Bishop was still Sea Mills Wood (or Comb Wood on some maps) that had survived from Saxon times. Fragments, running from Glen Drive to Druid

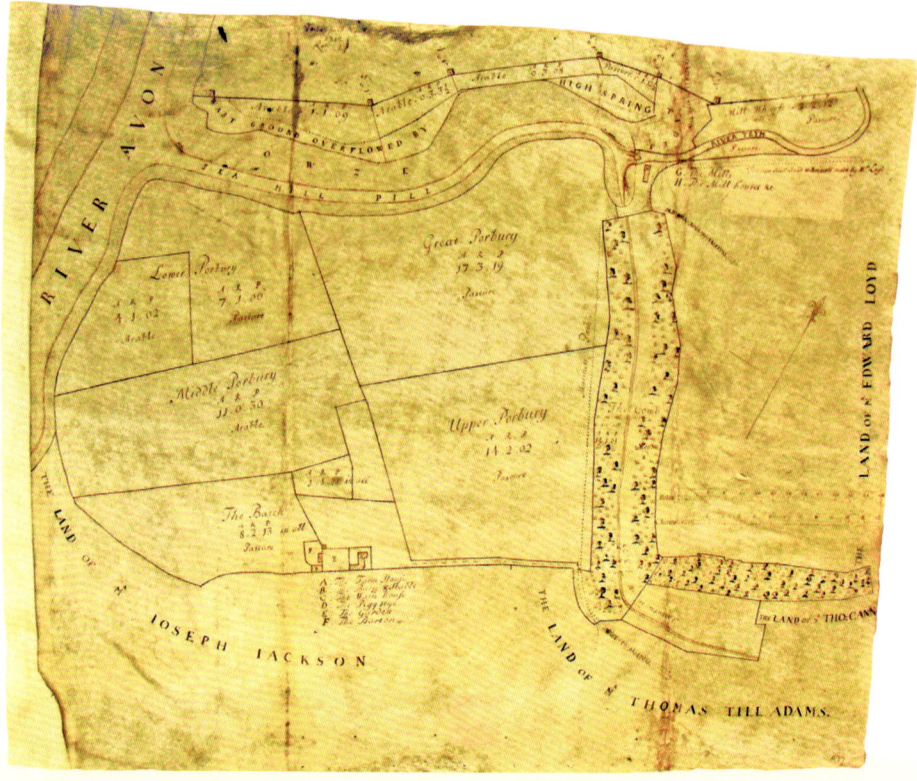

A 1712 Map (now in the National Archives) shows land around the mouth of the River Trym before the New Dock was built. Sea Mills Wood (Druid Woods) is on the right

Woods can still be seen. Whereas many farms in the country were growing to over 100 acres in size, Stoke Bishop seems to have bucked the trend with the majority of holdings being 80 acres or less. This is demonstrated by few farms being individually marked on the maps. The Parliamentary Map of 1840 mentioned only Sneed Park Farm and Sea Mills Farm. On a 1712 map, drawn before the Dock was built, a small farm is featured, most likely the holding of a single yeoman or husbandman and his family. It lay between the Jackson estate and what was then called the Sea Mill Pill on the Kings Weston estate. The farm buildings are vividly drawn and show a farm house, stable and barn, a wain house (for housing a cart), a pig-sty and a garden. The surrounding fields are marked *pasture*, except for one set aside for arable. It is a good example of a unitary holding and probably provided its owner with a fair income. The farmhouse would have been stone or brick built, have two storeys with walls a foot thick and be furnished with 4-7 rooms.

We can get a glimpse of what a cattle farm might have held by way of stock from an entry in the probate inventories. In 1707, Susanna Jayne, a widow of Stoke Bishop, left the following animals: *'Fourteen cows, Fore young beasts, Two mares, Fore sheep, Five pigs'*. The probate inventories give an idea too of the contents a family would have enjoyed. In 1710, William Price, a husbandman of Stoke Bishop, left the following:

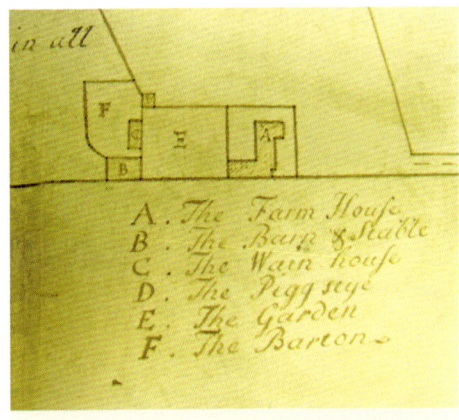

1712 map showing farm layout (detail)

> *'One bed, bedsteed and beding*
> *One chest of drawers and other lumber things in the parlour chamber*
> *Barrells, tubbs and other lumber things in the buttery*
> *One table board, one cupboard and three chairs in the hall*
> *One settle and tableboard, two chairs, one joyntstool in the kitchen*
> *Brass and pewter* (utensils) *and iron grate in the kitchen'*

Mills

In the Sadleir papers, mills were mentioned in the plural. There were, it seems, two mills on the lower Trym. The 1712 map marks one at the bottom of today's Avon Way where the river runs into the pill under Trym Cross Road. By the end of

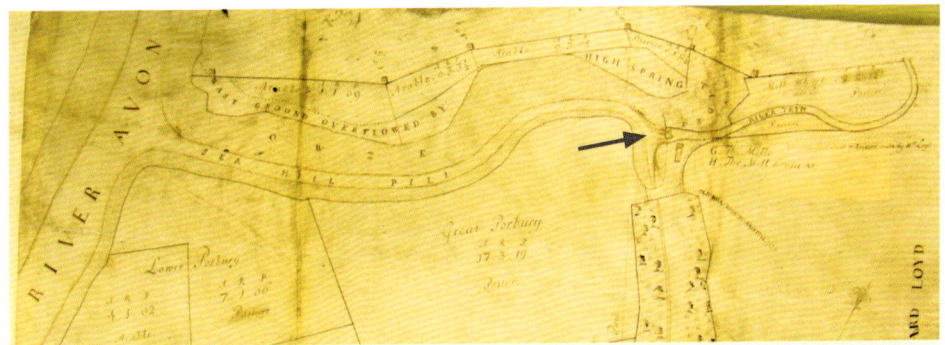

1712 map shows a mill and millhouse on the River Trym close to what was to become Trym Cross Road (arrow)

the century it no longer operated as a mill and had become the Sea Mills Tavern. Even later it would become a farm. The other mill was Clack Mill (sometimes called Black Mill), upstream of Shirehampton Road. This dated from the Middle Ages and went through a series of changes of use. An 1805 lease described it as *formerly a water grist mill, afterwards a cutlers mill, then a snuff mill, since a colour mill and now … used in the manufacture of sal ammoniac* (ammonium chloride used in pyrotechnics), *hartshorn* (from the antlers of red deer used as a leavening in baking), *glauber salts* (a natural laxative) and *ivory black* (paint pigment)'. The lease also included *'133 acres of land for turnip husbandry'*. It may also once have been used as a fulling mill in the 16th century producing a cheap serge cloth.

Historian Peter Harris has suggested the name Sea Mills derives from *saye* the medieval word for serge. Rudder certainly refers to it as *Say-mills*. Clack Mill survived until the 20th century manufacturing iron railings until it was demolished in 1937. The site was bought by Bristol Corporation as a rural space for £3,000 in 1939. The current course of the Trym follows the mill's leat.

Stoke Bishop in this period seemed already to have taken on the mantle of affluence and desirability that was to characterise it in the decades to come. But it did not escape poverty entirely. Towards the end of the 18th century the country was faced with a severe economic crisis. The Napoleonic Wars had resulted in higher taxes, inflationary food prices and high unemployment leaving many people facing starvation and eviction.

In 1793 the landscape painter Julius Caesar Ibbetson visited Sea Mills and described how the abandoned dock buildings had *'fallen to decay, scarce a roof remains perfect and those buildings that are occupied, the inhabitants are as wretched as the hovels'*.

In 1801 there was a census. It was largely a simple counting of heads. Stoke Bishop's population had now grown to 1,293 and, although not yet affected to any great extent by having Bristol on its doorstep, the latter's relentless expansion would soon have an impact.

Clack Mill stood beside the River Trym above Shirehampton Road and the Mill House. The site is now a green space

Chapter Seven

Land Sale

Part 1 1800-1840

Sometime in the 1830s a string of elegant villas appeared at the bottom of Stoke Hill.

They are still there and at the foot of the hill an older but more modest house called Oak Lodge. They were inhabited by a new breed of citizen, and one that would characterise those who settled in the area during the next hundred years. Bristol's professional and mercantile classes, crowded into a noxious smelling centre, looked towards the Downs and saw the possibility of a country life close to the city. Access had been made easier by the turnpike road that ran down Stoke Hill.

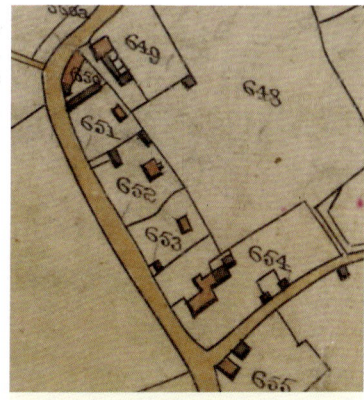

Left, 1825 map shows few houses on Stoke Hill. Above, the 1840 Tithe map shows a considerable increase

We do not know exactly when these Georgian and Regency style houses were built but at least two of them were on an 1825 map produced by estate agents, Y. & J.P. Sturge. One is oddly named *'Wise in Time'*. The others came a few years later, but they were all there by the time the 1840 Tithe Map was produced.

To us today they appear grand, but to the large landowners of the time they would have seemed modest, being narrow in dimension and having small gardens. They probably came about as a result of speculative development, contingent on the sale of parts of the Stoke House estate.

In 1829 Sir Henry Cann-Lippincott died. The terms of his will had stipulated that parts of the estate were to be put into trust ready to be sold to pay for death duties. This duly happened at an auction held by Y. & J.P. Sturge in August 1832. There was a scramble to acquire lots and those close to Stoke Hill had houses built on them.

Oak Lodge

Oak Lodge had the largest area of land and was the oldest. Historic England describes it as being built in a late Georgian style on the foundations of an earlier two storey 18th century building of around 1722 and it was certainly featured on the 1825 map. An early owner was the Hon. William Middleton Noel who had rented it to Thomas Burnell for £3 6s per annum. In the 1851 census a Thomas Crosby was living there and was described as an attorney at law. Modest though the house might have been, it still had all the facilities that a gentleman would require. In 1868 Oak Lodge was let and offered:

Oak Lodge with late Georgian front and a rural back, 2019

'nine rooms besides servants bedrooms with separate staircase, Pantries, Wine cellar, Stable, Coachhouses, large Yard, Greenhouse and most beautiful and productive Walled Garden well stocked with choicest fruit trees.'

Look behind the Georgian front and the house has what Historic England calls buildings *'predominantly agricultural in character'*, suggesting it may once have been a small farmhouse.

The Regency façade of Mulberry House, Stoke Hill

Mulberry House

Although close together, the houses are all individual in style and would have given their owners a sense of exclusiveness for which they probably craved. The visitor looking at Mulberry House could expect to see Jane Austen emerge at any moment. In the garden there is a mulberry tree that may have been planted when the house was built. On the outside wall there is a more recent plaque commemorating Hannah Casson. She wrote a book on aesthetics and a trilogy of novels reworking the medieval romance of Tristan and Iseult. She was living here when she fell ill and died in 1953.

Danes House

Danes House was built in 1880 onto an existing medieval cottage. Alan Smith, a later owner, remembered his father telling him that Winston Churchill stayed at Danes as guest of his father, who was Conservative Party Secretary. Churchill was in Bristol to deliver an election speech at the Colston Hall. It was probably on the occasion of his sudden resignation in 1955.

Vashni Lodge (Evendine, also known as the Portuguese House)

Sat atop its grassy knoll, this is the most imposing of the group. It was originally known as Vashni Lodge, an indication that it was regarded at the time as a modest

Vashni Lodge (Evendine, also known as the Portuguese House) and, right, Danes House

building. Not so today. It stands out with its eclectic architectural style. Tudor chimneys contrast with a Regency *tented wrought iron veranda*, conical striped awnings and fretted bargeboards. But impressive though the building is, it has another claim to fame.

Between 1878 and 1888 it was the residence of José Maria de Eça de Queiros. He was the Portuguese consul in Bristol. But he was also one of the major novelists of the 19th century and has been called the Portuguese Dickens. Much of Os Maias, regarded by some as his masterpiece, was written at Vashni. It tells of the various affairs of a young aristocrat in 1870s Portugal and is a reflection on the Portuguese monarchy's decline.

The Portuguese Ambassador and his wife unveiled a plaque at the house on Tuesday 5 April 1960. In his speech he said of Eça de Queiros that,

> *'he succeeded in writing some of the brightest and sunniest pages in his works whilst living under the overcast skies and the fog of northern latitudes'.*

But he went on to say that,

> *'of all the cities, Bristol assuredly held a very special place in Eça's heart, on account of the happy days of his early married life which he spent here.'*

69

Above, Eça de Queiros relaxes in his garden in Portugal. Right, unveiling the plaque outside Evendine (Vashni) on Stoke Hill

After that, the party made a hasty retreat to Harvey's wine cellars for a stiff glass of port. Harvey's, with its long association with the Portuguese wine trade, had donated the plaque.

The Portuguese House, as it is now colloquially known, continues to be a place of pilgrimage for those devoted to the novels of Eça de Queiros.

Stoke Lodge

William Munro, the elder, could look out of the window of Druid Stoke House and see his fields stretching to the new turnpike road (Shirehampton Road). The magnificent tree-lined avenue that ran from the turnpike to his house (Druid Stoke Avenue) had just been planted and he was looking to expand his estate. Beyond the turnpike lay fields belonging to Sir Henry Cann-Lippincott, who had just died, and as we saw earlier part of his estate had been put in trust to be sold. This included the fields Munro gazed at and when they came on the market in 1832, he lost no time in bidding for them. He acquired, after some legal wrangling over entitlement, two plots of land and two years later a third plot called Brownfields on which sat a *'cottage, tenement or dwelling house with the garden thereunto adjoining'*. He now went to work creating a substantial mansion on the site (Stoke Lodge), in the popular Tudor Gothic style of the day (see also Howecroft and Downside). The original

Druid Stoke House, 1897, with avenue of trees (today's Druid Stoke Avenue)

cottage was incorporated into the design of the house and an additional storey added. Munro never lived in the house. Did he intend to or was it a speculative development? It was certainly designed for a gentleman of substance wanting a rural life close to the city having all the attributes of genteel living – fourteen rooms, servants quarters, stabling and 33 acres of land. A later brochure stated, *'to persons resident in the neighbourhood of Clifton, the situation of Stoke Lodge, and its peculiar beauties, need no commendation; but strangers who have only heard generally of the exquisite scenery between Clifton, Durdham Down, and the mouth of the Avon, can form but a faint idea of the charms of this most desirable property'.*

The next owner was Thomas Bowman, an upright Bristol merchant, who bought the property from William Munro in 1841. He died unexpectedly in 1848 *'to the inexpressible grief of his afflicted wife and son'.* Bowman's widow, Mary Anne, was forced to leave Stoke Lodge. As Helen Powell, Stoke Lodge historian, puts it, *'she was turfed out of her home and all her belongings sold from under her, because that's just how things were done back then'.* Married women were not allowed to inherit property, a situation only reversed in 1882 when the Married Women's Property Act was introduced.

The Lodge was sold to solicitor George Pope of Cotham. The property now included a new wall along the turnpike (which is still there). By 1861 George was clearly enjoying his new role as country gentleman, as in the Census of that year, he described himself as *'landed proprietor'.* He was rearing a herd of Kerry cows and selling specimen pelargoniums. In an advert dated 30 December 1865, he offered *'ten tons of capital swedes, topped and cleaned for immediate use'* at 21 shillings a ton.

Helen Powell notes that *'by 1861 the estate has reached 'peak staff' with a cook, parlourmaid and housemaid living in, but also three families in the new servants' cottages, a coachman and his wife, a 'Labouring Gardener' with his wife and five children; and the gardener and his wife and two children. Altogether 21 people were living and working on the Stoke Lodge estate'.*

The Tudor Gothic style of Stoke Lodge is clearly seen in its southern aspect

Mercantile Grandees

George Pope died on 6 January 1888 and the house was occupied by a succession of Bristol's great mercantile families. First to move in were members of the Budgett dynasty. They had made their money from the wholesale grocery business, which they ran with a strict observance of Methodist principles. Daily prayers were held in their Nelson Street premises. The founder's grandson William Edward Budgett lived at Stoke Lodge with his wife Georgina, daughter Evelyn and five live-in servants. Like his predecessor, he also kept cattle, in his case a fine herd of Jersey cows, whose dairy products quickly became popular locally. The Western Daily Press wrote,

'the beautiful neighbourhood of Stoke Bishop and Clifton Down being very populous, this dairy soon obtained a great local reputation, and a demand arose, not alone for the butter, but for the cows that produced it, and some of these were therefore occasionally sold'.

Sadly the herd outgrew the estate and William Edward was forced to sell his beloved cows, although he did eventually restock.

Next to move in was Edward Burnett James, a partner in the tobacco firm of Edwards, Ringer and Bigg, which was eventually to join W.D. & H.O. Wills and eleven other companies to form Imperial Tobacco. He held most of the civic positions, being Master of the Merchant Venturers, High Sheriff of Bristol and twice Lord Mayor. He was knighted by Edward VII on the occasion of the King's visit to Bristol to open the Royal Edward Dock in Avonmouth.

Stoke Lodge was host to numerous garden parties and charity events, where the cream of Bristol society was invited *'to a day in the country'*. In 1901 100 soldiers from the Bristol Crimea and Indian Mutiny Veterans' Association were entertained to a *'sumptuous tea'*, wandered about the grounds and gardens, and *'indulged in a number of outdoor amusements, the Formidable band discoursing popular music'*. In November 1900 adverts in the local press announced that Mrs James was at home to receive guests during Advent week and on the second and fourth Tuesdays of each month.

Edward Burnett James

When the James family moved out to Leigh Woods and then back to Stoke Bishop, they settled in Springfort, close to the Downs, while Claude Fry and his family took up residence at Stoke Lodge.

Claude was a member of the Bristol chocolate company J.S. Fry & Sons, and at the time he was living in Stoke Lodge the company was enjoying its boom years. Between 1860 and 1907 it opened seven new factories in Bristol and employed 4,500 workers. The staffing level at Stoke Lodge was as high as ever. Besides the Fry family of four there were six servants: a cook, kitchen maid, parlour maid, house maid, nurse and under-nurse. In the Lodge cottages lived Peter Painter, the chauffeur, and his wife Emma, and the gardener, Herbert Chard, with his wife Annie and two children. Social occasions continued although probably not in a riotous way.

Claude Fry

Opening of the Royal Edward Dock at Avonmouth on 9 July 1908. Sir Edward Burnett James as Lord Mayor (left) accompanies the King, Edward the VII, and Queen Alexandra. The Royal Yacht Victoria and Albert is in the background

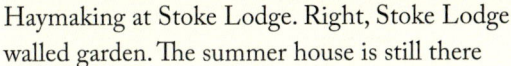
Haymaking at Stoke Lodge. Right, Stoke Lodge walled garden. The summer house is still there

The Frys were Quakers and in their factories they posted rules such as never use *'a profane oath or any other improper expression or a person who takes food in a disagreeable or noisy way is never a nice companion'.* When Field Marshal Sir Douglas Haig, commander of the British Expeditionary Force on the Western Front, visited Bristol in 1920, he was accompanied around the city by Mr and Mrs Claude Fry and was their guest at Stoke Lodge. *'The eminent soldier greatly pleased the children by visiting Stoke Bishop School.'* Groceries, tobacco and chocolate were three important products represented at Stoke Lodge. There was a fourth – brewing, but across the valley towards the Downs.

Downside

The biggest tranche of land, that was carved from the Stoke House estate in the Cann-Lippincott auction, was that purchased by Alfred George. He built Downside (later Wills Hall) around 1832 and his new demesne stretched from the Downs to what is now Shaplands. For 62 years he was partner in the Bristol brewery, Georges & Co Ltd, later shortened to Georges Brewery, which had been bought by the family in 1788. The Company was famous for its porter, a strong black ale, which took its name from the Covent Garden porters, who drank it copiously. An advert in Felix Farley's Journal for 1794 said that *'P. George, Bristol Porter and Beer Company will deliver in barrels and half barrels their Porter to all towns and villages within five miles of the City and is sold at Fourpence per Quart'.* Brewing was a lucrative trade. Water for the first half of the 19th century was often

A garden party in the 1890s at Downside (now the University of Bristol's Wills Hall)

not fit to drink, so people turned to beer which they drank at all meals. At one time Bristol had 240 inns, taverns and alehouses and that included Stoke Bishop.

In 1829 Alfred George married Eliza Oldham Edwards, daughter of a wealthy banker living at Redland Court. Her dowry gave Alfred the funds to build Downside, a substantial house in the Gothic style made popular in the 18th century by Horace Walpole's Strawberry Hill house near Twickenham. But for a man of such prominence Alfred George has remained elusive. No portrait of him has come to light. He eschewed public office and preferred to live quietly at Downside. But he is recorded on maps and on the deeds of property he bought and he worked tirelessly behind the scenes. When he died in 1878 the Bristol Times and Mirror wrote of him: '*He was a man of excellent judgement and good business abilities, but being indisposed to public office, he lived the quiet, retired, and useful life of a country gentleman, much esteemed by all those who knew him*'. David Wright, the new vicar of St Mary Magdalene praised him for being '*one of the first founders and foremost helpers of this church*'. His grave is in the churchyard.

He was succeeded by his son William Edwards George. The strange spelling of his middle name was in fact his mother's maiden name as we have seen. She

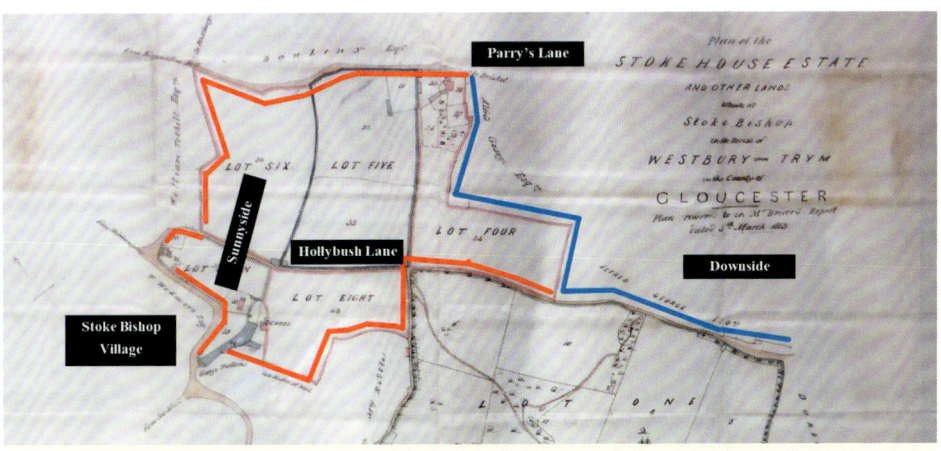

The George estate. The blue line shows the boundary of land purchased in 1832, the red line the enlarged estate created from the 1869 purchase

was of the Edwards family of Redland Court. William was a much more up front character. He extended the the estate to the boundary with The Grove on Druid Hill in 1869 and unlike his father used Downside as the venue for lavish social gatherings. In 1881 he hosted the West Gloucestershire Farmers' Club annual show and three years later the Stoke Bishop and Sneyd Park Rose and Fruit Show Society exhibition. Like his neighbours he kept livestock. An advertisement from March

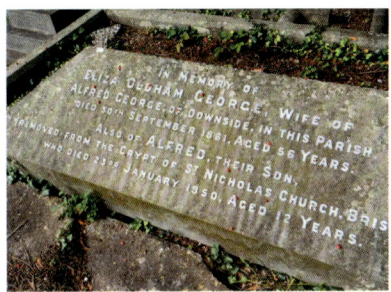

Alfred George's grave in St Mary Magdalene churchyard

1882 in the Bristol Mercury sought a man to take charge of a few cows, pigs and poultry *'upon a gentleman's grounds'* and his family, if he had any, must be *'small'*.

His diary shows the busy life that he led. In one week in July 1885 he attended a meeting of the Vice Presidents of the Bristol Conservative Union and a meeting of the School Managers of Stoke Bishop School. He inspected the connection of the Bristol water works company's mains pipe to *'my new Cottages'*. These probably referred to Sunnyside. Then later he noted *'Forgot Committee Meeting at the Brewery!'* He could be forgiven. He had eight children by two marriages. His second marriage in 1895 was to Thomasina (or Ina) Prittie Perry. The wedding took place in Ireland where William had property in County Antrim. The couple produced a baby boy, William John Hastings.

Family photographs of life at Downside in the 1890s

William Edwards George on the lawn at Downside

William Edwards George with second wife Ina

The terraced garden at Downside

The terraced garden at Downside (Wills Hall) today

Over the years a complex of gardens was created at Downside. Serpentine drives, paths meandering through woodland embraced an elaborate layout of formal gardens. There were pools and glasshouses to house William's collection of exotic plants. Downside became the epitome of a country gentleman's estate.

The Glen

On the 1840s Tithe Map, three other grand houses were featured, but all with smaller acreages. The oldest was The Glen erected around 1815, on a plot of land purchased in 1799, that covered roughly an area from Glen Drive to Old Sneed Avenue. Its first occupant was Clifton resident, Abraham Hillhouse, who owned the Albion shipyard, later to become Charles Hill and Sons. He was succeeded by an Alfred Claypole and then around 1875 by John Chetwood-Aiken, a director of Stuckey's Bank. He played a prominent role in civic life, being a JP and a member of the council. He also had aspirations to the peerage and in 1892 appealed to the House of Lords to become Baron of de Wahull (Bedfordshire). His claim failed and as the Gloucester Journal later reported, *'there was an absence of Parliamentary records showing that his ancestors sat in Parliament, but there was no question as to the pedigree'.*

Top, John Chetwood-Aiken; above, The Glen

The Pearman Family

For fifteen months between 1854 and 1856 the Pearman family rented The Glen. Alfred Pearman was a respected wine merchant in Wallingford in the Thames Valley. He was also a Quaker and a strong supporter of the temperance movement. His daughter, Emily, later wrote of her father's conflict of conscience.

> *'I cannot say that he ever came to the conviction that he was decidedly in the wrong… but he decided that as he certainly would not bring up his children to the same business, it would be well to enter upon some other line if a suitable opening offered.'*

A friend in Westbury-on-Trym secured him a partnership with a local man, Alfred Tuckett from Siston, who was planning to expand *'a large foreign trade in drain pipes, and in bricks for home demand'*. The firm's brickworks were at Shirehampton and so Alfred brought the Pearman family to Stoke Bishop. Emily wrote a vivid pen portrait of the village.

The Glen from Druid Hill

'Before Christmas, 1854, we were settled in the lovely village of Stoke Bishop, three miles out of Bristol on the road to Shirehampton. We were all delighted with such a lovely country home. The hilly rambling garden contained all the known English fruits, even quinces and medlars, besides a large fish pond well stocked with fish which was formed in a low part of the garden by a stream which ran outside the other parts of the premises, and divided them from the pretty hilly field crowned with trees which lay opposite to the drawing room window. An orchard stretched up the lane which divided it from Sneed Park, where at that time Alfred and Mary Waterhouse lived with all their family except their now famous son, Alfred Waterhouse RA, the great architect.'

Alfred Waterhouse was the designer of the Natural History Museum.

Emily Pearman's delightful drawings of the Glen (left) with its terraced gardens and (right) the walled pleasure garden and fish pond

Interestingly, one of his first commissions in 1854 was a set of stables for his father in Sneed Park. Sadly the Pearman idyll was not to last.

> 'Very soon after settling at Stoke Bishop, our father found that the whole business arrangement with Alfred Tuckett was a complete failure, and he was only too thankful to be able at once to dissolve the partnership and retire, leaving his money locked up in the concern never to see it again.'

Howecroft

In 1828 Jeremiah Hill of Down House in Westbury, Jeremiah Osborne of Bristol, a gentleman, Samuel Waring of Bristol, a merchant and William Ball of Bristol, a gentleman, took out a lease on a meadow called Howe Croft, bounded to the north east by Eastmead Lane. It cost them £642. By 1837 a house of the same name had been built on the meadow. Originally spelt How Croft, it was later elided to Howecroft. It was a grand edifice in the familiar Gothic style of the period and became the home of the aforementioned Samuel Waring and his family.

Howecroft in the 1950s. The Monkey Puzzle tree and Scots Pine survived until quite recently

The Guinness Connection

In the city archives there is a record of a mortgage for the lease of Howecroft being taken out in 1837. The names on the document included Samuel Waring. In addition were a number of names from Dublin, among them Arthur Guinness, William Lunell Guinness and Benjamin Lee Guinness. They were the sons of Arthur Guinness, the founder of the Dublin brewery. After their father's death they were running the brewery jointly. At first glance it is a mystery as to why they should purchase a lease on a property in Stoke Bishop, but the explanation lies in the activities of Samuel Waring.

The Guinness brothers had family connections with Bristol. Their sister and nieces lived in the city. It was also at this time that they were seeking to expand business outside Ireland and Bristol as England's second city, with good transport and trading links, seemed an obvious choice. They chose Samuel Waring, with his reputation for business preceding him, as their agent. For a time trade boomed. On 25 November 1825, for example, 75 hogsheads (large barrel), 25 barrels and 50 half barrels of Guinness porter sailed into Bristol in the Ann and not long after Waring was receiving consignments two or three times a week. All went well until 1837 when Waring invested a large sum of money in railway stock, which failed, throwing him into debt and an inability to pay his mortgage on Howecroft, hence the intervention of the Guinness brothers.

Interestingly another signatory on the lease was John Purser. He was the head brewer at Guinness, as had been his father and as was to be his son, both called John Purser! His name on the lease document suggested he might be seeking to set up a Guinness brewery in Bristol. But the Guinness archives in Dublin could not find any evidence for this,

An Austin car outside Howecroft, 1950s

which if so was probably a relief to Howecroft's influential neighbour, Mr George!

From 1905, Howecroft was the home of the Pratten family until it was demolished in 1969.

The Grove

The third house was built later, on a plot of land adjacent to Stoke Lodge. The Grove was completed around 1840 and was the home of the Tothill family for over sixty years. In style it eschewed the gothic and was more classical in appearance. William Tothill married Hannah Darby in 1818 at the Coalbrookdale Quaker Assembly. William, described in the marriage register as a Bristol merchant, had married into the Darby dynasty, the family of ironmasters, who, at Iron Bridge in Shropshire, pioneered the manufacture of iron, with their iron foundries becoming the cradle of the industrial revolution. There had been

The Grove

frequent contact between the Bristol ironmasters and Coalbrookdale and when William Tothill brought Hannah to live in The Grove he was described in the 1841 Census as *'ironmaster'*.

A number of letters written by Hannah from Stoke Bishop are in the Iron Bridge Museum. They illustrate the political world she brought to her safe rural enclave. They were written at a time of industrial unrest and agitation to repeal the restrictive Corn Laws, which were seen as responsible for the nation's ills. A new democratic movement called Chartism, which called for, among other things, annual parliaments, secret ballots and votes for all adult men, was seen as a violent threat to the government. Hannah was worried both for herself in Stoke Bishop and for her brother who was the ironmaster in Ebbw Vale, while showing sympathy for the protests. In a letter to her sister dated 26 August 1842 she wrote,

'My dear sister, must we not think of the legislators who have framed the cruel laws that have at length worn out the patience of the suffering people not only by taxing their very bread but restricting the commerce of the country and destroying the labour by which their lives can be sustained... We are happy and very thankful that those so dear to us have been preserved in safety and I hope from personal harm which thus far is our case in this neighbourhood. In the City there are many Chartists and upwards of 5000 persons destitute of employment who might naturally think it little harm to take from those who can well spare of their abundance, but the state of the Welsh iron works makes me even more anxious tho' happily the broad Severn rolls between us.'

In the event the repeal of the Corn Laws in 1846, and the torrential rain that dampened the great Chartist march against Parliament two years later, took the sting out of the threat and Hannah could return

'to the excitement of committees, meetings, flower shows and exhibitions of paintings with long walks and calls.' On 19 June 1851 she was again in crusading mood. She saw *'great benefits of Free Trade* (that) *seem to have given new life to our country at least. Would that they could emancipate the groaning nations of Europe from their present oppressors who seem bent on restoring both the military and ecclesiastical desolation of the dark ages'.*

Hannah clearly maintained a strong connection with her roots in Coalbrookdale as their three children were born there. Son William, who inherited the Grove, was described in the 1881 Census not as an ironmaster, but as a *'landed proprietor'*. Sarah, as we have seen, married William Munro of Druid Stoke. Rebecca, the second daughter, died unmarried. After living *'on own means'*, William died in 1906 without issue and the house was bought by a Charles William Allen, a manufacturer of corsets. Sadly he died shortly after arriving at The Grove in 1909. His son, Charles Edwin Allen, took over the business.

These had been the years when Stoke Bishop enjoyed to the full its reputation as a retreat from the commercial bustle of the city and where members of the mercantile class could live out their lives as country gentlemen. It was a settled and quiet place, certain of its position in society, but soon all that was to change.

Chapter Eight

Land Sale

Part 2 1853-1869

The Jackson family of Sneed Park never had a high profile.

Not much has appeared of their private lives and as the 18th century drew to a close the house and estate descended to Robert's daughter, Mary. She never married and when she died in 1811, without obvious heirs, she left Sneed Park to a number of relatives scattered around the country. One of these, James Martin of Ovebury, took on the tenancy of the house and the estate. When he died, the Martins remained there as tenants, but with so many parts of Sneed Park in the ownership of different members of the family, it became increasingly difficult to make the estate financially viable.

In 1850 the current tenant, James Thomas Martin, explored the possibility of developing the estate. But there was a huge obstacle. Mary Jackson's will had created a number of restrictive covenants that were designed to keep the estate from being broken up. Yet James Martin could see Bristol and Clifton approaching towards him across the Downs, hungry for new land to expand into. He had at his side William Baker, an ambitious builder, who could also see the potential for development. The solution the two came up with was to apply to Parliament to have the covenants on the will overturned.

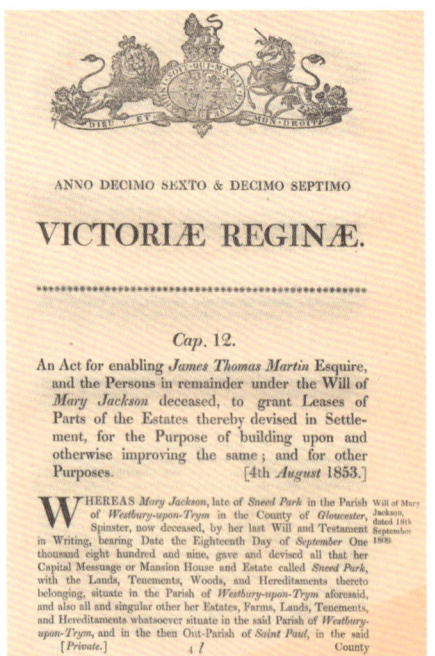

ANNO DECIMO SEXTO & DECIMO SEPTIMO

VICTORIÆ REGINÆ.

••

Cap. 12.

An Act for enabling *James Thomas Martin* Esquire, and the Persons in remainder under the Will of *Mary Jackson* deceased, to grant Leases of Parts of the Estates thereby devised in Settlement, for the Purpose of building upon and otherwise improving the same ; and for other Purposes.　　　[4th *August* 1853.]

WHEREAS *Mary Jackson*, late of *Sneed Park* in the Parish of *Westbury-upon-Trym* in the County of *Gloucester*, Spinster, now deceased, by her last Will and Testament in Writing, bearing Date the Eighteenth Day of *September* One thousand eight hundred and nine, gave and devised all that her Capital Messuage or Mansion House and Estate called *Sneed Park*, with the Lands, Tenements, Woods, and Hereditaments thereto belonging, situate in the Parish of *Westbury-upon-Trym* aforesaid, and also all and singular other her Estates, Farms, Lands, Tenements, and Hereditaments whatsoever situate in the said Parish of *Westbury-upon-Trym*, and in the then Out-Parish of *Saint Paul*, in the said
[*Private.*]　　4 *I*　　　　County

First page of the Martin Act 1853

On 4 August 1853 a private Act was passed *'enabling James Thomas Martin... under the Will of Mary Jackson deceased, to grant Leases of Parts of the Estates... for the Purpose of building upon and otherwise improving the same'*. The terms of the Act foresaw the opportunity for development. It noted how *'the devised Estates are near to the City of Bristol and to Clifton, and the Population of that City and of Clifton has of late Years greatly increased'*. Thus said the Act, proximity of the pastures of Sneed Park to the expanding conurbations made them the perfect place to erect *'detached villas and other houses'*. With the Act passing into law, William Baker lost no time in getting to work.

William Baker

We know little of William Baker's origins. Michael Morgan in his 1978 book Sneyd Park thought he was probably a self-made man. In the Directories of 1841 he appeared as a tiler, plasterer and house painter. By 1852 he described himself as a builder and contractor, with premises in Canons Marsh, where he owned a steam saw mill. Most importantly, the Act has him as signatory to the schedule of lands earmarked for development. It is clear that even before the Act was passed, he was identified as a principal developer.

William Baker came to live in Sneed Park in 1859, most likely to be on the spot to oversee his many building projects. He bought what in the schedule was described as Sneed Park Farmhouse, which he later renamed Sneyd Park Villa, presumably to distance the house from its agricultural roots. Although in the 1861 Census he was described as a *'builder employing 160 men and farmer of 160 acres employing three men and three boys'*, his agricultural acres quickly became building plots and the farm itself was relocated on park land close to today's Mariners Drive. When Baker died in 1882 Sneed Park Villa was renamed Downend. It was changed again to Braidlea in 1889 and is known today as the Well House, the only property on the west side of Ivywell Road.

Sneed Park Farmhouse or the Well House, Ivywell Road

First villas built in Sneyd Park on the junction of The Avenue and Hazelwood Road

Severn and Avon Houses

The first houses to be built under the new arrangement were surprisingly a pair of semi-detached villas. Severn and Avon (along with a detached house opposite) stood within spitting distance of the Well House. William Baker's name appeared on the original deed, dated 1861, leasing for 1,000 years to Ellis Lee Sanders a plot of land from the area identified in the schedule of the Martin Act as Down Leaze for the purpose of erecting *'not more than two dwellinghouses and an entrance or service lodges with suitable stables coach houses and outbuildings'*. Work began on the houses in 1863 and was completed around 1866. The houses soared to a height of four stories, but were spare and gaunt in appearance and seemed haphazardly placed in the middle of what was once a farm. Their most distinctive features were the decorative bricks around the windows and doors, reminiscent of the Byzantine style of warehouses in Bristol docks. This may have influenced William Baker as he could see the warehouses from his Canon's Marsh office. Another aspect of the building was the location of the entrances on the side of the house, which was to be a feature of later speculative building. It gave the occupants the illusion of entering their own detached house.

William Vachell, an iron merchant, leased Severn House and in 1893 bought the freehold to both properties from Ellis Saunders. He had a noted daughter, Ada Vachell. She devoted her life to helping the poor and *'handicapped'* and established a number of institutions to help the disadvantaged, among them social clubs for *'factory girls and crippled boys'*, an invalid children's school and an *'Apprentice Scheme for the Handicapped'*. She died in 1923. There is a plaque to her in Bristol Cathedral. In 2002 she was included in a book celebrating the lives of 100 Women of Bristol. The Vachells moved out in 1925 to be succeeded by Robert and Florence Everett. This family photograph shows the move taking place.

Removal wagons pulled by a steam tractor stand outside Severn House

In 1866 John Ellis bought the lease to Avon House, the other half of the building. He was another corset manufacturer.

Baker's Town

The next houses built were grand mansions and they naturally secured the best views overlooking the Gorge. The names of many are now only ghosts that have attached themselves to the lodges, roads, flats and new-builds of today's Sneyd Park. Drinagh, The Knoll, The Oak, Avon Grove, Avon Hirst, Seawall Villa, Locarno, Tower Hirst are all featured on the OS Map of 1844-1888. Other houses filled the hinterland, among them Towerleaze, Oakfield, Hillside, Woodside, Hazelwood, Avonleigh, and Manora. Such was the speed of development, the whole area became known ironically as Baker's Town. A tongue in cheek editorial in the Bristol Times, in 1855, talked of *fashionable refugees who will be flying to Baker's Town to escape the Bristol tax-gatherer'* and, the writer went on, *'should I myself live to be a Bristol patriarch I expect one day to buy my gloves in Cook Street, leading out of Sneyd Square'*.

To enhance the affluence of the estate, wide avenues were constructed between the houses, planted with trees to give the new residents the illusion they were still living in the countryside: limes in the Avenue, Scots pine in Church Road, horse chestnut in Mariner's Drive, plane trees in Hazelwood Road. Exotic varieties were planted in gardens and along drives, cedar of Lebanon, Wellingtonia, western red cedar, Japanese red cedar. They have all now grown to maturity and both enhance and cause problems for their neighbourhoods. As a tree expert has observed, *'if you plant trees of the same species along a road at the same time, they are likely to die at the same time'*.

Cycling along Rockleaze around 1900

After about 1880 a new type of house arrived, the speculative town-house, designed to attract the emerging professional class, which wanted a pleasant house in the countryside but which couldn't afford or didn't need a grand mansion. First to go up were the houses facing the Downs along Rockleaze, then from 1891 the construction of the Downleaze estate began. These semi-detached houses were built to similar dimensions. All had side entrances with a variety of external facades giving them the appearance of individuality. Accommodation was spacious, yet it was a dense development with small gardens and little stabling and few amenities.

A professional carpet beating facility was set up on the Downs to service the houses, plagued by dust from unmade roads, but there were so many complaints about the dust that the Downs Committee shut the operation down. Carriages to

Semi-detached houses in Rockleaze. Although built to the same dimensions, all the facades have individual features

This row of elegant semis runs behind the Downs and shows how tightly packed the Downleaze estate was

and from the estate churned up the turf and a road from Belgrave Road in Clifton to Ivywell Road was begun by Bristol Council to give easier access to Sneyd Park. This met a howl of protest and the project was abandoned. The residents of Sneyd Park saw it as an attempt by Bristol to incorporate the area into the City, which was the last thing they wanted. The road was turned back into a footpath and the turf replaced. As Michael Morgan observes: *'Why people with the money to afford these houses did not from the beginning insist on better access and gardens remains a mystery'.*

Stoke House 1829-1869

Across the Turnpike (Stoke Hill) Stoke House was also facing change. With no heirs to succeed him, Sir Henry Cann-Lippincott moved out of the house around 1820 and it became occupied by a R.B. Johnstone and then Isaac Cooke, a solicitor, until it was bought, on Cann-Lippincott's death in 1829, by Abraham Gray Harford Battersby of the Bristol banking family and owners of Blaise Castle. He sought to add new buildings and consulted with the celebrated architect and classical archaeologist, Charles Robert Cockerell, on the design of a classical styled conservatory. Cockerell was also responsible for installing a copy of the Parthenon Frieze in Blaize. The two seem to have fallen out and the conservatory never got built until much later. Harford Battersby died in 1851 and was succeeded by his son John Harford Battersby.

John Battersby Harford

The Harfords are a complicated family in that they were always changing their name. John Battersby Harford, on his marriage to Mary de Bunsen, daughter of the onetime Prussian Ambassador to the Court of St James, obtained a Royal Licence to change his name from Harford Battersby to Battersby Harford. The couple's arrival in Stoke House was to have a significant influence on the development of Stoke Bishop. J.B. Harford had never shown any interest in the family banking business and he devoted himself

John Battersby Harford as a young man

to the care of his tenants and property. He was among the first of Stoke Bishop's landowners to show a concern for social welfare and he was instrumental in the creation of Stoke Bishop's first church and its first school. But two events were to tear him away from Stoke House. First, he inherited Blaise on the death of his uncle in 1866. Second, he spent a lot of his time away from Stoke Bishop at Lampeter in South Wales where he had an estate and where he built a large Italianate house called Falcondale (hence Falcondale Road). In 1869, he decided to put Stoke House and the estate on the market.

Sale by Auction

The Times in an article on the 15 May 1869 wrote glowingly of Stoke House and spoke of '*the extensive views of Blaise Castle and the rich surrounding district of the Severn, Avon and Portishead*'. The views were more open then and to the residents of crowded Bristol they must have seemed breathtaking. The paper went on to describe the many facilities the house possessed and the beautiful pleasure grounds with their '*elegant conservatory, shrubberies, large and productive and well-stocked walled kitchen garden (the walls being clothed with choice fruit trees), vineries, storehouse, greenhouse, and other glass, potting and furnace houses and fruit rooms, also pine pit, ice-house and rookery*'. It all promised the ideal bucolic location for '*a Bristol merchant, banker or gentleman*'. But there was one other major attraction which an advert for the sale gave due prominence, stating that the estate was '*outside the City Boundaries and was free from heavy Taxes*'.

The auction took place at the White Lion in Broad Street at 12 o'clock sharp on Thursday 14 October 1869. The auctioneers were Messrs. Sherwood, Smith & Co. Over 90 acres of Stoke House parkland had been divided into 44 building lots. If we look closely at the prospectus we can see that, unlike the crowded development

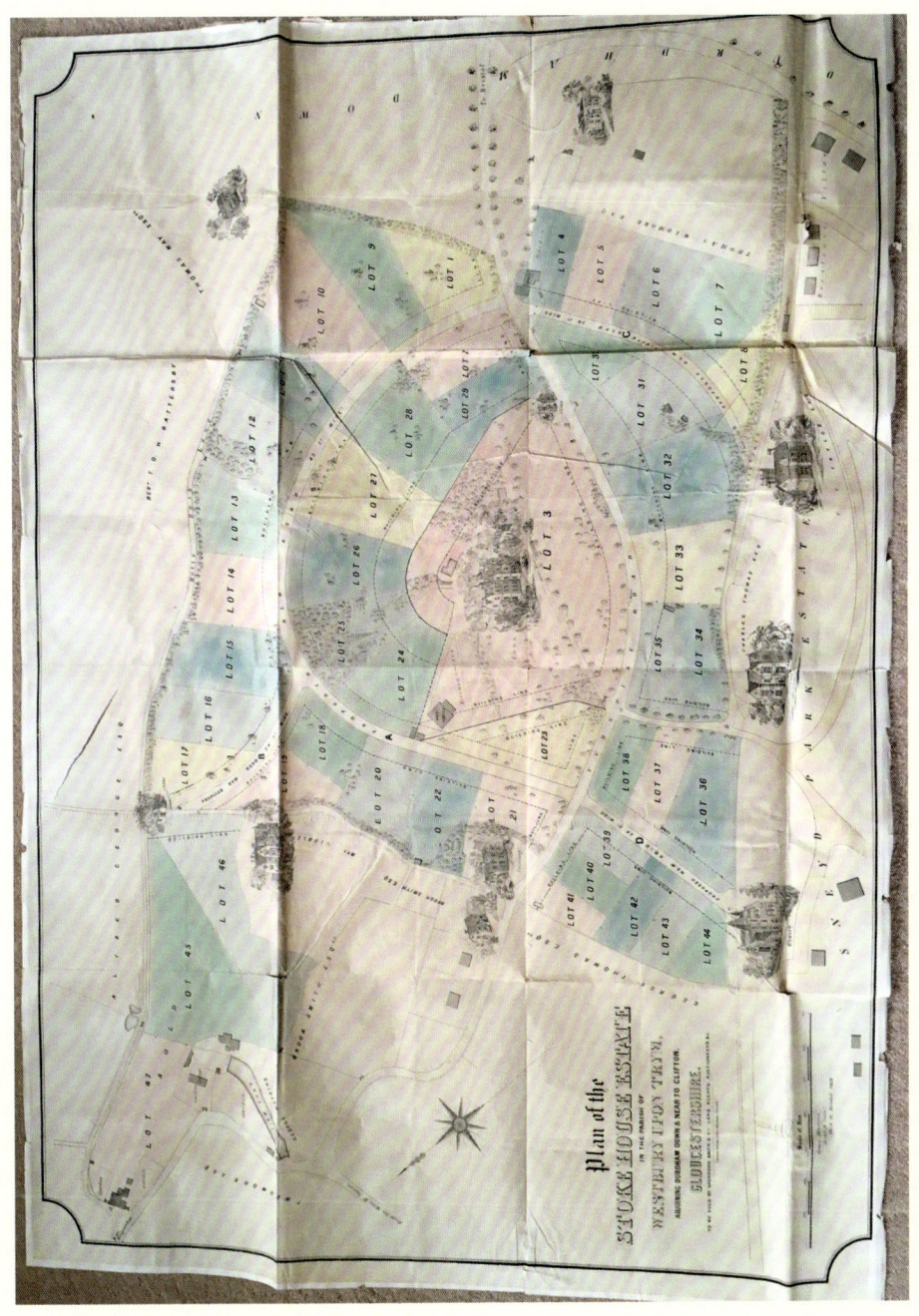

A beautifully drawn map of the Stoke House estate showing the exact division of the land into varying size plots. The Turnpike Road at the bottom of the picture is Stoke Hill and 'A' is the proposal for a new road which eventually becomes Stoke Park Road on the southern edge of Sneed Park, the plan here was to provide an estate of orderly and generously spaced villas. *'The Building Conditions'* were very strict. Only private residences could be erected. Each lot could have no more than two residences built on it and each residence had to be a good quality upmarket villa of no less than £1,000 in value. To enhance the appearance of the neighbourhood *'boundary fences... shall be built of good sound irregular jointed rubble masonry pointed and coped with bricks on edge'*, a requirement from which we continue to benefit today.

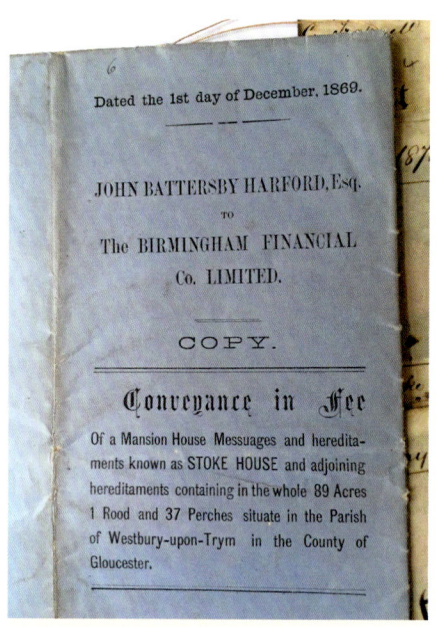

Stoke House conveyance Deed

New Houses

The house and estate was bought not by individuals but by The Birmingham Financial Co. Ltd., a holding company which then proceeded to resell the individual lots. It seemed to have only limited success and many of the lots remained vacant for many years. But a number of fine houses did get built. As we have seen, one purchaser was Battersby Harford's neighbour, William Edwards George. He acquired a plot on which in 1879 he built The Holmes as a dower house for his wife, should she become a widow, but it was never used. Other houses included Avonleigh, Marchlands, Stokeleigh, Severnleigh, Springfort, Waltham House and Claverton, all linked by a sweeping crescent (Stoke Park Road).

Mid 19th Century Stoke Bishop

We must now ask ourselves what effect this land rush was to have on Stoke Bishop. In the Census of 1841 the entries mainly related to rural occupations. Yeoman, agricultural labourer, gardener, blacksmith, farmer, the descriptions varied, but they all added up to an agrarian landscape. Only the larger landowners who had lately arrived described themselves by the trade they pursued in Bristol, for instance Alfred George entered *'porter brewer'*. Rockley House was headed by Edward Bevan who wrote *'butcher'*. In the same house lived John Brodie, *'grocer'* and James Culverwell, *'linen draper'*. If you were to look at a map for that year, you would see that buildings were thinly scattered with a small nucleus at the bottom of Stoke

Houses built on the Stoke House estate after the 1869 sale. Clockwise from top left, Stokeleigh, The Holmes, Springfort, Waltham House, Severnleigh

Hill. The Georgian houses aside, the cottages formed the main concentration of buildings in the centre of the village and these for the most part were inhabited by agricultural labourers.

According to the Victoria County History of Gloucestershire the population of Stoke Bishop in 1841 (including Redland) was 2,651. By 1871 it had risen to 10,187. The increase was of course the result of new houses that required servants to manage them. As early as the 1851 Census we can see *'agricultural labourer'* giving way to *'house servant'*, but soon the trickle became a flood. Even the most modest of the new semi-detached villas had room enough for two or three live-in servants. The Glen in the 1891 Census had five members of the family living there, attended by a cook, parlourmaid, housemaid and kitchenmaid. Up the road in Stoke House, the 1851 Census registered 19 persons. Beside the family of six, there was a housekeeper, lady's maid, laundry maid, two housemaids, kitchen maid, nurse, butler groom, two footmen and two children's nurses (not to mention the ground staff).

Stoke Cottages

Most distinctive of Stoke Bishop's surviving cottages is the row that once bordered Stoke Hill before it was by-passed. These were constructed at the end of the 18th century. A speculative date on one has 1786 as its origin. In the early days they were farm workers' cottages. The 1841 Census showed them being occupied by *'agricultural labourers'* and this changed little over the decades, although by 1891

18th century Stoke Cottages that are still lived in today

'*gardener*' had entered the list of occupations reflecting the needs of the big houses.

The 1891 Census has two interesting entries. John Board, brother of William Board, a gardener, described himself as a '*professional cricketer*'. Another referred to the end cottage in the row, called Glen Cottage. It had living there an Arthur Phipps and Henry Sansom, both described as '*Police Constables 1st Class*'. We have known there was once a police station in Stoke Bishop and it was most likely that it was in the centre of the village. Further evidence has recently come to light with the discovery of iron bars embedded in the wall of the end cottage, confirming the likelihood of this being the police station. Violet Watkins, growing up in Stoke Bishop remembered the police presence. '*Not sure how long the police station was there but it was there when I was small, Sergeant Barnes was there and after that it went to Sneyd Park. He would walk round on the beat every night*' and knock on the door '*if there was a light on*'.

Above, iron bars fitted to the window of Glen Cottage, confirming its former role as a police station; right, 1880s Ordnance Survey Map showing the strip gardens attached to Stoke Cottages and one outdoor privy

Gentrification by the middle of the 20th century had started to transform the cottages, but even in the 1960s some retained their original facilities as Christopher Smith remembers,

'*When Felicity and I first got married my father owned a* (pink) *cottage* (in the middle of the row of Stoke Cottages) *and he let us buy it at a very cheap price, £400, as a wedding present (we got married in 1967). He did it up, it needed doing up because when we first went round it with my father and the tenant, Mr Moss, whom my father was putting into much better accommodation, we found it had only electric light, no mains circuit, water was a tap outside the back door.'* (There was another surprise.) '*Mr Moss beckons me and says "Mr Smith, please come over here away from your intended" and he took me in one corner and said "the bucket's outside the back door." I didn't quite know what to say to that. What I discovered was that to flush the loo, which was an outhouse at the back shared by a number of cottages, you filled the bucket from the tap at the back! There was a tin bath hanging there as well and the gardens at the back didn't stretch out behind the houses, they actually ran parallel to the houses themselves in strips. Our garden was the end one of those strips.'*

New owners gradually added modern conveniences and updated the interiors. The most recent change has been to Glen Cottage itself, with the owner extending it using a galvanised steel frame rather than brick. This structure gives the interiors more space while keeping to the earlier footprint.

Above, extension constructed with galvnized steel frame; right, the partly finished restoration

Domestic Servants

With Stoke Bishop isolated from any centre of population, staff had to live in. From the records we find that servants, particularly young girls, could come from as far afield as Wales, the Forest of Dean or Somerset. In the 1871 Census The Grove had four servants, the cook, Mary Ann Lane, age 27, from Hereford, Elizabeth Court, a 55 year old lady's maid from Old Cleeve in Somerset, Rachel Groves, age 29, a parlourmaid from Penhow in Monmouthshire and Ellen Jarman, age 30, who was a housemaid from Porlock in Somerset. These women would have found themselves marooned in the houses they served. With its population growing, Stoke Bishop needed community facilities.

A carefully posed group of domestic and garden staff

Staff at The Glen

Chapter Nine

A New Church

1860

The owners of the big houses were wealthy, powerful and often men of faith.

Being in the parish of Westbury-on-Trym, their nearest church was a mile and a half away in Westbury, which meant every Sunday a three mile round trip along bumpy and unmetalled tracks. As more worshippers moved into the area, the idea of creating a church and forming a new parish locally became attractive.

David Wright, who was to become the first vicar, wrote *'to a certain number of resident gentry, the long distance of their homes and all the surrounding neighbourhood from their parish church of Westbury-on-Trym was felt as a serious disadvantage'.* Chief among these gentry was John Battersby Harford and it was to his house that a group of residents repaired in 1857 to consider the idea. They were men of influence and included George Pope of Stoke Lodge. They were often referred to as *'the Bristol Worthies'* on account of several of their number being included in two popular volumes of profiles entitled Bristol Worthies and Notable Residents compiled by A.B. Freeman that appeared at the turn of the century in 1907.

Despite their combined reputations, it must nevertheless have been an anxious gathering as they confronted the obstacles ahead of them. They first had to persuade the Ecclesiastical Commissioners that there were sufficient funds to build the church and then to endow the living. There were no grants. They had to do it themselves. Then came the tricky question: *'Does the incumbent of the parish in which the new church will be situated approve of the contemplated arrangements?'* The answer was a categorical *'No!'.* In fact William Cartwright, vicar of Westbury-on-Trym, was incandescent with rage, perhaps understandably. He was angry that he had not been consulted nor invited to the inaugural meeting and only learnt of it through the Bristol papers. He saw the whole scheme as a way *'to help a flagging building speculation... and second the wishes of a few wealthy individuals'.* It would deprive him of a good percentage of his already inadequate stipend, although the final agreement stipulated that he should receive the fees from weddings and funerals during his lifetime. His objections were overturned, but there was one more obstacle to be overcome. It was a requirement of a new parish that it had to have a population of over 300. In 1857 Stoke Bishop had 554 people living there, so it qualified.

First Steps

The estimated cost of the church was £2,500. It was planned to seat 350 with 200 seats being set aside for rental. William Baker donated a small plot of land for it to be built on, carved from an adjacent and much larger plot where he was to build Hillside (later called Heatherdale). The Conveyance Document, dated 30 October 1858, read *James Thomas Martin to the Ecclesiastical Commissioners of London: Conveyance of a land of Stoke Bishop in the parish of Westbury upon Trym in the County of Gloucester'* and was headed *'Stoke Bishop New Church Site'*. The postage stamp of

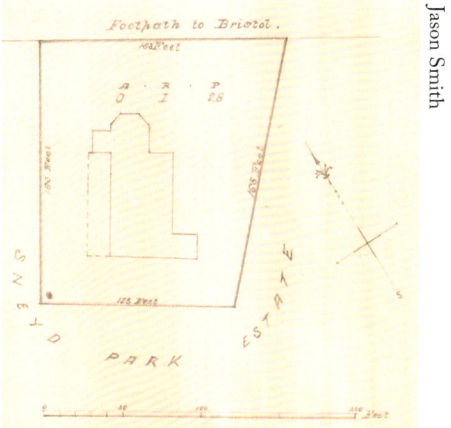

Jason Smith

Plan of proposed church on land donated by William Baker

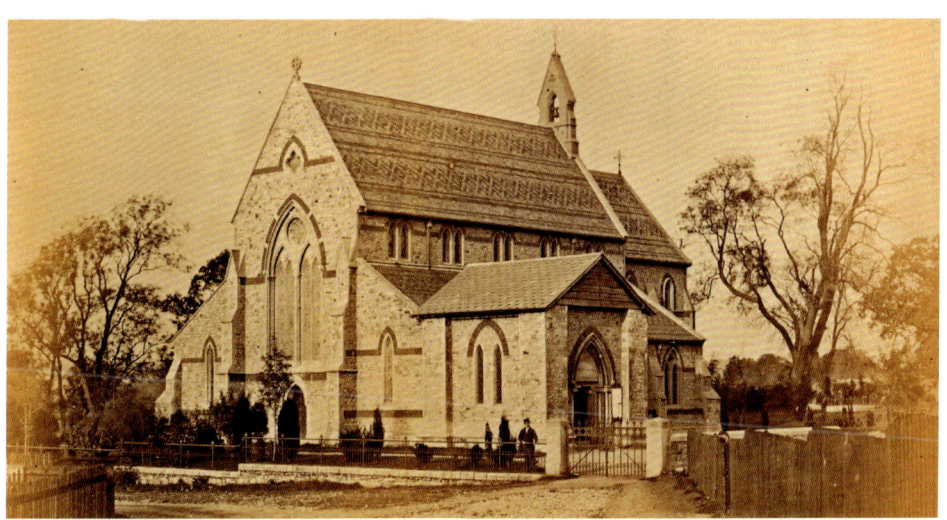

The Church in 1865 before the tower was built and the west end was extended

land overlooked the gates and lodge at the entrance to Sneed Park. Baker proposed the whole be enclosed by a boundary wall. The architect chosen was John Norton, formerly of Bristol and at the time practising in London. He was known for his high gothic style and he went on to design Tyntesfield, a huge mansion just south west of Bristol. The new church, which *stood alone among the fields'*, would look very different from the one today, but the later extended nave and graceful spire were always part of Norton's design, ready for when funds became available. The foundation stone was laid by John Scandrett Harford of Blaise Castle on 5 August 1858.

First Vicar

The land earmarked, the architect chosen, the next step was to choose a vicar. Battersby Harford suggested his brother the Revd. Thomas D. Harford Battersby, rector of Keswick, but he declined and advised his brother to extend his invitation to David Wright, a mutual acquaintance and a minor canon at Bristol Cathedral, *'because of his known character and the worth of his sermons as testified by many'*.

David Wright, Stoke Bishop's first vicar

At 43, David Wright became Stoke Bishop's first vicar. Related to the Wright family, who ran a Bristol publishing house, he was educated at Magdalen Hall (later Hertford College), Oxford, and was curate at St John the Evangelist, Clifton. He was a solid middle of the road Anglican, who was affable and much loved and who set the tone for the generations that followed. In the words of a later vicar, the Revd. Roy Henderson, *'he instinctively shrank away from controversial issues and it was in his nature to avoid them if he could'*. But there was one issue he felt passionate about and brought all his eloquence to bear in confronting it, and that was the ill treatment of animals. He was a tireless campaigner against the practice of vivisection and wrote often and eloquently about what he regarded as the evil of experimenting on live creatures in *'the interests of humanity'* (his italics).

> *'There must be a time coming when this great wrong... will have its place among those other dreadful things of the past over which the conscience of men... has at length prevailed and has afterwards looked back horror-struck and appalled that such things should ever have been.'*

He stepped down as vicar on 25 January 1895 after 35 years. He died on Ash Wednesday 19 February 1896 and was buried in the churchyard. *'The children of the school lined the road leading to the church. His friends from the cottages bore their vicar from the gates of his former home and he was followed by those who had sustained and helped him for many years in his work in the church'*. A fine Celtic cross marks his final resting place and on the brass plaque in the chancel are engraved the words: *'(He) embraced not only men but all creatures of God'*. On his death, his widow gathered his writings together in a book, published by the family firm, John Wright & Co, entitled Memorials of Stoke Bishop (the source material for much of this chapter).

The Vicarage

David Wright and his family needed somewhere to live close to the church. Again John Battersby Harford came to the rescue of the cash-strapped church trustees by donating a house from his estate on Stoke Hill at the corner of Eastmead Lane. The new vicar viewed it with mixed feelings. *'The first Parsonage,'* he wrote. *'was a small picturesque house, standing by the roadside, with its gardens, roomy stabling and coach house... In those days, from the garden, a wide-spread view was only bounded by the Welsh hills and the Bristol Channel'*. That was the up-side. The down-side was: *'The house was old, admitting freely the rain and infested by rats...'* A report by surveyors Forster and Wood found serious damp on interior walls from lack of drainage and a roof that was all but collapsed. They recommended *'entirely stripping off the present tiles, renewing the gutters, inserting proper lead flashings and re-covering the roof with slate'*. All the work needed was estimated to be £120. The church baulked at this and David Wright was offered £50 to go towards providing him with whatever

Above, the second vicarage on the corner of Stoke Hill and Eastmead Lane; right, Eastmead flats on site of the second vicarage

comfort he required, which must surely have included keeping his head dry. There is no record as to how the issue was resolved, but resolved it was as David Wright lived there until the building was demolished and a new vicarage was built on the site in 1870 at a cost of £2,000. The greenhouse was a gift to the vicar's wife from Alfred George. The garden overlooked a cricket pitch on the Stoke House estate, to the delight of the vicar and his friends. The new mansion was itself demolished in the nineteen seventies and replaced by a block of flats built on the site at the end of Eastmead Lane. A new vicarage was built opposite the church.

The First Years

The church was dedicated to St Mary Magdalene. Again there is no record as to why this controversial follower of Jesus was chosen. Perhaps in 1860 the elders saw a fallen woman in need of redemption as a symbol of their own need of repentance. The name was frequently in front of them in the Magdalene homes for women that were springing up around the country. But more often the church is referred to simply as St Mary's, a shortening that can lead to confusion. On one occasion a visiting preacher gave an entire sermon on St Mary the Virgin, the mother of Jesus, before it was gently pointed out that he had got the wrong Mary!

David Wright recorded the many firsts of a new church. The first baptism was of an orphan, Amy Elizabeth Bell, the orphan niece of Henry Goodeve; the first to be married, Miss Simmons of Howecroft and *the first grave was made for Richard Dingle, a gardener*', in 1861. Then on 14 December of that year the vicar announced the death of Albert, the Prince Consort. His eulogy was an example of his rich oration.

> *'It has come to the consciousness of the nation all at once – they had given slight, and almost slighting thought of it before – that he, who for the last two and twenty years has stood at the right hand of the throne of England, filled one of the noblest, but most difficult and dangerous positions in this world* (reference to an attempt on his life?), *with that masterly skill and upright purpose which are the elements of real greatness.'*

The vicar described the interior of the church as *'white and cold'*. At first it had no heating and the only lighting was oil lamps hung around the columns and wax candles. The gentry arrived in carriages or on horseback (the mounting block still survives) but the cottagers came across the fields.

The stark interior of the church which the vicar described as *'white and cold'*

'For some time the second service was held in the afternoon, as there was no arrangement for lighting the church and, when evening service was substituted, the roads were dark and many came with little lanterns to guide them through the wood and over the stiles which led to the church in those primitive days.'

'(Slush Lane) our old friend Mr Teast grimly called the best of the (paths), a mere hoof-trodden cattle track then, but long since become the main road to the church from Stoke Park (Church Avenue).'

Extending the Church

Memorials states: *'As the years went by, more houses rose up, more people came and a further church enlargement was needed. In the summer of 1871, the extension of the church was completed westward to its present dimensions and the west porch or narthex was added'*. John Norton's original design included a bell tower and spire, and work

The Church in 1874 now extended to the west and with bell tower and spire added completing John Norton's design

proceeded on these at the same time. The original porch formed the base of the tower onto which its top part and a spire were to be built. It must have been an impressive sight watching the slow emergence of the tower rise through a skein of scaffolding to its full height of 70 feet. But that would be nothing to the excitement of seeing the gravity defying spire soar heavenward clad in a bright mosaic of red and grey tiles. By December it had almost reached its full height of 100 feet and plans were afoot to celebrate its completion in the New Year. No one could have foreseen the disaster around the corner.

Stoke Bishop, with fewer trees, was then much more exposed to violent storms and one blew in on the morning of 20 December. The vicar witnessed *from the window of his study* what happened next. *'The spire, within a few days of its completion, was caught by one of those terrific gales which sweep up the valley from the Bristol Channel, and came crashing into the churchyard'*. Ewan Christian, the architect who surveyed the damage for the Ecclesiastical Commissioners, concluded that *'the spire must have been lifted bodily upward and overthrown by the force of the wind, doing no damage to the masonry'*. Nor, thankfully, was anyone hurt. When the storm came up the workforce was moved inside the church.

On Christmas Day, four days later, David Wright was able to promise *'that in all its unmutilated comeliness, the spire is to rise again'*. An offertory on that day raised £171 1s, enough for work to begin again. But for several years to come, anxious eyes were cast upwards whenever bad weather came in from the Channel. But the spire has stood the test of time, although its high Victorian decoration has been replaced with uniform red tiles to replicate the colour of the roof.

The Church Clock

Over the years, through gifts and bequests, many ornaments have enriched the original building's plain and austere appearance. To the tower were added six bells, cast by John Taylor & Co of Loughborough, and a clock. The latter was given by Henry Oldland of Avongrove and made by Potts and Sons of Leeds, who had supplied the clock for Lincoln Cathedral. The observant would notice that the clock only had three faces. The fourth was in direct line across open fields to Sneed Park (now called Old Sneed Park). The current owner, Francis Tagart, had been asked to contribute to the cost, with the carrot dangled before him that he would be able to read the time from his window, to which the apocryphal reply came that he had enough clocks in his house without paying for another one! On 12 April 1884 at 11.45am, a short dedication service was held outside the church. As the hymn, *'O God, our help in ages past'*, was being sung, *'Mrs Oldland went up to the clock tower and set the pendulum in motion. As the hymn ceased, the clock began to strike twelve'*.

The missing clockface on the tower

The James Chapel

In 1922, Sir Edward Burnett James, originally of Stoke Lodge, now moved to Springfort, a large house built on the Battersby Harford estate, sent a letter to the vicar in which he wrote: *'As you know, for some time my wife and I – and we know that other parishioners are of the same opinion – have thought the south chapel of our parish church in its present state hardly worthy of the services for which it is now needed. With this in view, we recently consulted the eminent architect, Mr J. M. Comper, as to what*

106

Sir Ninian Comper's altar and reredos in the James Chapel with a beardless alabaster Christ on the Cross

he would advise done to it'. Fred Norton, the current vicar, must have had mixed emotions as he read on. Plans were already fully formed, *'which we have discussed together on two or three occasions. I am now sending you plans, and would be obliged if you would submit them to our parochial church council'*. That a man of Sir Edward's influence had the ear of so distinguished an architect as Ninian Comper was good news but the tone of the letter suggested the plans were a fait accompli and had to be accepted without question, especially as David Wright's widow had already been consulted and had approved what was proposed. But the sugar on the pill was Sir Edward's offer to pay for the refurbishment *'as a thank-offering for the many blessings we have received'*.

The PCC unanimously approved the plans and expressed appreciation of Sir Edward and Lady James's generous offer. At the time Ninian Comper was one of the most prestigious church architects of the day. He was known for his High Gothic Revivalist style and introducing what he called the *'English Altar'*, a complex mix of curtains, poles and gilded angels before a low reredos. The altar, in what was to become known as the James Chapel, is a good example of this. The reredos is in alabaster and is unusual in depicting Christ on the cross without a beard. The curtain woven in gold thread surrounds the altar and above four gilded angels stand watch. Over all hangs a canopy, known as a Baldachino, so called after the canopy over the high altar in St Peter's in Rome. It gets its name from the Italian *'Baldacco'* (Bagdad) from where the materials came from for its construction. Whether the PCC really wanted it or not, it is without doubt St Mary Magdalene's finest treasure.

What was certainly not wanted was the large metal screen that in 1904 was erected between the chancel and the nave, effectively caging in the choir and the clergy and separating them from the congregation. It was the gift of Charles Cruddas and his wife and was a sadly misguided gesture. Over the years it remained a contentious issue, but it wasn't until 1966 that a small majority of the PCC voted to have it removed. In the arguments for and against, a choirboy argued that he and his fellows could not always pay attention for the entire service and he was *'frightened that the removal of the screen may give the congregation a clearer view of our activities, which the vicar kindly ignores most of the time'*.

Church interior showing the screen, the nave and the choir

Pew Rents

In the early days, St Mary Magdalene was blessed with a very wealthy congregation, but it still needed a regular income. One way to achieve this was through pew rents. Individuals purchased a particular seat, which was theirs for so long as they paid a rental fee. These seats were much sought after and were often included in the amenities of house sales. But the practice naturally led to problems. Visitors had to navigate where they could and couldn't sit and absenteeism among those who rented pews led to large gaps in the body of the church. In 1936 the vicar, Fred Norton, drew attention *'to the considerable number of Church-folk who had recently come into the Parish and the difficulty of seating them in Church'*. It was his successor,

Sydney Worters, who grasped the nettle. To many pew rentals were seen as obsolete and divisive and they wanted them abolished. This happened in 1939. On Easter Day all pews were declared free. It was of sufficient moment to be recorded in the local papers. But, as Roy Henderson writes, the system *'continued to make its influence felt because some people still wanted to be able to sit in what they regarded as their pew, their family having rented it for years, and resented it if they found somebody else already sitting there. It would be many years before the pews became truly free for all in the mind of every worshipper'.* A system of individual giving replaced pew rents.

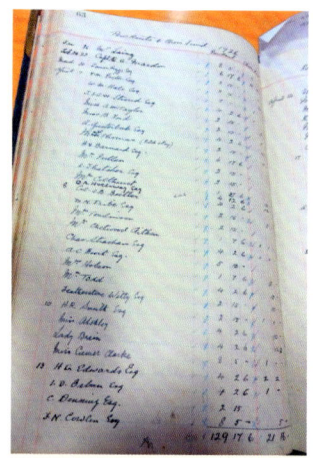

The Pew Rent Ledger

Churchyard Closed

The gentry lost their pews. They also couldn't be buried in the churchyard. By the turn of the 20th century, the churchyard had filled up and it was decided there could be no more burials. When the land for the church had been given by William Baker, it was barely big enough to accommodate the building and provided little room for a graveyard. Eventually an extension was found on the north side of the

The graveyard's Victorian tombstones enjoy a controlled wilding

church. Here families, like the Tagarts and the Goodeves, created family vaults with steps down into them. Today the churchyard stands as a silent monument to the wealthy and powerful of Bristol who crossed the Downs and created a leafy Victorian suburb.

Memories of a Verger's Daughter

In 1885 former army regular and verger at the church, Albert Tyler, applied for the job of live-in caretaker at Stoke Bishop Village Hall, a job he combined with his role as verger. He was successful in his application and remained in both posts until his death in 1925. He was helped in his tasks by his daughter, Violet (Vi) Watkins, née Tyler, who has left a vivid picture of church life and is interviewed here by her grandson, Dave.

'My father looked after the church as verger and put the people in the pews. He had to open the church and shut it at night after a service. There weren't so many services in those days as there are today'.

Albert Tyler, verger and Village Hall caretaker, and his daughter Vi Watkins

110

On pew rents: *'The church warden would work out* (the rents), *and they would pay every Easter. The gentry had their pews and the servants had their pews as well. My dad knew where to put the different people, that was his job. If people didn't pay pew rents, they could turn up and he would tell them where to sit'.* Collecting meant going round to the houses and Violet would help her father by knocking on the *'toffs''* doors.

Keeping the clock going meant a lot of work. *'It had to be wound up and would go for nearly two days. It wasn't the clock it was the chimes. The clock maker came every Friday and he did the clock. He went round to all the other parish churches and did theirs as well. The clock chimed every quarter, half, three quarters and hour. People* (complained)... *they didn't like it chiming all the time, so it just chimes on the hour now'.*

Christchurch

In 1878, a second church opened in Julian Road. This was the Congregational Christchurch, which although meant for a non-conformist congregation, was designed by its architect, Stuart Colman, on a scale grander than was probably needed. It was felt that *'God's house should not be inferior in quality or style to the surrounding dwellings'.* It had a highly decorated tower and spire of slender proportions, clearly aiming to vie with St Mary Magdalene. The arguments of its critics that its structure was too ambitious proved sadly prophetic. In 1962 it closed through lack of funds and poor Sunday attendance. It was demolished and replaced with a block of flats.

Congregational church in Julian Road

The architect's drawing of Christchurch which shows clearly the ambitious design

Chapter Ten

First School and Village Hall

The Early Years

The first mention of education in Stoke Bishop is to be found in Memorials. *About the year 1832, Mrs Daniel of Old Sneyd Park, collected five or six children at her lodge'.*

In 1841 Abraham Gray Harford Battersby of Stoke House gave his gardener's cottage over to the village with the purpose of turning it into a school. It was situated at the north end of the estate, adjacent to the fish pond in the village and was a simple one up and one down. An extra room was added, designed to be the classroom that *'sufficed for all the children of the hamlet'.* This later became the

The first school after its enlargement in 1856. The original cottage is to the left. Note the field in the foreground

school's dining room and the cottage, the headmaster's house. The first teacher was Miss Raynes. She was followed in 1848 by Miss Morgan (later Mrs Rake) and she was helped from time to time by Eleanor Harford, John Battersby Harford's sister, from the Big House. Another helper was the sister of the Revd. J.F. Wickenden, a curate from St Mary Magdalene. In the year Miss Morgan took up her post, she recorded 27 pupils in the register. They were referred to as *'cottagers'* children and clearly needed help as *'a small lending library... and a clothing club... were instituted early'*.

Stoke Bishop was fortunate to have a school from such an early date. In the first part of the Victorian period elementary education was a hit and miss affair and depended on enlightened benefactors. From the start Stoke Bishop was lucky in this respect. It was also a mixed school, which was not always the case, with the prevailing sentiment being that boys' education came before girls'. We don't have the evidence from the early days but given the smallness of numbers it was likely that boys and girls were taught together.

There was government inspection of sorts. In 1839 Her Majesty's Inspectorate came into being and Stoke Bishop School received its first visit on 4 May 1855. The inspector, the Revd. J.W.D. Herniman, wrote: *'Schoolroom too small at present, better accommodation will be provided. Playground fair. Deficiency of books and slates. Organisation, three classes in parallel rows. Discipline pretty fair. Instruction generally fair, in arithmetic imperfect. A pretty little school'*.

Following the inspector's report, plans were set in motion to enlarge the school. The foundation stone was laid in August 1856 and the extension completed the following April. It was at this time the ornamental windows and stone dressings were added, *'which make it so picturesque an object'*. Clearly with its Queen Anne gabling Stoke Bishop school was never going to be utilitarian in appearance, being located on a gentleman's estate.

In 1860 when St Mary Magdalene was established, the school moved out of secular hands into those of the church. The three Battersby Harfords (John, Eleanor and Thomas), for the sum of 5s, made over the school to a board of Trustees appointed by the church, with the vicar David Wright in the chair. Their instruction to the Trustees was for the building to be used for *'daily and Sunday schools, for the use of the working classes living in the district'*, with religious instruction given in the Protestant faith. It is interesting to note that the church's cramped site necessitated its Sunday school to be held in the school. The pupils of the school were expected to attend on Sunday but that didn't always happen. In 1886, of a total of 70 pupils, only 36 came on Sunday.

School Grows

As more houses were built, the numbers coming to school naturally increased and the need for more space became imperative. In 1874 additional land was purchased from William Henry Budgett, the then owner of Stoke House, to extend the building. It cost the Trustees £14. The school now assumed the appearance that later pupils remembered, although further buildings were to be added.

All through this period of expansion, the church was anxious to maintain control of the school. This became particularly critical after the passing of the 1870 Education Act which provided for a system of school boards to be set up. These were to be locally elected and draw their funding from the local rates. Religious teaching was to be non-denominational. Voluntary funded schools like Stoke Bishop were left alone provided sufficient money was raised. David Wright made several appeals to his congregation for support. He was successful as the school stayed close to the church even after numbers increased again with the introduction of the second Education Act of 1880. It now became compulsory for all children between five and ten to attend school. It was extended to eleven in 1893. In that year the intake had reached 235 and a large central room was created to accommodate the infants. A further extension was built in 1906. In 1899 a new Board of Education came into being and took a close interest in church schools. It replaced the board of Trustees with four foundation managers, of which one was ex-officio, the vicar, now David

The school after its expansion in 1874. The houses of Sunnyside can be seen behind

Wright's successor, Canon Josiah Alford. The arrangement was to continue for three decades until the 1944 Education Act when it was put under the control of the local authority, with its governing board compulsorily required to include managers appointed outside the church. Nevertheless as Dorothy Duddridge, the headmistress at the time, later wrote, *'the school has remained first and foremost a Church School'*.

Access

It was little wonder that the school was described as *'pretty'* and *'picturesque'*. It was in the middle of fields and in the early years proved difficult to get to. When the school was originally set up by the Harfords, no access path or road was provided. Getting to the school proved to be an ad hoc business. This came to a head in 1900 with an altercation between William Edwards George and Canon Alford.

There were three ways of getting to the school, none of them official. The first was a path that ran from Hollybush Lane along a fenced-off track to the school and then on through a wicket gate across a field and through a second wicket gate into Stoke Hill (today it is a public footpath). The second route, even less official, was through two gates at the back of the school into a garden and onto Butcher's Hill (Druid Hill). Rubbish and coal for the fires had to be dragged in and out from Hollybush Lane, but many pupils took advantage of the shorter route through the garden, which would take them straight into the village. That is until Mr George locked the gates. He wrote an irate letter to Canon Alford complaining that *'all my gates were left wide open, my water taps twice broken wantonly, recently and a daily run made of the place'*. He went on to seek assurance from the school managers that they *'will give me a letter saying no right of way is assumed, and that my property will have all reasonable protection'*. He goes on to protest that *'whenever Mr Miller* (the head teacher) *is told of these events, his one reply is that he has*

A side view of the school seen from the garden of 5 Sunnyside

no control over his pupils outside the classroom – but I think a little manners added to his curriculum would improve some of the rising generation of our parish!' Clearly he didn't get a satisfactory reply from Canon Alford who seemed to insist there were public rights of way. Mr George disputed this arguing that the paths had been created by trespass. *'Westbury children by trespass created* (a path) *from Hollybush Lane. This one I gravelled myself and put a fence of iron to protect my Tenant's field'.* He made one concession, a monthly opening *'to pass coal into the school'.* Otherwise the back gates stayed locked.

School Life

Penny Jetzer has compiled a pen portrait of the school from interviews she conducted with former pupils:

'On entering the porch, in front was a long dark corridor. On the left side was a door to the headmaster's house, to the right there was a large classroom/hall. At the end of the corridor where coats could be kept, there was a sink and cold water tap, and the girls' lavatories. The boys' lavatories were in the playground. From the main classroom, which could be divided by a folding screen, there were two more classrooms, which again were divided if required by another folding screen. The final two classrooms were not divided, and it was here that the head teacher taught. From these classrooms there was an entrance

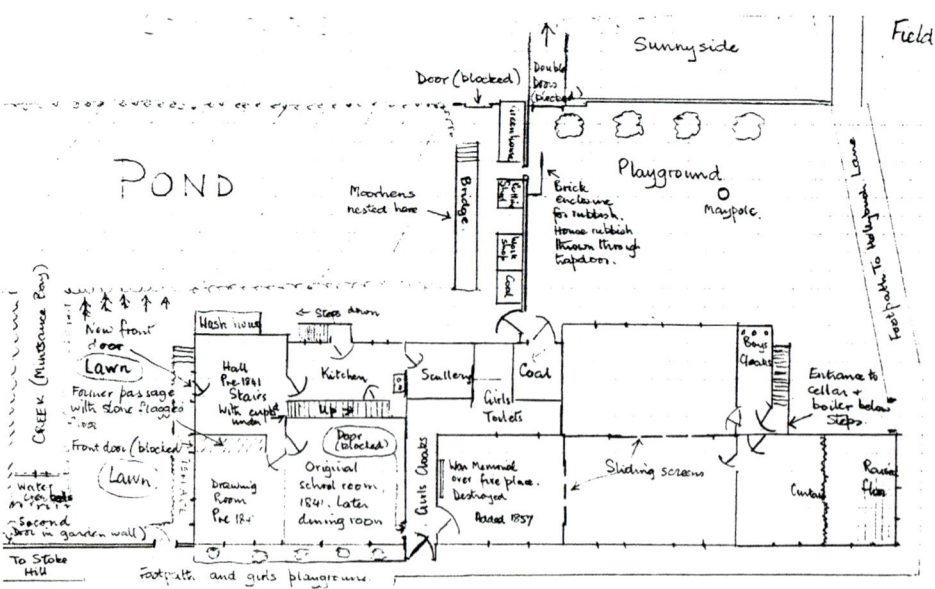

A later plan drawn from memory was made by a former pupil, Vera Horseman

Group of children at the village entrance to the school. The school building can be seen in the top left corner

to the rear playground. On the whole the boys played in the rear of the school and the girls in the front along the narrow footpath. The school was quite dark, the colour scheme brown. Lighting was by gas and heating was by large open fires.'

Past Memories: *'Our headmaster – Mr Tom Miller – was a very learned man with a first class knowledge of the subjects he taught us and an excellent musician. He nobly fulfilled his duties at the school for forty years'* (Ethel Griffin Watkins).

Learning. *'We learnt to write on special lined paper so that all the small letters touched the second line from the bottom and our capital letters the top line'* (Vera Horseman).

Punishments were often physical. *'The school master and his wife were Irish, the wife very quick tempered. She broke a ruler over my head once because I could not cut a pattern correctly'* (Alice Maude Gould). *'If one incurred Miss Kerswell's displeasure during needlework one was rapped on the head with a thimble. In other classes one's skirt was pulled up and one was slapped on the back of the leg with either her bare hand or a ruler'* (unknown writer).

Boys' mischief. *'We progressed to joined up looped writing... with proper inkwells filled in the desks into which the boys thought it great fun to dip the girls' plaits. Alternatively they tied our plaits to the bar along the back of the seat – and the girl always got the blame because she couldn't stand up properly!'* (Vera Horseman).

Walking was the order of the day. *'Children walked to school from as far away as Shirehampton and Westbury-on-Trym... and boys who attended swimming baths for lessons had to walk to Kingsdown Baths'* (Ethel Watkins).

The fields to the south of the School gave opportunity for outdoor lessons. *'In good weather we would hold our* (sewing) *class under the trees by a small lake'* (Alice Maude Gould). *'Kew Stoke Road was a meadow... And after the grass had been mown,*

Girls class 1890

Mixed class 1920s

The bridge that crossed the pond to the rear of the school is still visible today. Note the rail on the left

we used to have our lessons out of doors – sitting on bales of hay' (Ethel Watkins).

The pond bordered the School. In the 1930s *'there was an elaborate bridge at the east end of the pond. It was divided into sections by masonry dams... There were no fish in the pond then. There were always moorhens and sometimes wild ducks would stay for a while... The pond was emptied by sluices... And regularly cleaned of silt'* (unknown writer).

The annual treat. *'On a lovely July day, we boarded a train at Sea Mills – thence to Hotwells, where we found the pleasure steamer Britannia waiting to take us on our annual school treat to Weston-super-Mare. It was looked forward to weeks before and talked about weeks after'* (Ethel Watkins).

The Village Hall

As the population of Stoke Bishop grew in the second half of the 19th century, with the church strapped for space and the children now with their own school, there arose an urgent need for adults to have somewhere to meet. Parishioner Elizabeth Hooper, who was also the sextoness (or administrator) at the church, organised a reading room in her house, but the demand was getting too great for the small room she provided. Several influential members of the congregation decided the time had come to look around for premises suitable for a church hall. I am indebted again to Penny Jetzer for many of the details that follow.

Two of the leading gentry lived on Stoke Hill and had spotted the ideal place. The landlady of the Three Stars public house which was located at the bottom of the hill had found running the pub too much and had just given up and the opportunity presented itself to acquire it. The three men, responsible for pushing the scheme through, were Henry Fedden, business man and JP, John Colhurst Godwin, who ran a firm of iron merchants and Sir George Edwards, tobacco baron and twice Lord Mayor of Bristol. It is likely that the energy for the project came from Henry Fedden, as earlier he had raised the money to purchase an 80 gun warship, HMS Formidable, to convert into a training ship for homeless boys. It later became the National Nautical School at Portishead.

In acquiring the pub they saw an opportunity of killing two birds with one stone. There had long been a grumble that coachmen were spending time in the pub while their masters were in church. How true this was is a moot point. After all, rented pews were available for servants as well their employers. But whatever the reality, it gave the triumvirate the chance to get the Three Stars closed down. They somehow persuaded the Bristol Corporation, probably through the agency of Sir George Edwards, to purchase the pub and demolish it. Given that Stoke Bishop was still in Gloucestershire at the time, this seemed a strange thing for Bristol to do, but it was possible that it had an eye to the future and was getting a foot in the door.

The £400 to build a new hall on the site of the demolished pub was raised by public subscription. The architect was Edward Gabriel and it was crafted in a striking early Arts and Craft style, while its centrepiece, a great bay window with

An early photograph of the Village Hall from the field opposite, now houses

121

Edward Gabriel's architect's drawing of the Village Hall

stained glass, spoke of the moral high ground of its founders. In his penchant for understatement David Wright described it as *'a very pretty and suitable building... forming an attractive feature at the turn of the hill'*.

David Wright opened the new hall on Thursday 15 October 1885. The date is proudly inscribed in relief on the gable. Only a few days before, the great reformer Lord Shaftesbury had died. David Wright's sermon the Sunday before set the tone of earnest improvement that was to characterise the activities of the new hall.

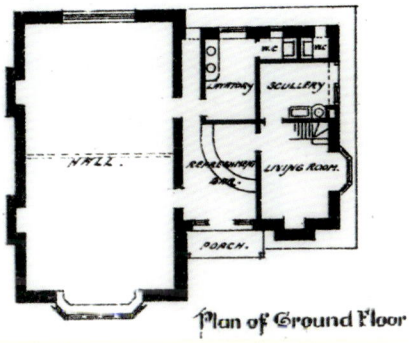

Plan of Ground Floor

The facilities proposed by Gabriel would make the Village Hall one of the best equipped of its day

'Lord Shaftesbury knew,' he said, *'that cruelties were committed in factories, and still more in mines, where women were yoked to horses, and children of six years old were taken from their beds, and made to do what poor feeble work they could; cruelties which the horrors of West Indian slavery have not surpassed.'* Wright went on. *'In politics he was a Conservative; in religion he was that which is known as an Evangelical ... Words were spoken by Lord Shaftesbury which would not seem unfitting now from the lips of those who are called Socialists.'*

In the beginning the events held were meetings and church gatherings. A lending library was established and there were facilities for tea and coffee. In January 1895 David Wright wrote in his paternal way of *'the last gathering in the Village Hall'* before he stepped down as vicar. *'We meet at our annual tea-gathering, it is one for all our cottage friends in the parish .... Well, the occasion is intended to be one of social enjoyment, first of a pleasant tea, and then of music and certain cheery passages. And last year I remember that this second part of the evening's engagements was supplied entirely by native or quite neighbouring talent. But just between the two parts it has always been my custom to throw in one or two pastoral words...'*

Eliza, second wife of Albert Tyler, lived with her caretaker husband in the Village Hall

The hall had provision for a live in caretaker. Albert Tyler, who was the church verger, was appointed to the post and he moved with his wife, Susannah, son, Albert and two daughters, Mary (known as Maud) and Clara into the accommodation provided in rooms above the hall. Susanah died in 1895. Albert married again. His new wife, Eliza, gave birth to Violet Norah, married name Watkins, in the upstairs flat on 3 July 1897. Albert lived there until his death in 1925.

Chapter Eleven

Pubs, Inns and Taverns

There has long been a local saying that Stoke Bishop is dry because much of it was built on Quaker land.

It is the first thing newcomers hear when settling in the area. Is there any truth in the statement? The answer as with all historical questions is yes and no.

18th and Early 19th Centuries

During this period a number of drinking places can be identified. We have already seen that beer was available for visitors to Cook's Folly. This was almost certainly served from an old cottage which stood next door to the tower. Once the area had become *'a popular place of amusement'*, the cottage was converted into a tavern, known as Folly Cottage. It closed around 1859, probably on the agency of Henry Goodeve, the new owner of Cook's Folly, and perhaps as the result of the notoriety surrounding a terrible happening a few years earlier. It is described in

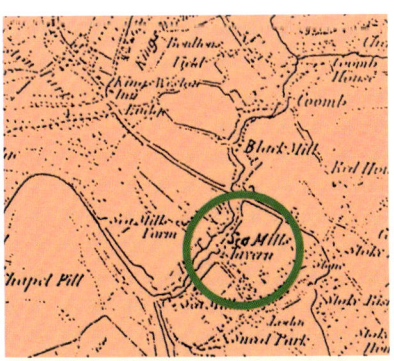

Sea Mills Tavern on 1712 map beside the River Trym

John Latimer's Annals of Bristol. *'On August 18th, 1855, a little girl named Melinda Payne, living in one of the cottages which then stood on the right bank of the Avon, near the ravine, was sent by her father to this house for some beer, and was murdered whilst returning homewards. The perpetrator was never discovered'*.

The Sea Mills Tavern was featured on a 1712 map and was still there in 1836. It would have been a popular watering hole for dock workers and seamen while the floating dock was operational, although as we have seen a second tavern was opened for a short time closer to the dock buildings. But once the dock fell into disuse, customers must have fallen away with the workers at Clack Mill and from the farms being the

Beer was sold to visitors to Cook's Folly from a cottage next door

only clientele. By the end of the 19th century the tavern had become a farmhouse, known as the Hermitage.

Stoke Bishop village had a pub called the Three Stars (now the Village Hall) which stood at the bottom of Stoke Hill. In the 1841 census the pub was being run by John Griffin who was 68 at the time. Later we find the landlord was a Charles Bevan and when he died his wife Eliza took over as landlady. Quite what the

THREE STARS,	GRIFFIN, John	Head	68		Beer seller
STOKE BISHOP	John	Son	26		Labourer
	TICKAM, Sarah Rose	Niece		13	
	HILL, Jane	Servant		17	House servant

citizens of Stoke Bishop thought of a woman running a pub, we don't know, but it was clearly hard work and it eventually got too much for Eliza, who in around 1884 announced she was retiring. As we have seen a group of influential and high minded churchmen took the opportunity of ridding the village of this *quaint little public house*.

But it wasn't done without protest. Thomas Cox of Redland applied for a licence to replace the Three Stars, which was now in quite a dilapidated state, and put up a new alehouse elsewhere in the village. But in any contest between the cottagers and the gentry there was little doubt as to who was going to win. The licensing magistrates turned down the application and the Village Hall was built. Part of the wall of the old pub can still be seen along the left side of the present building, no doubt bringing to the faces of the former drinkers, denied their watering hole, a wry smile.

Embedded in the wall of the present Village Hall, the remains of the Three Stars are still visible

Not all supplies of liquor came from the pubs during this period. People sold beer from their cottage doors. David Wright wrote of his first vicarage: *'The house had a quaint charm of its own, with its bow window and outside shutters; so suggestive of a wayside inn, that, though the door was not habitually standing open to invite the weary wayfarer, there would come an enquiry from a passer-by, 'Please do you sell beer?''*

Two Ostrich Pubs

David Wright painted a contrasting picture of the Downs at the time the church was consecrated in 1860,

> *'not levelled to monotony, but of uneven surface, broken up into delightful surprises, ferny tangles and fragrant hollows... The dainty close-cropped grass on which the sheep fed was bespangled... by sweet-scented thyme and yellow coltsfoot, wild strawberry plants and little golden cistus... yet it was very lonesome at night, in fog and snow impassable* (with) *legends of spectral hearses and clanking chains'*

Located on the north side of this wild land was the Ostrich pub and, although it was only a stone's throw from the Clifton to Shirehampton turnpike, it was never a coaching inn. *'It stood,'* said David Wright, *'upon the turf, having no carriage access except by a thread-like road which crossed the Down to it obliquely from Black Boy Hill.'* It still stands today and is now a private dwelling. But once it made capital of all that took place on the Downs, *'notorious for its horse races, its two cockpits, its fine bowling green and its high play; also for the gentler pastime of archery, to which Maria*

126

Edgeworth, in one of her novels, escorts her young ladies' (David Wright).

Horse racing on the Downs began in 1718, so the Ostrich must have been established at least by this date. Farley's Bristol Newspaper, dated 9 October 1725, reported that a velvet saddle worth £5 was the prize offered to the winner of a three mile race *'sponsored'* by the Ostrich. As Clifton's fashionable terraces spread, so its elegant citizens sought nearby amusement, which, at least during the day, they could find on the Downs, much of it courtesy of the Ostrich. In his Annals of Bristol Latimer records that

> *'a cockfight on the largest scale took place at the Ostrich Inn in February 1778, and was attended by great numbers of West Country squires, the match having been arranged between the gentry of Somerset and Devon. Fifty one birds contended on each side for prizes amounting to 350 guineas.'*

Particularly popular was backsword fighting. This combat involved bashing heads with either a wooden sword or the flat side of a duelling sword. On one occasion the Ostrich announced that it would offer a prize of five guineas to the *first best*

The Ostrich today, renamed the Old Halt, is a private house facing the Downs

man, *who breaks most heads, saving his own'*, and added, *'Vinegar by J. W.'* The Inn was grateful for the patronage of its fashionable visitors, who came in daylight, and would provide lanterns for their return at night.

In 1749 the racecourse on Durdham Down was enlarged, the ground levelled and stands erected. Greater numbers than ever flocked to the Downs and to boost its trade the Ostrich laid on extra attractions during the race meetings. On one occasion two men ran against each other naked, after which it was

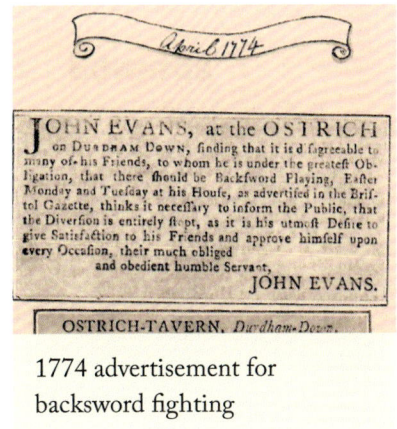

1774 advertisement for backsword fighting

announced that *'a laced Holland smock would be run for by'* (fully clothed) *maidens'*. Such was the popularity of these events a second Ostrich Inn opened in a building on a site of what became Down House (Saville Manor Nursing Home).

There had long been a debate as to exactly where the Ostrich was located on the Downs. The mystery was solved by the ever curious vicar of Westbury-on-Trym, the Revd. H. J. Wilkins. From the Westbury book of tithings he discovered

Horse racing on Durdham Down, c1813. Bristol artist, Rolinda Sharples, shows the chaotic nature of the event. Note Cook's Folly in the background

An early photo from about 1852. The Clifton Cricket Club plays on Durdham Down with the Ostrich (now a private residence) behind. Note: the houses of Downleaze had not been built

1770-1.—Rate 2d. in the £ :
David Friew for the New Ostrich ....
Mrs. Stokes for the Old Ostrich ....
1774-5.—Rate 1s. 3d. in £ to, inter alia, "defray expenses of re-casting church bells":
John Evans for New Ostrich ....
Mrs. George Hart for the Old Ostrich ....
1775-6.—Rate 9d. in £ to, inter alia, "defray the expences of erecting a new clock":
John Evans for the New Ostrich ....
Mrs. Franks for the Old Ostrich ....
1776-7.—Rate 3d. in £ for, inter alia, "repairing the churchyard wall":
James Evans for the New Ostrich ....
Mrs. Franks or tenant for the Old Ostrich ....
1781-2.—Rate 15d. in £ for, inter alia "repairs of Shirehampton Chapell":
As in 1776.
1785-7.—Rate 6d. in £ :
David Evans, New Ostrich
Joseph Shapeland, Esqr. Old Ostrich ....

H. J. Wilkins' letter to the Bristol Times and Mirror demonstrating two Ostrich pubs from the Westbury-on-Trym tithings

that, in the year 1775-6, rents were being paid by *Mrs Franks for the Old Ostrich* and by *John Evans for the New Ostrich*', conclusive evidence that there were not one but *two* Ostrich inns. They traded together for a number of years until the Old Ostrich converted to a private dwelling in 1778. The New Ostrich carried on for a few more years, until it too became a private house in 1797. The forces of decency, reacting against increasing rowdiness and drunkenness that were bedevilling the entertainments put on, succeeded, in 1838, in getting all racing and games banned. They came back in a controlled way when the Downs Act of 1861 was passed, protecting the green expanse as a permanent place of recreation for all.

A curious question mark has long hung over the Old Ostrich. Was it, as some have claimed, ever used for smuggling? It lay outside the boundaries of Bristol Corporation and could avoid Bristol's licencing tax. In the cellars below the house there is a door that now leads nowhere but which could once have been the entrance to a tunnel that led to the Avon Gorge, allowing contraband liquor to be smuggled into the Ostrich. With the inn's change of use, its cellars were sealed up. It wasn't until 1877 that they were re-discovered. The daughter of a later owner, Thomas Turner, described how this happened. *'After we had settled in, my father... said to me one morning, 'I should like to investigate the cellars'. So we found an old cellar leading downwards and I was the first to venture on the very unsafe stairs, which gave way under me. However we procured a ladder and were rewarded by discovering a considerable store of wine, the bottles being very heavily encrusted. It proved to be a very fine Madeira.'* It is a good story, but then on this wild frontier between fashionable Clifton and discreet Stoke Bishop anything could have happened.

The cellar that may once have led to a smugglers' tunnel

Covenants

Where once there had been a plethora of pubs in the area, now one by one, for whatever reason, they had all closed by 1884. The mid-Victorian residents of Stoke Bishop, locked away in their big houses, had no wish to have a raucous tavern in their midst. Whatever they might do privately, in public they needed to present to the world an exemplary life of abstinence and forbearance. As lots were sold,

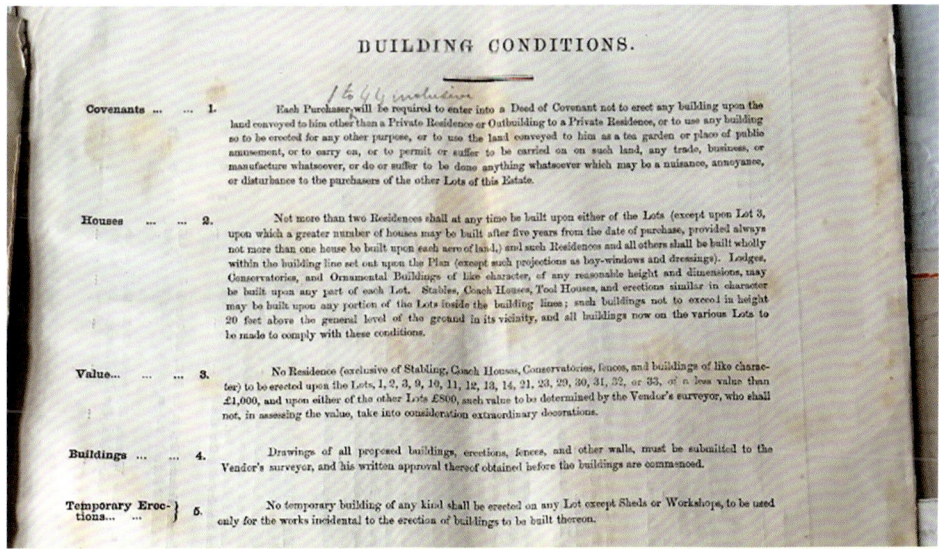

Stoke House Estate Sale's restrictive covenant forbade any place of public amusement

covenants were placed on them that restricted their use. There was to be no selling alcohol by the back door. For example the properties erected on the Stoke House estate had in their deeds the clear stipulation that the buyer was not *'to use the land conveyed to him as a tea garden or place of amusement'*. Although there was no blanket prohibition, for many years there was a strong feeling against any inn being built.

The Mill House

Stoke Bishop was to remain 'dry' until 1972 when a new pub opened its doors at the old Millpill Bridge (on Shirehampton Road) beside the River Trym, a short distance from where the 18th century Sea Mills Tavern had stood. The pub probably started life as a private house but by 1925 it had become a grocery store. It was owned by Cecil Smith, who also started to sell teas. At the time tea gardens were popular along the Trym and people from Bristol travelled out to the area to enjoy a day in the country. It was a natural step to apply for a licence to sell beer. Smith was unsuccessful, but a new owner of what became known as 'The Stores', Thomas Jeffrey Prestidge, had more luck. Over 1,000 people signed a petition and, despite opposition from doctors and the church, he was granted a licence to sell beer and cider in 1929. Five years later, in 1934, he secured a licence to sell wine. A third owner, William Tucker, renamed the premises The Mill Pill House and ran the off licence until his death in 1970. By this date there was growing demand for a pub in the area.

Interestingly, Bristol Corporation actively discouraged the sale of alcohol on its council estates, so Sea Mills, like Stoke Bishop, had no pub. It was ironic, therefore, that the nearest pub would be in 'dry' neighbouring Stoke Bishop. In 1972 Courage's Brewery (which by now had subsumed Georges Brewery) took over the Mill Pill House and opened it as a new pub. They renamed it Mill House, not as it is commonly believed after the mills on the Trym, but after a

Mill House leads at Cheltenham

famous racehorse of the day called Mill House. The horse was considered a rival to Arkle, the undisputed champion of the time, and in fact the two horses fought it out for the Cheltenham Gold Cup in 1964, Mill House losing to Arkle by five lengths. Clearly the horse was considered worthy by the brewers to be the ideal

131

The Mill House as a grocery store and tea shop in the 1920s

The Mill House as an off-licence in the thirties, with Georges Brewery supplying the beer

The Mill House today

name for their new themed pub. In an advertising feature in The Evening Post a Courage spokesman wrote: *'It's basically a very smart local with tasteful décor, but we have followed through the race horse theme with pictures of the horse and details of its racing career, together with other mementos of this great sport.'* None of this survives in today's pub, which has now added the definite article to its name.

Chapter Twelve

Stamps, Steam and Jubilee

Queen Victoria's Last Years

Occasionally during the latter half of Queen Victoria's long reign, Stoke Bishop was referred to as a village, but more often and more accurately as a hamlet.

Although houses were built, its population was slow to grow. The 1861 census gave the number of residents as 554. Forty years later, in the 1901 census, it had only increased to 1602. It had a church, school and village hall, but no purpose built shop. Other amenities arrived at infrequent intervals, the first being the post office.

The Post Office

The first postage stamp, the Penny Black, was issued in 1840 and Post Office records show a stamped letter was sent from Stoke Bishop to Bristol on 1 January 1847. Henry Pinker was the first postmaster. He lived in No 3 Ivey Cottage, one of a group of cottages in the centre of the village. He was described in the 1841 Census as a plasterer and carter, ten years later in the 1851 Census as a painter. He

must have assumed postal duties in addition to his trade. He died in 1862. David Wright in his eulogy on 5 October said that he discharged his duties with *'unvarying alacrity, courtesy and*

Esther Pinker, postmistress, outside the cottage that served as the post office (now the entrance to Tunstall Close) 1880

The 1892 post office appears to have been located in the room to the right of the front door along the side of the house

obliging cheerfulness'. At the time the post office must have opened on Sunday mornings as David Wright went on to describe how *'there was no neglecting the duties of his responsible office on the Sunday morning... but it required planning and arrangement'* for him to complete his work and still get to church on time. *'As it was it would be rare for anyone to come to the church, however early, without finding that one place filled'*.

The business was carried on by Henry's wife, Esther, and their daughter, also Esther. But it became more than just a post office. It became Stoke Bishop's only shop. In Kelly's street directory of 1889 the entry read *'Pinker, Esther (Mrs) grocer and post office'*. Vi Watkins recalled: *'There was just the one shop in the village – the post office, which would sell milk, butter, a few groceries and stamps... Miss Pinker ran the post office and was a bit deaf. She gave up just after the* (First World) *war and then went over to Canada with her niece'*.

In 1892 the post office moved into the large red brick house opposite the Village Hall. The three acre plot of land on which it was built was called Court Hay and had originally been part of The Glen estate. It now belonged to a builder, William Edward Studley, who sought planning permission to build a house and post office on the site. Studley's initials and date of the building are on the side gable and it is in this side part of the house that the post office and shop were located. When the new road was constructed at the bottom of Stoke Hill in 1922, the post office moved across the road into the new parade of shops and Studley's house became a men's club.

The Railway

On 6 March 1865 the railway came to Stoke Bishop, lucky enough to be on a new

Above, station staff pose in front of a train at Hotwells Station in the 1890s; right, single platform at Hotwells

line being built from Avonmouth to Hotwells. A station was constructed near the Sea Mills harbour, served by the new Bristol Port and Pier Railway. The latter ran its single engine on a standard gauge single track and was unique in the country at the time in being the only railway line that did not feed into the national system. It had been built in anticipation of a new dock being created at the mouth of the Avon after the failure of the Sea Mills Dock project. As this did not happen until 1877, the first trains carried only passengers from Sea Mills station on a day trip to Hotwells where they connected with transport into the city. In the other direction

136

they could enjoy a day by the sea at Avonmouth.

To begin with there were six trains a day in both directions, but the Railway's isolation meant it was never going to be profitable. The Port and Pier company knew they had to connect up with the rest of the country. Pushing on beyond Hotwells would be difficult and expensive, so they opted for a line driven from Sneyd Park through the Downs in a two and a half mile tunnel to Clifton, where it was hoped an extension would link it with the Great Western Railway to London and the Midland Railway to Birmingham. After considerable delay through lack of finance, a frustrated Great Western and Midland took over the project and completed the extension. It became operational for passenger travel on 1 September 1885. Now Stoke Bishop residents had an untroubled way of getting into the city.

The Station

The original station was a timber building, but when the track was doubled at Sneyd Park Junction, where the two railways merged before approaching Sea Mills Station, it became necessary to re-design the station layout. A stationmaster's house was built in 1894, at a cost of £240, and 10 years later, in August 1906, a new station was opened. It had two platforms and an elegant station building of brick and stone in the domestic style. A decorated portico gave onto a ladies waiting

A steam train pulls into Sea Mills Station. Note the double track (left) and the neat station building (right)

room and booking hall.

The stationmaster's duties were not always that onerous. One kept pigs and poultry and took his pony and trap to fetch swill from the docks. He sold eggs to the passengers and provided his Superintendent in Bristol with eggs and butter.

A subway was constructed to connect the platforms, but this could flood at exceptional high tides. It was the porter's job to clear the passageway of rubbish after an inundation. He could claim *'dirty money'* for doing this and may well have exaggerated the number of high tides. That was until the Shirehampton stationmaster, who had overall responsibility for the section, was provided with a set of tide tables and could check up on his porter's claims!

Decline and Rise

The opening of the Avonmouth dock gave a boost to the Clifton link both in freight and passenger traffic, but the Hotwells section, still single track, declined. There was a spike from military use during the First World War, but numbers fell dramatically after hostilities had ended. The line from Sneyd Park to Hotwells closed on 30 June 1922, its demise accelerated by the proposed new road along the Gorge, whose plans utilised part of the track bed as the course of the road. The Clifton section, however, received a further boost in 1928 when it was extended beyond Avonmouth to Severn Beach, which was enjoying a short lived boom as a seaside destination.

1900 train steams over wooden trestles before the iron bridge was built

Village Life

Vi Watkins remembered how quiet Stoke Bishop was,

> *'not many people around. There was just the one shop in the village – the post office, which would sell milk, butter, a few groceries... the butcher, grocer, baker and milkman would all call.'*

Samuel Loxton

Samual Loxton was a Clifton born illustrator whose pencil recorded the many facets of life in and around Bristol at the turn of the 20th century. Through his friendship with George Frederick Stone, editor of the Western Daily Press, his drawings became a popular feature of Bristol newspapers. He visited Stoke Bishop in 1919 and left a memorable picture of life in the village.

> *'Dr Parsons would come by bike or walk. He came from Sneyd Park. He came and saw everybody. You had to pay in those days, a lot of people used to doctor themselves.'* Traffic was horse drawn. There was no danger of being knocked down. *'You could hear them coming! They had horses and carriages then. People had to walk, the working class. Gentry walked a good bit as well, they did not always have carriages out.'*

Village Occasions

'Everything going on was always at the Village Hall. Gentry would have fancy dress balls and (they) *might be at any time. They would have cards with a pencil hanging on to it and would write down who they wanted to dance with. The pencil was pink for ladies and gentlemen blue, on a little holding thing'*. (Vi Watkins)

There were special days. Oak Apple Day was 29 May: *'You had to have an oak apple in your lapel or they called you a shick-shack. We didn't all have oak apples, but most of us did.* (We got ours) *down by the shops, by the fountain. In the woods just beyond there, there were oak apple trees by the wall and we would climb on the wall and pick the oak apples'*. (Vi Watkins)

'St George's Day was always recognised at school. A huge Union Jack was draped across the room and a special song sung, enthusiastically, 'Flag of Britain Proudly Waving Over Distant Seas', and later on where it said, 'we salute thee', all the boys gave a military salute'. (Ethel Watkins)

Above, George Frederick Stone, editor of the Western Daily Press. When he and Loxton visited Stoke Bishop, Loxton drew the church, right

Queen Victoria's Diamond Jubilee, 1897

Queen Victoria was the first monarch to celebrate 60 years on the throne and celebrations were held throughout the country. Stoke Bishop's event was a very controlled affair. It was entitled The Stoke Bishop Diamond Jubilee Celebration and took place on Wednesday 23 June 1897 *'by kind permission of the Executors of the late Mr Thomas Wedmore in the Grounds of Druid's Stoke'*. Admission to the ground was by ticket only, although there was no charge, and tickets were available to *'residents and persons permanently employed in the Parish'*. Clearly Stoke Bishop was promising an exclusive event that might well have attracted gate-crashers.

The Committee organising the celebration was 30 strong and as would be expected was drawn from a cabal of house owners that included William Edwards George, William Budgett and J.C. Chetwood-Aiken. In the printed list men came first, women (all wives) second. Celebrations were never going to get out of hand.

Festivities kicked off at 1pm with a *'Dinner to those who have been specially invited'*. A crowded afternoon followed. The Band of the Gloucestershire Artillery Volunteers played throughout with a wide repertoire, much of it popular music of the day, including such titles as 'Sally In Our Alley', 'Home, Sweet Home' and 'Darling Mabel'. At 3pm there was a procession of children. Earlier at 2pm the sports had started and were to go on all afternoon and into the early evening. There were all the

Samuel Loxton's drawings of Stoke Bishop

View from Druid Hill. The Glen is to the right, Stoke Hill in the middle distance and St Mary Magdalene at the top

View across the Trym at high tide with the signal station on the right, the railway bridge on the left and Sneed Park beyond

141

Stoke Hill running
between the Village
Hall and the red
brick post office

Footbridge over railway into Sneed Park

Parry's Lane and Stoke Abbey Farm

Bridge over the Trym in
Sea Mills Lane upstream
of Trym Cross Road

usual events but also some novelty ones such as the *'ginger beer and bun race'*, where ginger beer and buns were consumed at the half way point and the *'floral bicycle ride'* for *'ladies only'* riding their own flower festooned bicycles. The day finished with dancing to the military band.

Francis Tagart

The celebration was a memorable occasion, but it was missing one important element, the gift of the Jubilee Fountain, promised by Francis Tagart, the owner of Old Sneed Park. Following the Martin Act, Sneed Park House appeared to be renamed Old Sneed Park. During this period it had several owners, the longest being the first, Francis Tagart, a man of forthright opinion, who was both careful and generous with his money. *'It was his custom when making a contribution to any good work, to tender his cheque by hand, instead of sending it by post'*

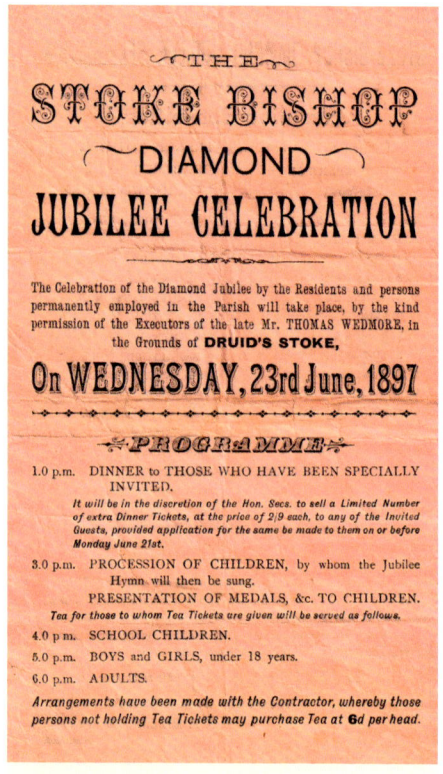

Jubilee Celebration programme

(Bristol Times and Mirror). We have already seen his apocryphal response when asked to contribute to the St Mary Magdalene clock. He chose his projects carefully.

Francis Tagart was born in 1819 in Barnstaple, was twice married and spent most of his working life in London. He ran mercantile businesses, travelled extensively and put his experience of marine engineering to use in chairing a number of related companies, including the Grand Junction Waterworks Company, which supplied water to west London, and the Surrey Commercial Dock Company. He had a wide range of interests as evidenced in his membership of the Linnean Society and the Royal Geographical Society. He was also a member of the Reform Club and although he never got entangled in civic politics, he was an *'ardent liberal'* most of his life and on one occasion stood for Parliament. This was in 1868 after Benjamin Disraeli, the Tory leader, had passed his Reform Act extending the voting franchise. He lost and never tried again. His London House was in Queen's Gate, but he sought a house in the country and when Old Sneed Park came on the market he bought it, an indication of how rural Stoke Bishop was still regarded.

Children posing in the centre of the village close to the Jubilee Fountain, more commonly known as the Tagart Fountain. Glen House can be seen in the background

The Country Gentleman

Like many of his contemporaries, Francis Tagart showed a tireless energy and was soon involved with local projects. He shared a common interest in Bristol's mercantile and maritime future with the newer owners of Stoke Bishop's big houses. Just as Louis Philip Nott, newly arrived in Stoke House, was involved with the development of the city docks, so Francis Tagart became director of the company set up to build the new dock at Avonmouth. He was also a justice of the peace for Gloucestershire. But his great passion was to live the life of a country gentleman. He rode with the Duke of Beaufort's hounds and lavished time and care on his estate and garden. He revived the deer park and stocked it with a fine herd of red and fallow deer.

The undulating and sloping nature of Old Sneed Park allowed his gardeners considerable scope in achieving a variety of horticultural delights, a patchwork of terraces, a statuary garden, secret rooms and always a triumphant display of colour. Annually a vast carpet bed exploded into a dramatic tableau, one year the Union Jack, another, Tagart and his wife's golden wedding initials and dates. An array of glasshouses were stocked with cooler ferns around an indoor pond, while vines, exotic peaches and pineapples grew under the hotter glass. In her book *Old Sneed Park Nature Reserve* Eileen Stonebridge suggested that the lake in the lower valley was adapted for outdoor bathing. There are steps at the head of the lake and *the*

Above, watercolour by Alfred O. Townsend shows the flower garden at Old Sneed Park as it follows the steep slope from the house and merges with the parkland, right

water would have been considerably cleaner in those days as the lake was fed by streams rather than road run-off'.

Garden Visits

Tagart did not keep his garden to himself, but was generous in allowing others to see it. On a number of occasions he hosted the annual shows of agricultural and horticultural societies which he supported. On 1 August 1887, the West Gloucester Farmers Club held its *'26th Annual Exhibition of Stock, Cheese, Butter, Cut Flowers etc'* in *'the picturesque grounds'* of Old Sneed Park. Among the events staged was *'the jumping of the horses over water, stone wall, gate and gorsed hurdles'* competing for Silver Cups.

Two views of the undulating gardens at Old Sneed Park

Another regular visit was from the boys of the Bristol Telegraph Messengers, who, as their name suggested, delivered telegraph messages around the city. On Saturday 18 August, the youngsters marched behind a fife and drum band from Blackboy Hill, across the Downs, to Stoke Bishop, where they enjoyed an afternoon in Tagart's garden, exploring the estate and playing cricket on what the newspaper report described as *'a nursery ground for such players as the Graces, C.L. Townsend, Ernest and Noel Tagart etc'*. The cricketing days of Ernest, Tagart's grandson, may have been over as he was introduced as having just been wounded in the war against the Boers in South Africa. It must have been a lively occasion as *'very hearty cheers were given by the messengers for the host and hostess'*. But this was nothing, perhaps, to the thousands who spilled across the park on open days, which happened twice a year, always on a Wednesday (early closing day) and Saturday, to maximise the numbers who were able to come.

The Tagart Fountain

Francis Tagart was reported to have said that *'from Shirehampton to Redland there was not one spot where a carter could refresh himself or water his horse'*. To rectify this omission, he offered to present a public fountain in honour of Queen Victoria's Diamond Jubilee. But its opening missed the due date. Tagart showed his forthright character by withholding his gift until he was certain that an initiative by Bristol Corporation to absorb Stoke Bishop within its boundaries had gone away.

A year later on 15 August 1898, the fountain was officially opened by the Duchess of Beaufort. In attendance were her husband, the Duke of Beaufort, the High Sherriff of Bristol, the vicar Canon Alford and most of the Tagart family. A

146

reporter from the Bristol Mercury described how the Duchess *'turned on the water and drank some of it from a silver cup. She expressed a hope that the fountain would be a comfort for man and beast'*. As ever the school children lined up waving flags and a military band played throughout. The reporter wrote a pen portrait of the new fountain that now sat beside the large oak tree in the centre of the village. *'The design is of rustic character, harmonising well with the surroundings. The fountain is of Aberdeen granite... The roof of the shelter is covered with Boseley tiles surrounded by a lead apex and finial... At the foot of the structure are four dog troughs of pennant stone.'* The water came from an underground spring. The fountain still stands, although no longer connected to a water supply and the dog troughs have gone.

One curious question is exactly how much Francis Tagart contributed to the cost of the memorial. Money for the fountain was raised

The Tagart Fountain. The inscription reads: 'Presented to Stoke Bishop in Memory of the 60th year of Queen Victoria's Reign by Francis Tagart of Old Sneed Park'

by public subscription and Tagart was always described as having *'presented'* the fountain. Perhaps being the oldest man of importance in the village it was felt an honour that his name should be associated with the fountain. He died on 25 November 1911 aged 92. In his will he gave £300 each to his butler, William Attwell, his coachman, Charles Garrett and his gardener, Edwin Binfield. Although officially called the Jubilee Fountain, it will be forever known affectionately as the Tagart Fountain.

Cook's Folly: the Later Years

Before we leave the 19th century, we should continue the story of Cook's Folly, which we left enjoying its status as a popular tourist attraction. All this was to change in 1855, when a Dr Henry Goodeve and his wife Isabella bought the tower from the Martins and built onto it a substantial Gothic villa, a private residence that became a family home.

Wedding albums of the Pethick family of Woodside, Tagart's neighbours

The Dream

Over 25 years before, around 1830, the Goodeves were on their honeymoon in the Bristol area and must have visited Cook's Folly, as the young Henry, about to embark on a medical career in India, confided to his *wife 'his desire, if successful, to build himself a house on a certain "coign of vantage" overlooking the Avon, on which there stood a tower of uncertain date'* (John Beddoe, a friend). Another even more romantic version of the story was told by Frances Power Cobbe, feminist writer and social reformer. *'As they were descending the turret-stair and taking, as they thought a last look on the loveliness of England, the young wife perceived that her husband's head was bent down in deep depression. She laid her hand on his shoulder and whispered, "Never mind Harry. You shall make a fortune in India and we will come back and buy Cook's Folly."'*

Henry Goodeve indeed made that fortune and realised his dream. He joined the Bengal Medical Service in 1831 and when the Calcutta Medical College was established in 1835, he became the first professor of midwifery and anatomy and used his position to push for improvements and reform in Indian medicine. He took a great interest in children's diseases and in training new Indian doctors. In 1844, back in London, he was awarded a Fellowship of the Royal College of Surgeons. Ill health forced him to retire in 1845, but he was back in service again in 1853 in the Crimea where he was appointed inspector of civil hospitals at Renkioi. He was mentioned in a Times despatch: *'the* Imperador *steamed into sight with*

Henry Goodeve in middle age

215 sick and wounded from Balaclava. The two inspectors, Drs Goodeve and Robertson, stationed themselves at the extremity of the corridor to sort out the cases as they arrived...'

The House

Isabella joined her husband in the Crimea and it is while they were there that they purchased their dream house. When the war was over they returned to Bristol and began enlarging Cook's Folly. An article in the Bristol Mercury in 1884 described in detail the Goodeve's new residence.

'As he jealously preserved the legendary name, so did he faithfully keep intact the rooms of the old tower... It is now more than a quarter of a century since the modern building was erected and its main front is like the tower, entirely mantled in ivy... (From the smoking room in the tower), *a staircase leads to the western side of the tower, from which the most charming view of all can be obtained, of the winding river, the gleaming waters of the Channel, the meadows of Sneyd Park and Sea Mills...'*

Although childless themselves, the Goodeves filled Cook's Folly with nieces and nephews and the children of ex-India servicemen. They adopted Amy Bell, the baby daughter of a niece who had died of a fever in Bangkok (she was the first to be baptised at St Mary Magdalene). Henry involved himself in Bristol civic life, became a justice of the peace and was a trustee of the Bristol Royal Infirmary for 25 years.

Soon after his return to Bristol, he became captain of a company of a volunteer corps known as the Bristol Rifles. One day in 1860 a shooting match took place in Sneyd Park at which the Bristol Rifles participated. Goodeve's No 7 company won the coveted bugle donated by *'Mr and Mrs Pritchard'*. His speech of acceptance was

Cook's Folly after Goodeve's Victorian residence was added. The original tower is to the right

reported by the Bristol Mercury. It was full of the bombastic militarism that was characteristic of the day and an ominous portent of what was to come.

> *'He trusted that the bugle might never summon men whose deeds would throw a tarnish on it, but, whether on the parade ground or on the sterner fields of battle, they might be ever ready to do their duty and defend their hearths and homes, which English women had rendered such that they were willing to fight, or if need be, to die for* (cheers).' Goodeve had seen the battlefield in the raw.

Isabel Goodeve died on 29 May 1870 and was buried in a family vault on the north side of St Mary Magdalene churchyard. She was followed by her husband ten years later. Goodeve's will was generous to relatives and staff. To Amy Bell he gave a piano and set up a trust for her.

Into the Future

The house failed to sell in 1884 and, when it did, it had a number of owners, including two Lord Mayors. One owner, Horace Walker, held an event that must have been very lively indeed. It took place on a hot August Saturday and was a theatrical garden party. All the artists who had been performing in Bristol that week were invited and the po-faced report by the Western Daily Press, that was little more than a catalogue of stalls and stall-holders, hardly did justice to the high jinks that must have occurred. What would members of the D'Oyly Carte make of *'Chalking the bull's eye'* or *'Guessing the weight'* run by *'Miss Nancy of the Klu-Klux-Klan Company'*? But that was nothing to guessing the number of programmes sold. *'Success in that entitled the winner to the possession of the delectable young thing called Dolly Daydream.'*

John Cook's folly came to an end in 1933, when the tower was demolished and the house divided into two. Goodeve's house still stands and he is commemorated in a road in Sneyd Park named after him as well as in a block of flats.

Chapter Thirteen

Change and Protest

The Edwardian Years

The decade, after Queen Victoria's death in 1901, heralded a period of change and uncertainty.

The country experienced a foreboding that could not be shaken off. Political turmoil at Westminster, the ongoing fight for Irish Home Rule, legislation that threatened the status quo of the landed gentry, strikes and trade union agitation, the campaign for women's votes, all contributed to a sense of unease. Hanging over everything was the arms race (the baying cry for the Dreadnought class warships: *'We want eight, we won't wait!'*) and the almost inevitable drift towards war. Stoke Bishop was not immune from this growing sense of dread.

New Housing

Development continued to chip away at the edges of the estates. Following the building of the Downleaze and Rockleaze houses on the southern side of Sneyd

R. Milverton Drake's striking Edwardian house and his Whiteladies Road bank (next door to St John the Evangelist church)

Park (about this time Sneed changes to Sneyd as the favoured spelling), there was a smaller development on the northern edge of the parish on Druid Stoke estate. When Willian Munro senior died in 1856, his son, also William, later sold the estate to a Quaker and wholesale grocer, Thomas Wedmore, another luminary in the Stoke Bishop firmament. As we have seen Wedmore's executors arranged for the grounds of Druid Stoke House to be used for the Jubilee celebrations. His son, Frederick, was a distinguished art critic and man of letters. When Wedmore died in 1897, the estate was put up for auction. Houses rose along what became known as Druid Stoke Avenue. They were striking villas in the Arts and Craft style. The architect was R Milverton Drake, who from his practice in Bristol, embraced a range of architectural styles and created such diverse buildings as the soaring edifice of Stuckey's Bank in Whiteladies Road, the imposing perpendicular façade of Horfield Baptist Church and the Empire Theatre in Swindon.

Sunnyside

A humbler development was the initiative of William Edwards George who requisitioned part of his own estate for housing. He chose the hillside above the school where he established a small collection of twenty-one cottages. As we have seen, he referred to them as 'my cottages' and it is possible that he intended to house his estate workers in them. Originally they were called Georges Cottages, but had become known as 'Sunnyside' by the time they

Little girl in Hollybush Lane in front of nos 5 and 6 Sunnyside

were sold in 1922. Construction began around 1885 and they were built in stages. That they were well built is attested by the fact they still form a thriving community today.

Although the basic plans for each were the same, building materials and decoration varied. The early houses tended to be of a stone and tile construction, the latter ones sported red brick. They were generously appointed, all with three bedrooms, a sitting room, kitchen, scullery and other offices, plus a small garden. It was an idyllic setting, surrounded by fields, pasture and grazing cattle. At the bottom of the hill a stream burbled on its way to the Trym. The slightly haphazard way the paths led to the various cottages made for neighbourliness. One hundred

Cows graze in front of the school. To the right can be seen the first cottages built in Sunnyside. Later ones filled the gaps

and three year old resident, Flora Nash, speaking in 2023, remembered how she could be *'throwing out a pail of water and a neighbour would pop her head out and invite her in for a cuppa tea'*. Rebecca Clevett remembers Flora. *'She used to give my brother and I a polo mint to see how small we could get it. We also used to visit her cuckoo clock close to 'the hour' so that we could see the cuckoo make an appearance!'*

But that friendliness could be taken advantage of. The Western Daily Press ran a story in 1905 about how William Jones of No 4 Georges Cottages had a pair of trousers stolen It happened the day a young 14 year old Italian boy, Thomas Geravace, was serenading the cottages with a melodeon. *'Mrs Jones stated... that she gave him a penny and a crust of bread and cheese. Soon afterwards she missed her husband's trousers which were hanging on the line.'* The police were called and went in hot pursuit of the boy. *'PC 54 stated that he received information of the missing trousers and found the accused wearing them.'* In court Geravace *'said he had no father nor mother and his uncle*

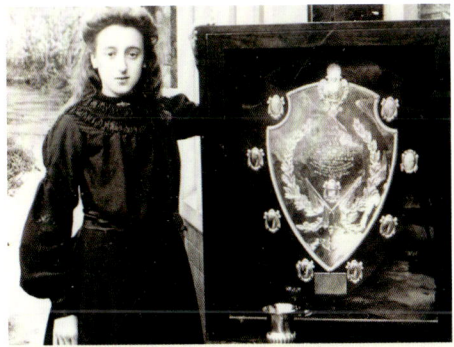

Kate Brocks of No 2 Sunnyside proudly displaying a sporting trophy

Number 5 Sunnyside

Mrs Hayward outside the front of No 5 around 1900. Note the fields beyond towards Kewstoke Road

Connie and Arthur Hayward in the garden

Rear of No 5

brought him from Italy, but was a long distance away now.' The *'bench'* let him go on the condition he left the city that very day.

Youth

More houses meant more families, meant more children. Apart from the school there were no organised activities for young people, nowhere to let off high spirits and what there was at church was invariably instructional. Clearly there was concern as in 1893 a Stoke Bishop Youth Club was created under the presidency of the vicar, David Wright. It met in the Village Hall and was for boys only (girls were invisible) from 13 years of age. To start with it may have been quite relaxed as later card playing and smoking were banned. But there was still an emphasis on improvement in what was organised. It cost three pennies a month to learn shorthand and four for leather punching. When David Wright's successor, Canon Alford, became vicar in 1896, the rules tightened. In addition to cards and smoking, whistling and bad language were added to the list of prohibitions. It is recorded that a John Kent was dismissed for improper language. There was a reading room where draughts, chess and dominoes could be played and wood carving was added to the practical activities.

In 1898 men over 18 were allowed to join the club, which for us today may seem surprising. It meant smoking returned, but not cards. A small billiard table, a quoits wall and table tennis were among the new attractions introduced. Members of the gentry joined, often sitting on the committee, making the Village Hall a more egalitarian social centre, where different classes could meet. When Canon Alford left in 1909, the rules were further relaxed, with card games, such as bridge and whist being allowed.

Scouts

But what the Youth Club couldn't provide was an outlet for physical activity. When the church noted that the behaviour of boys at evensong left a lot to be desired, it provided a weekly gymnasium class in the winter months. It was this sense of moral improvement through exercise that infused the arrival of the first Scout troop in Stoke Bishop.

Formed soon after Lord Baden-Powell inaugurated the Scout movement in 1908, the troop, from the start, was closely associated with the church. Its first leader was a curate at St Mary Magdalene, the Revd. Ralph Whytehead. The new movement emphasised self-discipline, loyalty to king and country and a strenuous pursuit of outdoor activities. Baden-Powell had become a national hero through his defence of

First Scout troop with the leader Revd. Ralph Whytehead in the centre

Mafeking during the Boer War in South Africa and many of his training techniques of tracking, mapping and field craft that he had learnt in South Africa found their way into the handbook, Scouting for Boys. For the youngsters in that first troop it would have been an ironic preparation for the battlefields of Flanders.

Boys during this period may have displayed high spirits, fought with each other and engaged in practical jokes, but they did not indulge in what we today would call anti-social behaviour. Crime was petty and opportunistic, as we have seen in the case of Thomas Geravace, and more often than not committed by an adult. One newspaper report told of a man arrested and convicted for stealing daffodil bulbs. But for everyone a new danger lurked.

The Horseless Carriage

Motorcars began to make their appearance on Stoke Bishop roads. *'The Georges had a small car, one which sits two with driver who used to sit at the back'* (Hence 'back-seat driver'). *'The first to have a car in Stoke Bishop was Halliwell, lived in one of the cottages and half the time they had to push it. It wasn't very reliable'* (Vi Watkins).

Stoke Bishop's steep, narrow and twisting roads were a major problem for the new vehicles. In the early years accidents were plentifully and often gruesomely reported. A particularly nasty one occurred on the evening of Tuesday 29 August

1911. It happened on Butcher's Hill (now Druid Hill), an incline described by the Western Daily Press as *'being known in the neighbourhood as dangerous for practically all classes of traffic'*. On the evening in question a traction engine pulling two wagons, laden with grain from Avonmouth, started to descend Butcher's Hill. A young woman stopped the driver and pointed out the steepness of the road and that an accident had happened there only the week before. The driver assured her his brakes were sound and he had known steeper hills. The convoy had a crew of three, the driver, the steersman, who had the wheel, and a brakeman, who operated the brakes on the wagons.

All went well to begin with, but then as, the traction engine approached the sharp bend at the bottom of the hill, it started to speed up, causing the wagons to go out of control. *'They overran the engine pulling it completely round and in a moment the engine and truck next to it had toppled over against the wall at the sharpest part of the bend'* (The Bristol Times). The steersman was pinned under the engine and died before he could be extricated. The driver and brakeman survived. At the inquest it was pointed out that the crew, who were from Burnham-on-Sea, did not know the area and should have been advised to go via Parry's Lane, a straighter route to the Downs. The verdict was *'Death from shock sustained by the accidental overturning of a traction engine on Butcher's Hill'*.

The aftermath of the fatal accident on Druid Hill in 1911 in which one man died

Sir Roy Fedden in his office

Speed and the conflict between car and cart was also a problem. On 5 April 1909, Roy Fedden, son of Bristol sugar magnate and philanthropist, Henry Fedden, was accused of using the road between Stoke Bishop and Shirehampton as a racetrack. It was said that he was an experienced racing driver and had won at Brooklands, but that didn't help his case. On the day in question James Robinson, of Druid Stoke Farm, was driving his cart on Shirehampton Road and was approaching another cart near the junction with Sea Mills Lane. The two vehicles drew abreast of one another and had no time to avoid Feddon's automobile, as it shot towards them. The car squeezed through the gap between the carts at speed and avoided colliding with them by a whisker. Feddon claimed he had slowed down, that he was an experienced driver and could have stopped if he had needed to. The magistrate didn't accept his defence and he was fined 40 shillings. Feddon went on to enjoy a distinguished career in aeronautical engineering and developed aero engines for the

Bristol Aeroplane Company, most famously the Bristol Jupiter, a man of speed at odds with the leisurely horse-drawn conveyance of the day. He was knighted in 1942.

But perhaps the most macabre of the early accidents happened on Stoke Hill on a rough, drizzly night in 1913. It involved the brother of Emily Pinker, the Stoke Bishop postmistress. Sixty-nine year old Charles Pinker was walking back from the Coach and

The Coach and Horses today

Horses pub on Blackboy Hill to his home at the post office, when he was apparently knocked down by a taxi in horrific fashion. The Bristol Times reported that

'at 12.10am John Chaney, taxi cab driver, arrived at the Cottage, Druid Stoke, Stoke Bishop, with a fare, and on going to restart the cab found the body of a man hanging from the starting handle, which had passed through his head. The driver stated that he felt a thud going down Stoke Hill and assumed the man was struck then and dragged to Druid Stoke, about one mile distant'.

Those were the bare facts, but how exactly it had happened mystified the authorities. At the inquest Douglas Moore, who was the passenger at the time and himself a motor engineer, estimated the car was going at about fifteen miles an hour. The jolt happened opposite the lodge to Springfort at the top of Stoke Hill. *'The driver pulled up immediately, and getting down, went to the side of the cab to investigate what had happened. Looking back along the road, he could see nothing to account for the jolt and he remounted and drove on.'* The road at that point was badly lit and it was raining, but Chaney noticed *'nothing dragging or impeding the progress of the car'*.

When they got to Druid Stoke both saw *'a man's head impaled on the starting handle, and his body under the car'*. The shocked driver *'released his handbrake and pushed the car back about a foot, the deceased's head falling from the starting handle to the ground'*. The situation was further clouded when the police went to the scene of the accident and *'found the deceased's hat and coat lying beside the road, whilst in the middle of the road there were marks of a body having been dragged along and smears of blood extending for about 10 yards'*. There was no evidence Charles Pinker was inebriated when he left the pub, *'his speech being clear and his gait perfectly steady.'* It was thought most likely that he was already in the road when he was struck. Had he had a heart attack? Then, why was his hat and coat lying, on a rainy night, beside

View of Sneyd Park. DURDHAM DOWNS.

The top of Stoke Hill where the accident happened

the road? The jury must have been bemused, as they returned a verdict of *'Killed by being accidentally struck by the starting handle of a taxi-cab'*. They exonerated John Chaney of all blame.

Keep Bristol Out!

Many of the changes that were taking place must have horrified the owners of some of the big houses. The development they feared most was being absorbed into Bristol. Although, ironically, a number of them had earned their fortunes from running businesses in Bristol, they had chosen to settle outside the city in what they considered to be a rural Gloucestershire enclave, to allow them to live a country life, but which, conveniently, enabled them to avoid paying the heavier taxes they would have incurred had they been residing in the city. But Bristol Corporation was always looking for ways it could infiltrate its *'country'* neighbour. To fight the threat, a group of landowners led by Francis Tagart banded together to resist any encroachment. As we have seen, Tagart held back his donation of the Jubilee Fountain until he was assured the threat had gone away. But it hadn't.

The Bristol Extension Bill, which among other matters, included a provision to extend the city boundaries to include Shirehampton, Horfield, Stapleton, St George and Stoke Bishop, when presented to the House of Lords in 1895, was fiercely contested. A counter bill, entitled the Opposed Bill, was delivered to the House of Lords by the local parish councils of the above mentioned and *'the owners, lessees and occupiers of the tything of Stoke Bishop'*. The arguments were instructive in the light they throw on the continuing belief that Stoke Bishop was still in the middle of the countryside. A picture that has recently come to light, painted in 1900, by noted landscape painter, William Tippett, could serve as the emblem for the anti-Bristol group. It shows a Victorian house on the Stoke House estate, the centre of a rural idyll, part of a farm with cows and geese quietly grazing.

But Bristol was having none of this. Its population had grown substantially and had spread over into districts like Horfield, where people worked in the city but lived outside it. But Mr Pomber, the barrister representing Stoke Bishop, argued this was not the case with his client. Stoke Bishop was largely agricultural, was separated by the Downs and contained no overflow of the working population of Bristol. Nevertheless replied the Town Clerk for the Corporation *'most of its inhabitants are more or less connected with Bristol, most of them get money from works or trade or commerce in Bristol'*. Not so, retorted Mr Pomber. The arguments swung back and forth and embraced topics from rates to amenities. The Town Clerk pointed out that Stoke Bishop had no provision for treating infectious diseases

William Tippett's painting of a house in Hollymead Lane marked the northern end of land owned by William H Budgett and later Louis Philip Nott of Stoke House

and when the retort came back that the parish never suffered them, he was able to cite the case of a servant in Sneyd Park who had to be treated for smallpox in the city's hospital.

Bristol's muscle won the day and in 1897 the Extension Bill passed both Houses of Parliament and by 1904 Stoke Bishop had been incorporated into the city. One of the first improvements was a proper road across the Downs, which made the prospect of commuting to and from Bristol a viable option. Already the tram network had crossed the Downs and there was talk (never realised) of it reaching Stoke Bishop.

Tramway across the Downs

Votes for Women

Stoke Bishop often conservative in outlook was not however

immune to progressive ideas. In the genteel drawing rooms of the Victorian mansions radical notions circulated away from prying eyes. At the 1884 annual meeting of the Bristol branch of the Women's Suffrage Association held in Park Street, it was noted that *'a series of drawing room meetings were given in or near Clifton in the spring, by Mrs Bruce in Sneyd Park... By Mrs Charles Thomas at Pitch and Pay, where Miss Todd of Belfast gave an address... There was a full attendance of ladies'* (Bristol Mercury). The tone of the speech was paternalistic. Miss Todd argued that the women who might qualify for the vote would be small in number, but their voice would speak up for the underclass of working women who had no one to whom they could turn to redress their grievances. *'Their object would be to draw the attention of members of Parliament specially to great social questions.'* And specific ones. *'If women obtained the vote, they would find it a material protection... against brutal attacks on wives by wife-beaters.'* Throughout a very long address the emphasis was on argument and verbal persuasion. What would have been the reaction of those assembled to a call for direct action? Alas reasoned debate failed and soon women resorted to a bitter campaign of violence and destruction in an attempt to make their voice heard.

Stoke Bishop Torched

In 1903 the Women's Social and Political Union was set up by Emmeline Pankhurst with a view to bringing the women's suffrage movement onto the streets. The rallies were often attacked, ending in brick throwing and assault. The WSPU resorted to more drastic protest. Stoke Bishop experienced it directly on 23 October 1913, when the University of Bristol sports pavilion at Coombe Dingle, built two years before at a cost of £2,000, was burnt down with suffragette literature found nearby demanding the release of a woman member arrested in London. The students response was angry and disproportionate. That evening undergraduates, numbering some three hundred, poured into Queen's

MORE ARSON BY WILD WOMEN.

The shell of the University's sports pavilion

The student damage inflicted on the suffragettes' headquarters in Queen's Road

Road and ransacked the WSPU headquarters. They piled up furniture, papers, books and pamphlets in the street and made a huge bonfire, dancing around the blaze to the applause of onlookers. The police did nothing. No arrests were made. Two women were trapped in the shop and feared for their lives. The Lord Mayor applauded the actions of the students and the Vice-Chancellor of the University, Sir Isambard Owen, made light of it at a dinner speech he made that evening, *'remarking that it seemed that the undergraduates had mistaken the calendar and had been celebrating the fifth of November a little in advance'* (The Yorkshire Post).

The next attack came a few weeks later and was reported in the suffragettes' own newspaper. Intruders got in through a downstairs window of Severnleigh at the top of Stoke Hill, one of the mansions created from the Stoke House estate. It was empty at the time. A fire was started at the base of the main staircase and destroyed much of the fabric of the inside of the house. *'The staircase was destroyed and several of the rooms downstairs and upstairs were very badly disfigured... The suffragette literature that was found... included a copy of the Suffragette on which was inscribed a message protesting against the arrest of Mrs Pankhurst.'*

The final recorded incident was part of a co-ordinated plan to disrupt services in a number of churches around Bristol on the evening of 15 March 1914. St

Mary Magdalene in Stoke Bishop was one of the churches selected. A man and a woman slipped into the service. At an appointed moment the woman stood up and recited a prayer, while the man stood guard. They were escorted from the church, most probably refusing, in suffragette fashion, to move and being dragged forcibly from the scene. The prayer left in the seats read *'O Lord, we beseech Thee, save Thy servants, Emily Pankhurst and Mary Richardson, and all who are enduring torture for conscience sake'*.

The Web Snaps

The barbaric practice of forced feeding, the violence inflicted, the jeers and the stones, all failed to give women the vote. What turned the tide was their war service and the way they were prepared to step into men's shoes on the domestic front and to take over when their menfolk went to war.

After a series of international crises, the complex web of alliances and ententes became so tightly bound that a major incident was certain to snap it. That happened in Sarajevo in Bosnia on 28 June 1914, when Archduke Franz Ferdinand, heir to the Austro-Hungarian Empire, was assassinated by a Bosnian separatist. The web unravelled and within days mobilisation had begun. Armies, subject to the dictates of railway timetables, moved with inexorable speed towards one another. Once the clock had started ticking there was no turning back. Within a few days of the assassination, Germany invaded Belgium as part of its grand strategy to overrun Europe. Britain gave Germany an ultimatum to withdraw or it would declare war. At midnight on 4 August, no assurance had been given. It was announced at 11pm (Berlin was one hour ahead) that Great Britain was at war with Germany. *'The lamps are going out all over Europe, we shall not see them lit again in our life-time'* (Edward Grey, Foreign Secretary).

Chapter Fourteen

The Great War

1914-1918

This chapter tells the story of the Home Front. The lives of the soldiers who left Stoke Bishop to fight are told in a companion book published by Stoke Bishop Local History Group, Leaving Home To Fight by Liz Tomlinson and Jenny Weeks. I am indebted to the fleeting glimpses that book gives of life back home.

On the Sunday after war had been declared, the vicar, Bishop Alfred Clifford (he had been Bishop of Lucknow in India before he came to Stoke Bishop) preached on the text *'God is our refuge and strength, a very present help in trouble'*, prescient words in view of what was to come.

We have few records of what the people of Stoke Bishop felt when the announcement was made. We can only surmise that it was a mixture of apprehension and excitement at the prospect of being part of what was seen as a great adventure. Vera Price was only eleven at the time and remembered being at Temple Meads as the troops were leaving for France.

Bishop Clifford vicar of St Mary Magdalene

'I could see all these men with colossal loads on their backs, wondering how they could possibly carry so much it was so heavy. But on their feet were little white spats – all brilliantly pipe cleaned or whatever they rubbed on them to make them very white. And I watched them marching until they all went through and was so intrigued by the little spats.'

There was an impatience to get to the front as reflected in Gilbert Ackland's wartime diary (the entry has been adapted). *'I couldn't wait to get over there. Mind you the French are a funny lot. They do things different from us. We had lumps of bread without plates, hard boiled eggs and – would you believe – tea in basins. We were all eager to get to the trenches and the fighting. After all that's why we'd come'.* For many, only a couple of years before, they had been schoolboys. The sons of the big houses invariably became officers, most from Stoke Bishop school went into the ranks.

Refugees

If the mood of the moment was one of hope that *'it would all be over by Christmas'*, harsh reality came with the arrival of refugees from Belgium. This small country had been rapidly overrun in the first days of the war and stories started to circulate of the brutal treatment meted out to the population by the occupying German army. Headlines denouncing the rape of women and the bayoneting of children were everywhere, atrocities seemingly confirmed when the refugees started to arrive. Of the 2,000 who came by steamer to Avonmouth, 50 were settled in houses around Stoke Bishop. The Village Hall was set aside for their use and they were taken on outings in the area. A photograph of them on the Downs has survived. Volunteers delivered food parcels and clothing. As the war progressed the men were encouraged to return to Flanders by enlisting in the British army. Those who stayed were urged to seek work and it wasn't until February 1919 that they returned

Belgian refugees photographed on the Downs

to Belgium. On Saturday 15 February, 600 mainly women and children, including 100 children born in Bristol, boarded a special train in Temple Meads bound for Tilbury and Antwerp.

Road Difficulties

As we have seen, roads in Stoke Bishop were inadequate for the mechanised age and were quick to prove an obstacle to military efficiency. Armaments destined for the Front were shipped from Avonmouth. To get to the port, traffic had to go through Stoke Bishop, but as the Western Daily Press reported on 12 April 1915, this direct route *'was practically barred on account of the very steep gradients'*. Heavy traffic, including caterpillar-tractors, had to be re-routed via Parry's Lane, but even that was difficult as *'there was a deep descent* (and) *the road is at times very narrow and the two practically rectangular corners, before the Shirehampton Road is reached, are about as bad as anything...'* Some tree felling and widening at the top of Butcher's (Druid) Hill helped, but no major improvements to the roads were made until after the war. Another difficulty was navigation. Drivers were getting lost in the lanes. Special signs directing them to Avonmouth had to be erected.

The Nott Boys

In 1914 communication systems were developed enough to ensure that news travelled fast. It wasn't long before letters began to arrive announcing the names of the dead and wounded. A letter posted in western France would arrive the next day, telegrams even quicker. Soon households across Stoke Bishop were mourning their loss. Some were hit harder than others, none more so than the Nott family of Stoke House.

We have followed the fortunes of Stoke House from its beginnings. After John Battersby Harford left in 1869, the house had several owners, among them William Henry Budgett of the grocer family. In 1896, Louis Philip Nott, his wife and their large family of three sons and seven daughters (one died young), moved into Stoke House from Manchester. Louis was born in Portsmouth and trained under Thomas Andrew Walker, a noted civil engineer who rescued and completed the Severn Railway Tunnel after it had flooded in 1879. Under Walker, Nott supervised a number of high profile contracts including the construction of the Manchester Ship Canal. When Walker died, he took on his own contracts, which he continued when he came to Bristol. These included harbour and dock works as well as railway and sewage projects, both in Bristol and South Wales.

In 1883 Louis married Walker's daughter, Mary Elizabeth, who had been born

From left, back row: Jeanette Mabel, Winifred, Thomas Walker, Marjory, Louis Cameron, Brenda; front row: Henry Paton, Mary (wife), Louis Philip, Margaret Audrey, Dorothy

in New Brunswick in Canada. The Notts had three boys: Thomas Walker, Louis Cameron and Henry Paton. All were educated at Clifton College and Emmanuel College in Cambridge. All joined the 6th Battalion of the Gloucestershire Regiment (Louis and Henry were still at Cambridge). All became officers. All were in France by March 1915. All were dead by April 1917. In their short time in France, they gave, through their letters, a vivid picture of life on the Western Front. The following is a small sample of what they were writing home to Stoke Bishop.

Henry Paton Nott *'We are now within sound of the guns. The French people are very different from our own. Everywhere the men salute or take off their hats. The women smile and clap and the children cheer and shout 'Biscuits – souvenir'. Our men chuck them halfpennies. The Bully Beef is really excellent. The people are very peculiar, there seems very little privacy. You may be half stripped washing, when in will come your hostess and her daughter without knocking or anything.'*

Thomas Walker Nott *'Yesterday we marched 18 miles in pouring rain. Imagine a column of infantry, each man loaded to the full and the column well over* *a mile and a half long. Alongside it perhaps a battery of artillery lumbering along driving the foot sloggers into the slimiest and beastliest mud while they rumble along the pave. Very different from our route marches at home. The owner of our billet has been killed but his widow carries on. The farmer nearby is said to have been hanged by the Germans.'*

Henry Paton Nott *'I was sitting talking to some of the men when a great tall young sergeant put his head over the parapet. I said to him: 'If you don't keep down you'll have a hole through your head.' Within 10min he had one and 10min later he died. Poor fellow – he wasn't three yds from me when he was hit. I think the most awful part of this war is the absolute callousness with which one looks on death.'*

Thomas Walker Nott *'I had a bath yesterday evening. In a brewery or wine factory here. There are large vats and these are filled with hot water, which is disinfected with creosote. You stand up to your neck in this; in fact you can just swim. After this you can get your clothes washed and put on clean ones. After 100 hours without your clothes off and living in straw, muck and filth you can imagine what this means to us and the men. I've only had 10 hrs sleep in five days.'*

Thomas Walker Nott sending a letter no mother wants to read. *'Pat (Henry) was with Fowlie going up the Communication Trench to my Firing Line in order to look out for a spot in the German line to which he could lead a patrol*

Thomas Walker Nott Louis Cameron Nott Henry Paton Nott

tonight, when a shrapnel shell burst right in the trench and when Fowlie turned round Pat was dead. It was absolutely instantaneous, as he was fatally hit in several places. As the sun was setting last night we laid him to rest where so many of the 6th Gloucesters lie in peace, while overhead the shells scream.'

At approximately 4am on 18 April 1917 a delayed-action fuse, which had been left by the retreating Germans in a cellar where Louis Cameron, Thomas Walker and others were sheltering, exploded.

The War Memorial in Bude, Cornwall

April 20th 1917
Dear Mrs Nott
You will have heard already from the War Office of the death of your sons Lt Col T W Nott, DSO and Capt L C Nott. They were both killed with four other officers by a German mine which exploded where they were living early yesterday morning. They were buried this morning in the village cemetery. Nearly all the Regiment and many other officers of the Division were present.
Yours sincerely
R Fanshawe
Major General
Commander of Division

Henry Paton was buried at Hebuterne Military Cemetery in the Pas-de-Calais and Thomas Walker and Louis Cameron at Villers-Fauçon Communal Cemetery, all in France. They are commemorated on the war memorials of Clifton and Emmanuel Colleges and Stoke Bishop. The are also remembered on the war memorial in Bude, where the family had a house.

We cannot imagine the depth of grief the Notts must have felt at their appalling loss. But they were not alone. The Robinson family of Springfort, who had inherited the paper and packaging company, lost three boys, as did the Hosegood family of 6 Downleaze. Stoke Bishop's big houses produced a higher percentage than elsewhere of young men who became junior officers and it was they who led their men into battle with the concomitant risk of getting killed.

The Nott Sisters (Audrey in a wheelchair)

But what of the women at home? The Notts were again representative of the effort many women contributed to the war effort. The six Nott daughters, Jeanette, Dorothy, Marjorie, Brenda, Winifred and Audrey were all engaged in various wartime activities. Two, Marjorie and Jeanette, were working at the Red Maids division of the 2nd Southern General Hospital, Marjorie in dispensing and Jeanette as secretary to one of the doctors. Winifred continued her medical studies at Bristol University and went on to become one of the first women GPs in Bristol.

Jeanette also did a spell in an Avonmouth munitions factory, while Audrey worked at Filton on aircraft manufacture. She was in the assembly hall of the Bristol Fighter, operating a jig that had been especially made for women to handle. It involved stretching the canvas over the wing frames and then coating the fabric with dope, a glue-like substance that gave off intoxicating fumes and caused the women to suffer terrible headaches.

The contribution of women during these years turned public opinion in their favour. Before the war ended, the Representation of the People Bill was passed giving married women over 30 the vote, the first step towards full suffrage in 1928 for all women over 21.

Grief took its toll on Louis Nott. He died at Stoke House in July 1916 a few months after the death of his son, Henry Paton. Mary Nott and some of the girls remained in the house until 1926 when it was sold and became a school. Mary moved to Cook's Folly where she died in 1930.

An imposing view of Bishop's Knoll with parkland running down to the railway as it enters the Avon Gorge.

Bishop's Knoll at War

Perhaps the biggest story in wartime Stoke Bishop was that of Bishop's Knoll, which became a hospital for wounded Australian service men.

Bishop's Knoll was one of the big houses that overlooked the Avon Gorge. William Baker acquired the land, a part of the Martin estate, and built the house around 1861. Its massive proportions were designed to impress, its medieval-like tower dominating the knoll on which it stood. It was sold in 1870 to Peter Dowling Prankerd, who had made his fortune as a land agent in Australia. When he died in 1902 the house passed to his two sons, one of whom, Percy John Prankerd, was at Clifton College with a Robert Edwin Bush. Percy never lived at Bishop's Knoll, but we find that on his death in 1908, the house was bought by the same Robert Bush, who was to live there until his death in 1939.

Robert Bush

Robert Edwin Bush was born in 1855 in Redland into a family of merchants (the Bush Warehouse in Prince's Street, now the Arnolfini, was the centre of their operations) and went to Clifton College, where he acquired a love for cricket. As a member of the Gloucestershire County team he played alongside W.G. Grace. Not sure what to do with his life, Bush decided to chance his luck in Australia. After several unsuccessful enterprises, he bought the lease on some land which he converted into a sheep station. This proved a shrewd decision and by 1905 he was owning two million acres on which he ran 100,000 sheep. He became part of the political elite of the new State of Western Australia, but in 1896 his wife died and in 1905, he returned to England, probably because of his children's education. In the same year he bought Bishop's Knoll. Two years later on 27 May 1907 he married Marjery Scott, the daughter of an old Australian friend. She was 21, he 51. The wedding took place in St Mary Magdalene church.

Robert Bush in his characteristic quasi colonial dress

Not well known in Bristol, Bush remedied this by actively courting civic life. In 1911 he was elected High Sherriff and he served on the committee that funded the Edward VII Memorial Wing of the Bristol Royal Infirmary, which was opened by King George V and Queen Mary on 28 June 1912. But Robert Bush never forgot Australia and when war broke out, he and his wife wanted to repay the country that had made them so wealthy. They immediately sought to convert Bishop's Knoll into a 100 bed hospital. This astonishingly was accomplished within three weeks of the announcement of hostilities. It was no doubt helped by the fact that Bush's younger brother, Lt Colonel Paul Bush, was in charge of the 2nd Southern General Hospital, under which Bishop's Knoll would operate. The letter of acceptance noted that Bush's *generous and patriotic offer... will*

Bishop's Knoll from Leigh Woods on the other side of the Gorge seen here flying the flag of the Red Cross

be taken advantage of when the need arises'. Neither were to know how quickly that *'need'* was to become a reality.

Archie Powell of the Western Daily Press, described the transformation:

> *'I remember visiting it on a glorious day in mid-summer. The scene even now is fresh in my memory – the gay throng scattered about lawns and terrace, the superb view of the winding Avon with the woods of Leigh across the river and the Bristol Channel and Welsh hills in the far distance, making a picture of peculiar charm. How changed is the scene when I next cross the Downs and visit the Knoll.'*

The ballroom had been stripped of its treasures and had joined the drawing room, the dining room, bedrooms and billiard room in becoming wards.

> *'Fortunate indeed are the lads who come battle-scarred to Bishop's Knoll. Not only are they set in the midst of natural beauty that will be hard to beat anywhere in our British Isles, but the whole atmosphere of the place is comforting.'*

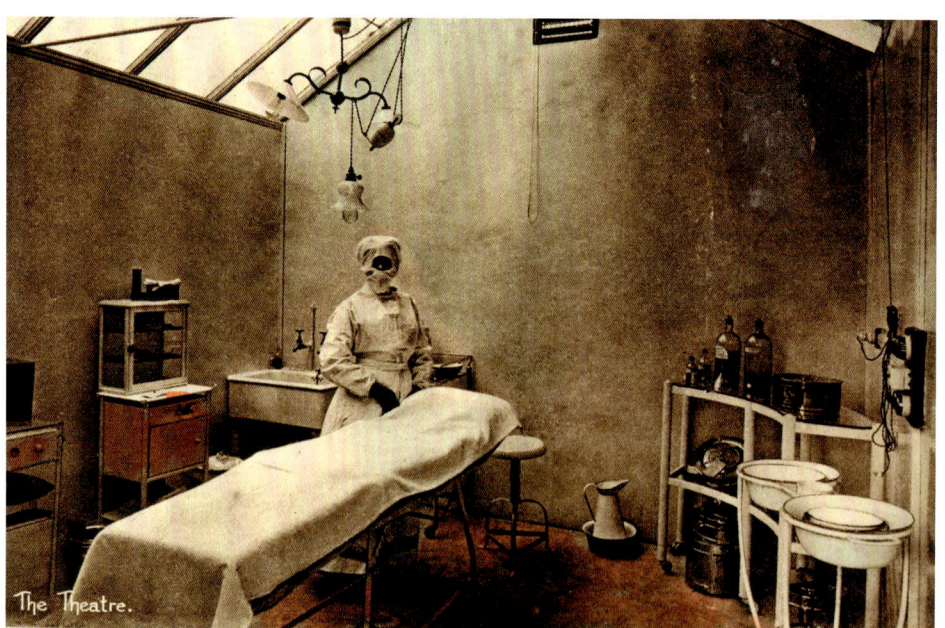

The operating theatre at Bishop's Knoll

Pictures from a photograph album given to staff

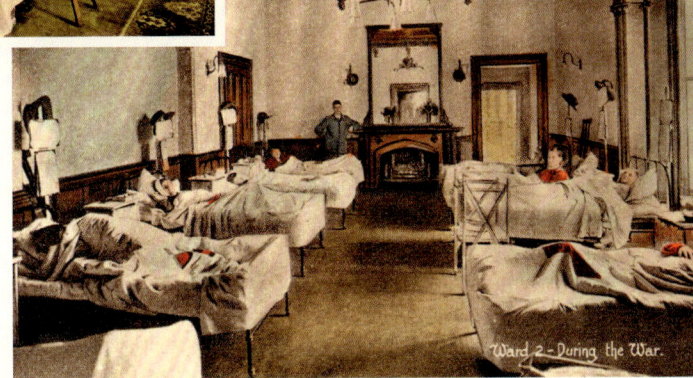

Above, dining room
pre-war; right,
dining room during
the war

Above, entrance
before the war; right,
casualties arrive by
ambulance

Title Page of Coo-ee, the newspaper edited by Archie Powell for Bishop's Knoll patients and staff

The new hospital contained a dedicated operating theatre and the whole was equipped and staffed at Bush's expense. It has been estimated that over the entire war period it cost him £100,000 (around £10 million today).

The first wounded arrived in Bristol after the battle of Mons (23 August 1914), but soon contingents were pouring in by rail to Temple Meads and ship to Avonmouth. It was clear that there were not going to be enough beds and Bishop's Knoll was quickly called into service. Bush would have preferred to take in only Australian wounded, but because the hospital was part of the British 2nd General Hospital the Australian government would not accept Bishop's Knoll as coming under its jurisdiction. This was to change after Gallipoli. Churchill's attempt to open up a second front by attacking the soft underbelly of Turkey misfired tragically. The assault on the Dardanelles and the abortive landings at Gallipoli resulted in a huge number of Australian casualties. On 30 September 1915, the War Office consented to allow only Australians to be treated at Bishop's Knoll, resulting in a cultural interaction that had not been seen before in Stoke Bishop.

The Commandant, Staff and Patients

We have a vivid picture of what life was like at the hospital through an album of photographs given to staff that depicted before and after scenes and via a regular

A promotional picture of Robert Bush working in the kitchen with Marjery, his wife, in VAD uniform, opposite him

newspaper, edited by Archie Powell and written by the staff and patients. Called Coo-ee after an Australian bush call, it was a compendium of jokes, poems and writings, with titles like *What I think of English Girls* by Private F.G. Hull or *What I think of the Australians* by Sister Sylvia, as well as more serious articles on the soldiers' war experiences.

Robert Bush took charge of running the hospital. He was known as the Commandant. But he was also hands on, working as an orderly and collecting the wounded from Temple Meads. His wife, Marjery, was the Quartermaster and took charge of the kitchen. The nursing staff included seven trained nurses, Red Cross auxiliaries and volunteers from Bristol 12th Detachment of VADs (Voluntary Aid Detachment). The latter were volunteer medical assistants (mainly women from the middle and upper classes, distinctive in their newly designed long blue cambric dresses) who, although they only had 10 days first aid training and a three months probationary period, provided valuable support on the wards. Just how valuable is shown by this poem written by Private Angel Davis and published in Coo-ee.

> *'They're called 'the Pillow Smoothers', they have another name,*
> *The 'Very Artful Darlings', and well they play the game.*
> *I'm but a shy young ANZAC, not used to women much,*
> *I've always dreaded nurses, and hospitals, and such.*
> *How was I going to stick it, until my wounds were well?*
> *A crowd of them all fussing – far worse than shot or shell.*

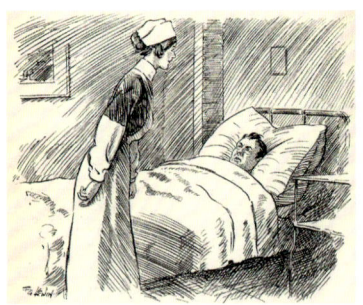

> *I lay upon a stretcher, a little girl tripped up,*
> *My cigarette she lighted, and held my coffee cup.*
> *And 'Could she write a postcard to send to any friend?'*
> *Or 'Would I like a pillow?' she bucked me up no end.*
> *I had no friends in Blighty, and when the pain got worse,*
> *I never could have stood it, without that little nurse.'*

Fresh air was thought to be a great healer as these pictures show of patients convalescing in the garden

To begin with there were four doctors who lived locally. Dr Henry Lawrence Ormerod of Westbury-on-Trym acted as surgeon until a resident one was appointed. The chaplain was the vicar, Bishop Clifford, assisted by the curate Revd. R. Whytehead.

Bishop's Knoll was described as *'more of a home than a hospital'* and certainly there appeared to be a wide variety of diversions available, from sporting activities to concerts and other musical entertainments. For those able to go, outings were organised to local beauty spots or, if confined to the house, there were the extensive gardens to enjoy. Trooper J. Lennox described a typical Bishop's Knoll Christmas.

> *'Mr and Mrs Bush carved the huge turkey, and all the other Sisters were busy helping. Then came plum pudding and after that fruit... After dinner there was the great excitement of dressing up in different costumes. The Sisters all dressed up too, mostly in Dutch Costumes, and we all joined around the laden Christmas Tree, which was covered with presents for all, and were given out by the Commandant. Afterwards we had games, then supper, and then to bed very late.'*

The writer wondered whether he would see another Christmas Day at Bishop's

Knoll or would he have to content himself with the *'book of memory... which we shall have to read over and over again long after the war is over, when we are back in our own quiet homes, in all parts of the Empire'*. Some were not to see their home, as one nurse remembered:

> *'Before the end came, he was wandering in his mind. I found from his talk that he had a wife in Australia, and that after a quarrel he had left her hastily and then enlisted. He never saw her again, but in those last days of his life his thoughts were constantly of her. Now in his delirium he has mistaken me for his wife and he has made up the quarrel with her and has died quietly, soothed by my voice.'*

The Oak

Having moved out of their spacious mansion, the Bush family had to find alternative accommodation. Fortunately the Oak, a smaller house, but big enough for their needs, lay unoccupied next door and they leased the house for the duration of the war. It had a lodge occupied by Henry Sweeting and his family. Henry and his two sons ran a market garden business on the estate and travellers along the Port and Pier railway would comment on the sea of glass cascading down the side of the Gorge. For Bush this was fortuitous as vegetables grown at the Oak combined with the fruit from his own walled garden were sufficient to supply the kitchen at the hospital with fresh fruit and vegetables for much of the year. He

VAD nurses working in the garden during their off duty hours

also kept a Jersey cow whose milk was stored in pans in the cellar. There were also piggeries in the area of today's Bramble Lane providing a ready supply of pork. It was reported that before the war the gardens had as many as eighteen working in them, but many would have volunteered. To make up for this depletion VADs were put to work in the gardens during their off duty hours!

Robert Bush: the Later Years

Within months of the Armistice being signed on 11 November 1918, the 2nd Southern General Hospital was wound down. The last patient left Bishop's Knoll

Robert Bush (standing left) with patients and staff. The nursing sisters have plain aprons and the VADs wear a red cross

in February 1919 and the Red Cross Flag was lowered from the tower.

Robert Bush maintained his close links with Australia and always attended Gallipoli Day (later renamed ANZAC Day) at Arnos Vale Cemetery. He kept his sheep station in Western Australia, having to divide its two million acres in 1928, when a law was passed restricting any one holding to one million acres. In Bristol he continued to play a major role in society. He became Chairman of Gloucestershire Cricket Club, President of Bristol Savages and President of the Old Cliftonian Society. In the New Year honours, January 1918, Marjery Bush was awarded the OBE. Strangely not her husband and when he was put forward for a CBE, he declined. Was he expecting a knighthood which is eventually what he got in 1923 when he was made Knight of the Order of St John of Jerusalem?

The Bushes returned to Bishop Knoll, where Robert lived until his death on the 28 December 1939. His granddaughter, June, remembered visiting him just before he died. He had two Australian birds in the Conservatory, a white cockatoo and a green parrot and he carved the meat at lunch wearing his Australian hat. His body was cremated at Arnos Vale where his name is on the family memorial.

The Memorial at the top of
Stoke Hill

Stoke Bishop Remembers

Bishop Knoll hospital ran itself down efficiently, with its patients returning to their homeland, but around Stoke Bishop there were painful gaps at the meal tables. In common with other towns and villages up and down the country, a growing desire to create permanent memorials to those who had been lost, began to emerge. Over 100 were killed or were missing from Stoke Bishop out of a population of 1382 (1911 Census). The Village Hall was the focus through which the campaign to raise money was organised.

There were three projects, a shield to be given to the school, with the names of the 32 boys killed inscribed on it, the purchase of the post office opposite to be turned into a men's club and the erection of a war memorial. Unsurprisingly the money came in to fund all three projects. It was sent to the War Memorial Committee via R.F. Budgett, often with touching notes. Harold Clark was a labourer and lived for a time in Stoke Cottages. He gave half a sovereign *'for the memorial for the dear ones who have gone from us'*. Mrs Clark wrote a letter to the Committee explaining that ever since *'our dear boy fell'* she and her husband had put the money aside *'on purpose for such a time as this'*. George Extence, a coachman, gave a ten shilling note. *'I feel I would like to make a small donation towards the memorial which is to be constructed in the memory of our fallen lads'*.

Sadly one man refused to give because he didn't like the design of the Memorial. The cross stood 17 feet tall, had on four sides space for the names and was constructed of Stancliffe stone, a warm coloured limestone quarried in Derbyshire. It was designed by Bristol architect, W.H. Watkins, and placed in what, in 1918, was a centre of population at the top of Stoke Hill. The Memorial was dedicated by the Bishop of Bristol on 16 May 1920. The photograph that was taken at the time shows a large crowd that must surely have constituted most of Stoke Bishop. An endowment fund was raised to the sum of £100 and put in the hands of the Merchant Venturers, the money from which was given to St Mary Magdalene for the upkeep of the Memorial. This transferred eventually to Bristol City Council.

Stoke Bishop School's Memorial Shield, which was sadly lost during a bombing

Dedication of the Memorial at the top of Stoke Hill by the Bishop of Bristol

raid in the Second World War, was unveiled at the school by the vicar, Bishop Clifford, on 29 September 1920. Mr Miller, the headmaster for over 40 years, read the lesson. Ethel Watkins witnessed it. *'Mr Miller knew us all by name and... as each name was read out our Master as we called him – wept unashamedly at their memory.'* The shield had been designed by Arnold Wathen Robinson, eldest son of Kossuth Robinson, of the Robinson packaging company. Arnold, whose three brothers died in the war, had survived and had devoted himself to pursuing his career as a stained-glass artist. His creations can be found in Tyndale Baptist Church and Bristol Cathedral and he was instrumental in setting up the Bristol Guild in Park Street.

The Men's Club opened its doors in its new premises in October 1920. It had been funded by public subscription. One man sent £25 to the War Memorial Fund *'to be divided equally between*

Stoke Bishop School Memorial Shield

A STOKE BISHOP MEMORIAL.

LYCH GATE FOR THE PARISH CHURCH.

Artist's sketch of the proposed
lychgate at St Mary Magdalene

the cross and the Village Hall Extension'. There had also been an injection from the Belgian Refugee fund, the money being no longer required as the Belgians by now had gone home. The new club was intended as a welcome home gesture, but whether those returning were not ready to return to society or were too busy getting back into work, the club was not a success and within ten years it had closed and the building sold as a private house.

One other memorial is worthy of mention and that is the lychgate at the entrance to St Mary Magdalene. This was given by Charles and Bessie Strachan in memory of Charles's cousin's son, Aubrey Strachan and Bessie's nephew Leslie Fry. It too was designed by W.H. Watkins and was dedicated on 14 December 1919. Charles and Bessie had no children of their own and Aubrey and Leslie were only sons. Giving the lychgate, which traditionally was where the body lay before entering the church, allowed people to pause and reflect as they passed through on those who had been lost.

A Coda

Amid the grief and sorrow that infected the community, there were occasionally happier moments. On the Sunday following the signing of the armistice, the vicar took as his text Psalm 98 v1 *'O sing to the Lord a new song, for He hath done marvellous things'.*

A peace celebration was organised in the village. *'Where the garage now stands at the bottom of Stoke Hill was a large field and it was there that our peace celebration and our sports days were held in that year. I as an eighteen year old participated'* (Ethel Watkins).

Then on the 16 July 1921 four officers, from

Anette Lennard arrives at church
holding her baby son, Thomas Jay

the 6th Glo'sters, and their wives brought their newly born babies to be baptised at St Mary Magdalene. The Bishop of Bristol, resplendent in his top hat, presided over the service, a unique occasion as all four babies had been born in 1921, a new birth for the future.

From left, Captain Peter and Mrs Lowicke; Captain and Mrs Calvert-Fisher; the Bishop of Bristol; Lieutenant and Mrs King; Major Ernest William and Anette Lennard

Chapter Fifteen

Twilight of the Farms

1918-1939

When the men returned from the war in 1918, the Stoke Bishop they came home to would have looked little different to the one they had left behind.

A map of the period would have shown a concentration of housing in the southern part of Sneyd Park and a cluster of cottages in the village, while the greater two thirds of the parish appeared as farmland, most of it, pasturage. The most common sights in the summer months were cattle grazing and the horse drawn harvesters making hay. Operating in the parish were around eight farms and a number of market gardens in Coombe Dingle. By 1939, all that was left of Stoke Bishop's agriculture was a scattering of horse paddocks, some piggeries and a residue of market gardens. Only two farms were left clinging to the fields beside Sea Mills harbour and in Old Sneed Park.

Information about the farms has been hard to glean, but a series of photographs that have survived show what a returning Tommy would have seen.

Stoke Abbey Farm

Abbey Farm (later Stoke Abbey Farm) was the largest and perhaps the most productive of the farms in the parish. It was a dairy farm producing milk for a large part of Bristol and its distinctive green carts and later vans were a familiar sight in the area. The farmhouse and milking sheds were off Parry's Lane. There had been a farm on the site from at least the end of the 17th century.

Stoke Abbey Farm was by 1852 part of the Harford / Stoke House estate with, according to the 1851 Census, 62 acres leased to John Harding, a 76 year old widower. He had three farm labourers to help him. By 1861 his son, Henry, was farming 100 acres and was employing five men. When William Edwards George bought the farm from John Battersby Harford in 1869, the Hardings continued to

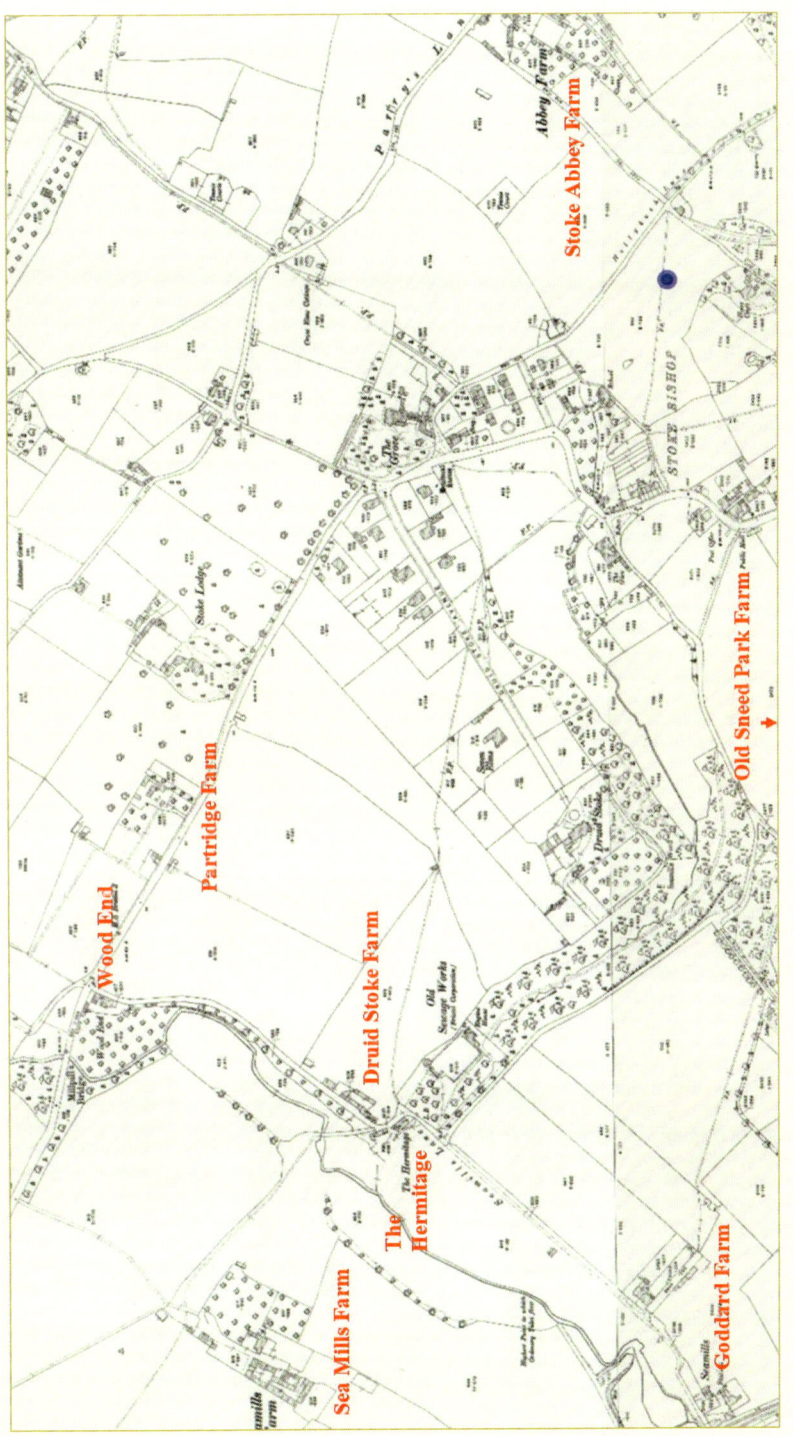

Farm map

A farm ramble

Walking up from the Avon along Sea Mills Lane, the first farm reached would be the Hermitage. In the photograph (above), the farm buildings are to the left of the farmhouse. This was originally the Sea Mills Tavern. (The Hermitage was probably demolished when the road was straightened and a main sewer constructed along Sea Mills Lane in the 1920s.) Up ahead the road took a sharp S bend around the entrance to Druid Stoke Farm, whose barns can be seen in the distance.

Boys play on the stone bridge which carried a track to Sea Mills Farm. Druid Stoke Farm is behind them.

Leaving Druid Stoke Farm, top, a walker would reach Wood End, above, at the intersection of Sea Mills Lane and Shirehampton Road. In 1938 a dairyman Charles Belben lived there. The farmhouse to the right has been demolished, but the cottage to the left still exists.

Turning right into Shirehampton Road and just before the Stoke Lodge estate lay the Partridge Farm, left.

Cows graze in the meadows in front of Stoke Abbey Farm. The pasture would later be the site of Ormerod Road

farm it. Henry now had 130 acres and a staff of five men and two boys.

In 1880, Edwin Albert Green, from Somerset, took over the farm, leasing a reduced acreage of 32 acres from the George estate and settled in the old farmhouse with his wife Mary Louisa. They had been married at Doulting parish church, near Shepton Mallet, and set about establishing a thriving dairy herd and raising a family. They had ten children, of whom eight grew to maturity. Tragically they suffered the loss of Ethel May, their three year old daughter, when her dress caught fire in the nursery and she died from her burns. She is buried in St Mary Magdalene churchyard.

Edwin quickly established himself as a leading figure in the Bristol agricultural establishment. He was a Downs Commoner and a well known figure at the Bristol Cattle Market and at the Corn Exchange. He was a member of the West Gloucestershire Farmers Club and the Gloucestershire Old Spot (a breed of pig) Society. The family had a rich social life and enjoyed all manner of sport. They had a tennis court on their land and stabled horses.

In 1922 they were able to buy the lease on the farm and increase their acreage after the George family had put the Downside estate up for sale. Earlier in 1915, Edwin had moved out of Stoke Abbey Farm putting the business into the hands of his eldest son Albert. He and his wife rented and moved into the nearby Cote Grange farmhouse in Cote Lane. The farm was managed by Albert, from Stoke

Abbey Farm, who grazed his prize herd of 32 Guernsey cattle in its fields. In 1927 he raised money to extend this pedigree herd by holding a farm sale at Cote Grange. The items on offer included 11 milking cows, three horses, farm implements, harness and dairy equipment. At the same time he developed the dairy side of the business.

Before the Great War, the Greens sold their milk locally from carts, but by the twenties Green's Dairy Farms, as they came to be called, used mechanised transport to deliver their bottles of pasteurised and Jersey milk, along with clotted and whipping cream, all over Bristol. Soon the local farms could not supply enough milk for the dairy and the Greens began using lorries to bring milk in churns from other farms. In all their advertising, which was extensive, they were at pains to stress their attention to hygiene and modern cleansing practices. They used *the latest approved steam apparatus* and were *under the direct supervision of the medical officer of health*. An advert in the Western Daily Press in 1926 promoted *a demonstration of a new bottling machine* at the farm.

But delivering milk by horse and cart carried on. Heather Pelmear, who lived in Woodland Grove in the 1930s, remembers another farm on the Kings Weston estate, bringing fresh milk to the house.

Edwin and Mary Louisa Green taking tea on the farmhouse terrace with some of their family

Green's Stoke Abbey Farm dairy cart before mechanisation; right, Edwin Green shows off one of his new motor vans

'Farmer Smith came with his horse and cart twice a day, the churns of milk behind him in the cart, and the householders would take out their jugs and he would fill them with a large ladle, probably a measured half pint size. Most wives were not out working in those days so there usually would be someone in, if not the wife, an elderly relative or in some homes a daily maid. In our home the milk would be put on a cold marble slab in the pantry and it usually stayed fresh until the next milking unless the weather was hot and thundery. Sometimes my mother put some of the milk in a wide shallow bowl and added some rennet and it would set into junket which we ate with nutmeg sprinkled on it. Another time we would have clotted cream. The milk was very slowly heated until the cream on the top formed a thick crust. This was left to cool then carefully skimmed off the top and we would have a bowl of clotted cream to enjoy with bread and jam, the cream always on the top, Cornish-wise. For some reason this bread, jam and cream was called thunder and lightning!'

In 1924, Edwin Green died and the family decided to sell Stoke Abbey Farm, although they kept Cote Grange and the milk distribution business. In 1941 Hornby's Dairies joined them after the latter's city premises had been bombed. When Hornby's Dairies went into liquidation in 1956, the Green family continued to run it until 1973, when the depot was taken over by first Cow and Gate, then Unilever and finally Dairy Crest as an important milk delivery depot. It was sold for housing in 2010.

The Last Farms

As we have seen pockets of land on the edge of estates and farms began to be sold off and agricultural lands found themselves tucked away behind new developments until eventually they were squeezed out of existence. Two farms did survive and stumbled on into the 1950s. One was the Home Farm of Old Sneed Park. In 1881 its 75 acres were being managed by John Codrington of Chipping Sodbury.

The other farm was the residual part of Sea Mills Farm that hadn't been swallowed up by the new Sea Mills estate created after the Great War. The fields of this

The Home Farm of Old Sneed Park with the house in the background

remnant ran from the Trym to the Avon and were the passion of a retired dentist, Henry Goddard, who lived in Roman Way. The farm buildings were the original milking sheds of Sea Mills Farm and sat behind Riverside House. Keith Horley grew up in the area and remembers the farm and how Henry Goddard had two cart horses, Bob and Dinah, stabled at the back of the two cottages near the railway station. *'Round the back there it was like a farmyard itself – there were ducks, fowls all running around. We'd go round and harness up these horses and go up to the fields, one hay and one corn. We had an old fashioned hay cart for the horses to pull and a mower to cut the hay.'*

The best pasture of Goddard's farm lay on the other side of the Portway and the railway line, alongside the river. Normally the cows were moved on a path under the bridges, but there was a problem when the spring tides arrived.

'When the tide was in we couldn't take them under the Portway so we'd drive them up the slip road to the road and take them across and a porter would come up from the station open the level crossing and we'd drive them across the track and he'd close the gate and there they were grazing out on the wharf (the field beside the river).'

On another occasion, Keith was told, Mr Goddard drove a flock of sheep all the way down the Portway to the Bristol Cattle Market near Temple Meads.

But perhaps the most haunting of Keith Horley's memories were the times he was helping with the hay making in Old Sneed Park. *'The fields were so quiet. There was no traffic on the Portway – all the freight went by train. All you could hear was the snorting of the horses, the chiming of St Mary's clock'.*

The rural and tranquil landscape of Old Sneed Park is evoked in this colourful watercolour by Alfred O. Townsend

Chapter Sixteen

A Postwar Housing Boom

1918-1939

On 22 November 1916, Sir George White died at his home in Old Sneed Park, aged 62.

In what he had achieved, he represented one of the great pioneers of the modern age. He had founded the Bristol and Colonial Aeroplane Company in 1910 and established a factory in Filton to manufacture commercial aircraft. Before that, and more importantly for Stoke Bishop, he had created the Bristol Tramways Company that brought the electric tram to the Downs and Westbury-on-Trym. It never got to Stoke Bishop, but it was an easy walk from the Downs into the village.

The distinctive figure of Bishop Clifford stands beside the tomb of Sir George White in St Mary Magdalene churchyard

A few days after Sir George's death, a funeral service was held at St Mary Magdalene, where his body was laid to rest beside his wife in a tomb that had been erected close to the church tower. The service was conducted by the vicar, Bishop Clifford, and attended by a gathering of sufficient size to attract the attention of one of London's more popular newspapers, The Daily Sketch.

Sir George White's transport empire now made it possible for Bristol to ease the pressure on the city's housing by taking advantage of its newly expanded boundaries. The professional classes saw that it was possible to work in the city and live in the 'countryside'. And a new generation of builders was going to make this happen.

A New Vision

After Francis Tagart's death in 1911, Old Sneed Park was bought by Cecil Wills (of the Wills tobacco family) and then by Sir George White, whose family were to be the last private owners of a house that had stood since the 18th century. After Sir George's death, it fell into disrepair, as happened to so many country houses after the Great War, drained of staff and afflicted by new punitive taxes. In 1923 the house and 130 acres of the estate were put up for sale. The buyer was a Catholic organisation which converted it into an orphanage. Eight years later, in 1932, all but 32 acres of the original purchase were sold. The Stride Brothers Ltd, a firm

A Stride house in Church Road

197

of family builders from Shirehampton, bought plots along what was to become Mariner's Drive. This allowed them to put into practice a new vision for the area, which they outlined in their sales brochure.

'The design of the residences is intended to meet the demand of the professional or city man in business in Bristol who wishes to have his house in the country where he and his family can enjoy the advantages of sunshine and country air, channel breezes and beautiful views, situated in the most select district, yet served by the advantageous services of a city in the way of transport, water, gas, electricity and drainage.'

And there we have it, a utopian dream, not for the bosses of commerce and industry, but for the affluent middle class, who, if they came in numbers, would destroy the very thing they strove to acquire. But not yet. Most of the amenities described were not fully in place and the Strides themselves saw the dangers of mass housing. They planned that each house built would be individual in design and sit on half an acre. *'Our ambition is to multiply the beauties of Old Sneed Park and not to destroy them.'* They insisted that trees would be preserved.

The Stride Brothers

The Stride family had had a long history of house building. Originally from Somerset, some members of the family, from humble beginnings, taught

The Stride Family in Station Road, Shirehampton. Brothers Arthur and Fred far left with their sister Lucy, her husband Bertram and their son Gerald. On the right of the pillar, their father Jared, his wife Mary-Jane, their brother Ernest and their uncle Jethro

themselves building skills and moved first to Cardiff and then across the estuary to Shirehampton, where a company was formed in 1848 by Edwin Stride and his two sons Jethro and Jared. They built houses locally on Park Hill and Station Road in Shirehampton and were involved with the building of Avonmouth docks.

Jared's sons, Arthur, a carpenter and Fred, a bricklayer, were to carry on the business but not before new horizons

Fred and Arthur Stride

beckoned. In 1910, with trade slack, they decided to chance their luck abroad and took ship to Canada, settling in Medicine Hat, Alberta. For the first few years they lived on the frontier in a tent. They tried cattle ranching but were unsuccessful and turned to the trade they knew, building houses. They met and courted their wives in Canada but a worsening economic climate made selling houses difficult. Arthur's son, Leslie, takes up the story:

'So they decided they'd better come home and see their mother, so, in 1920, they packed up their bags and me with them, six months old, and set off to see their mother. Things were getting better here, so they stayed much to the chagrin of

The Stride Brothers in Canada. Left, Arthur on horseback; right, Arthur standing, Fred bending down

their wives. They had left all their furniture behind and a barrel of salt pork which mother never forgot'.

The Houses

It proved to be the right decision. The brothers bought substantial plots in Sneyd Park and elsewhere in Stoke Bishop and set about creating houses of distinction.

Neither brother was a trained architect, but each had an eye for design, incorporating Canadian ideas and inventions into their houses. They used a lot of good quality wood, particularly oak, roofs were deep pitched and in the cold Canadian winters they had seen how important central heating was to the buyer and embraced the latest techniques for heating houses. Equally they massaged their clients' ego by assuring them of an individual look to each house. The company stressed that *'there are no hard and fast rules to the size and design of the houses'.*

The Strides put great emphasis on their attention to detail and it was in the detail that they could satisfy the buyer's desire for individuality. They also went out of their way to include new ideas of interior design and modern convenience accessories. They introduced double doors between reception rooms, fitted dressing rooms, tiled kitchens and bathrooms with sunken baths and chromium plated fittings. Novelties like two way drawers between kitchen and dining room

From top: Houses in Old Sneed Park, Church Road and Mariners Drive

enlivened the interiors and new colours, oyster pink and turquoise green, brightened the porcelain enamelling of bathrooms and kitchens.

The houses were wired for electricity, with two way switches in the hall and landing. Kitchens were fitted with Ascot gas heaters to provide hot water and an electric point to run a refrigerator. *'Every fresh idea is considered, and if thought practicable and reasonable, is put into operation wherever possible.'* They took great pride in making all the wooden parts of the house, the panelling, staircases and wardrobes, in their workshop in Shirehampton. In a later sale of a Stride house in Church Road the prospectus read *'the convenient layout was planned by the late owner and built, under Architects supervision, by the well-known Builders, Messrs. Stride Bros'.*

But never far away in all their literature was the lure of country pursuits *('there is hunting with both the Earl of Berkeley's and the Duke of Beaufort's hounds, and golf at Shirehampton and Henbury'),* combined with proximity to the city by regular public transport. In the beginning Old Sneed Park was advertised as an exclusive estate. New roads, Roman Road (later renamed Mariner's Drive), New Road (Old Sneed

Some surviving fittings. Note the quality woodwork, colour co-ordinated bathroom and elaborate fireplace

Park) and Church Road, had been put in, and it was noted that *'omnibus routes pass within 100 yards of both the Upper and Lower entrances and the Railway Station is but ten minutes walk away'*.

Old Sneed Park estate was perhaps the Strides' most prestigious building project in Stoke Bishop, but it was not the first. They erected bungalows in Bell Barn Road from as early as 1927. These had a distinctive Canadian look, being low in build with deep pitched roofs to protect against the west country weather. Another early

The Strides' drawing of a proposed dwelling for Bell Barn Road. Note the steep pitched roof and dormer windows, reflecting a Canadian influence

development was close by in Cheyne Road (1929) and Stoke Paddock Road. The firm boasted its houses would not depreciate. They did more than that. They set the tone for the way Stoke Bishop was to look in the next decade. Today an estate agent's description can still state *'a classic Stride family house in leafy Sneyd Park'*.

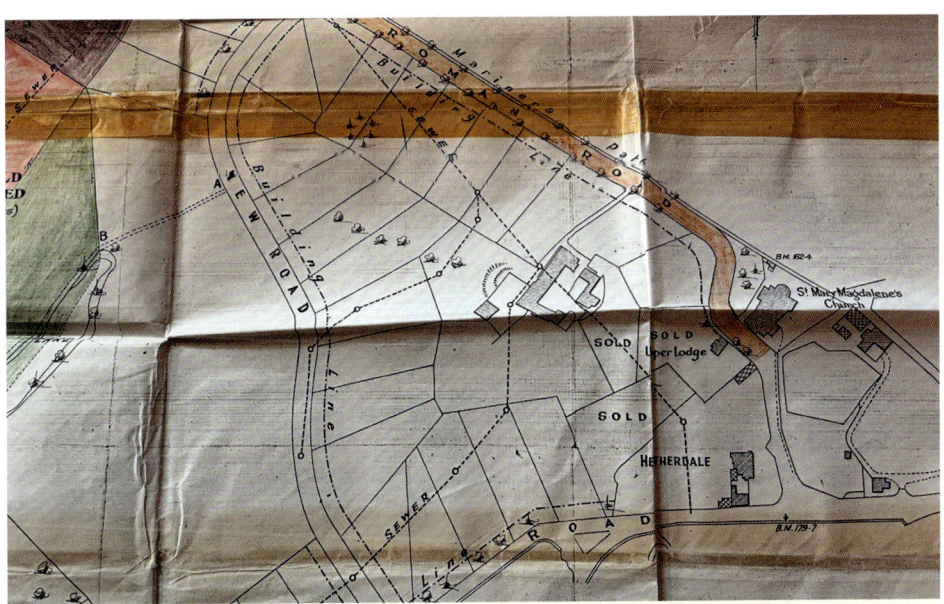

An estate map showing the layout of the new roads across the parkland of Old Sneed Park

A Second Sale

In 1922, one year before the sale of Old Sneed Park, an advertisement appeared announcing the sale of the Downside estate. The previous year, at the age of 79, William Edwards George had died. His will failed to appoint any individual member of the family to succeed to Downside and so it was decided to sell the estate. Through the agency of the Wills Tobacco family, the house, the Home Farm and the southern part of the estate were sold to the newly created University of Bristol as a *'residential college for men'*. The remaining 50 acres were sold separately. These included Stoke Abbey Farm and the twenty one Sunnyside Cottages.

As we have seen, Edwin Green, who was leasing Stoke Abbey Farm, bought the farm and increased his acreage by buying most of the other northern half of the estate. His farm stretched from what is now Shaplands to the edge of the Grove near the top of Druid Hill. But when he died in 1924 the family decided to sell Stoke Abbey Farm, keep the milk distribution business based in the farm yard and

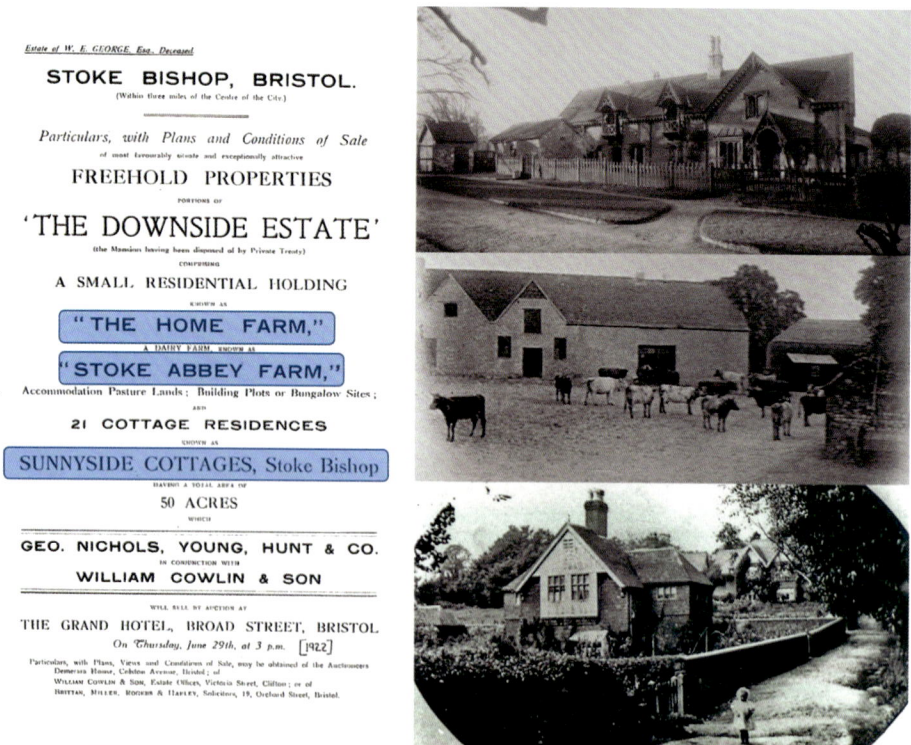

The sale notice advertising the sale of (top) Home Farm, (middle) Stoke Abbey Farm, (bottom) Sunnyside Cottages

the lease on Cote Grange Farm and put the fields on the market for development. What had been a trickle of housing became a flood. Where cows once grazed, whole estates appeared.

Joseph Smith

One of the first builders in the area was Joseph Smith. He had recently come south from Lancashire to seek his fortune. He was the seventh son of a publican in Burnley in Lancashire. His grandson, Christopher Smith, takes up the story.

> 'In those days public houses were basically staging posts for coach horses at the end of the nineteenth century. As he was the seventh son he had the joy of getting up early in the morning and getting the horses ready for travel. He really had an affinity for horses. He then grew up and started a small carting firm of his own. I've got memories of him saying that he made a reasonable amount of money and for a reason I don't know he moved south and bought a farm in Hallen and he brought down his horses and his carts about the time of the First World War and he said these motor lorries'll never catch on and he went bust!'

But this didn't stop him and he took a gamble at trying his luck at house building. He and others followed the practice of buying plots of land, putting in unmade roads, drainage and other services and then building on a few plots themselves and selling on the remainder to other builders. Joseph Smith laid out Ormerod Road, Birbeck Road (where he built himself a house) and Reedly Road. As was common practice, he named them himself after places he had visited in Lancashire and the Lake District. *'Birbeck was named after a stream in the Lake District, in Shap Fell,*

A Joseph Smith built house in Ormerod Road

204

where they call them becks and not streams. We used to go on holidays up there. Spelt Birkbeck. He took the k out because he thought these southerners would pronounce the k whereas the locals pronounced it without the k!' (Christopher Smith)

The Vokes

A Voke house in Little Stoke Road

William and Leon Voke, father and son, were responsible for much of 1930s Henleaze including many of its shops, but they did stray into Stoke Bishop. Houses in Little Stoke Road and Kewstoke Road are examples of their work. Like the Stride brothers, William Voke made his fortune abroad. He was an ornamental plasterer by trade and went to Africa in his twenties. He was responsible for the rococo work in the Court Rooms of Bulawayo in Zimbabwe. On his return before the Great War, he started building in Bedminster and then moved to Redland. After the war he bought a farm in Henleaze and began building extensively in the area. He was joined by his son. During the thirties they spread their operations across north west Bristol.

It must have been a frenzied period of activity, but the first builders attempted, if not always successfully, to create individual styles. Michael Brooks, who had a long career with the estate agents, Chappell and Matthews, has collected photographs of the houses being built, which give a vivid picture of the transformation from farmland to urban street. He himself grew up in Kewstoke Road. His parents, like

Michael Brooks in front of the house he grew up in in Kewstoke Road

205

many who came, had the desire to live in this new leafy paradise, but often found it a struggle to raise the capital to buy.

A building site in Kewstoke Roadd

> *'My parents bought the house in 1932 and I was born here in June 1933. They didn't move in straight away having bought it. They couldn't afford to do so at that time. The price was about £600, a great deal of money. The road was unmade, lots of rubble about.'*

The half-tamed landscape was a playground for children as Heather Pelmear remembers.

> *'It was a whole new suburb... just waiting for the builders. This is where we... made dens and climbed trees. We had plenty of materials from the pile of building equipment left by the builders, including bricks. Scaffolding then was made up with long wooden planks and strong wooden poles. We used clumps of grass stuffed between the bricks and poles to make a sturdy den. Big sister Ce joined in from a distance by leaving coded messages and drawing Skull and Crossbones in our den when we were not there! She was probably reading Arthur Ransome's Swallow and Amazon books at the time.'*

Wyndham Rossiter

Another local builder was Wyndham Rossiter. He lived on Butcher's Hill (Druid Hill). Among his developments were the Arts & Craft style houses in Druid Road. He bought the land there in 1930, built the houses and was selling them between 1932 and 1934. The process of development followed the usual pattern.

The land purchased was called Lower Westfield and was part of the 1923 sale of Old Sneed Park lands by Sir George White's family. It was bought by H.W. Giffin of the Shire House in Beach Road, Weston-super-Mare, who sold it on to Rossiter in 1930.

Although there was a builder's yard at the bottom of Butcher's (Druid) Hill, Rossiter's yard was in an old farmhouse on Parry's Lane at the junction with Stoke Lane.

Houses being built in the 1930s
(from the collection of Michael Brooks)

Kewstoke Road with fields behind

Cranleigh Gardens with fields behind

Voke houses in Kewstoke Road

Ormerod Road

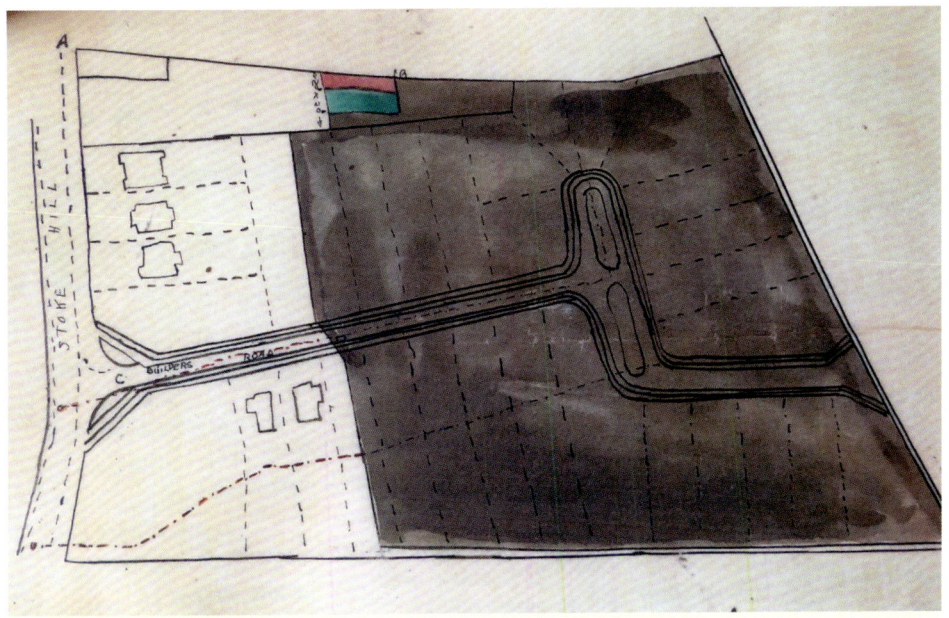

Rossiter's plan for Druid Road, showing the attractive island layout in the middle of the development

Rossiter's business occupied the old farmhouse on the junction of Parry's Lane and Stoke Lane, now a block of flats

A Case History

It is possible to see, through a study of one house, how convoluted was the process of moving from pasture to suburban dwelling. When Stoke Abbey Farm was broken up, its many parts were willed to different members of the family. Gwendoline Hannah Weston-Stevens, described as a spinster living in Abbey Gate off Parry's Lane, was bequeathed 32 acres, which were marked pink on the deed map. These

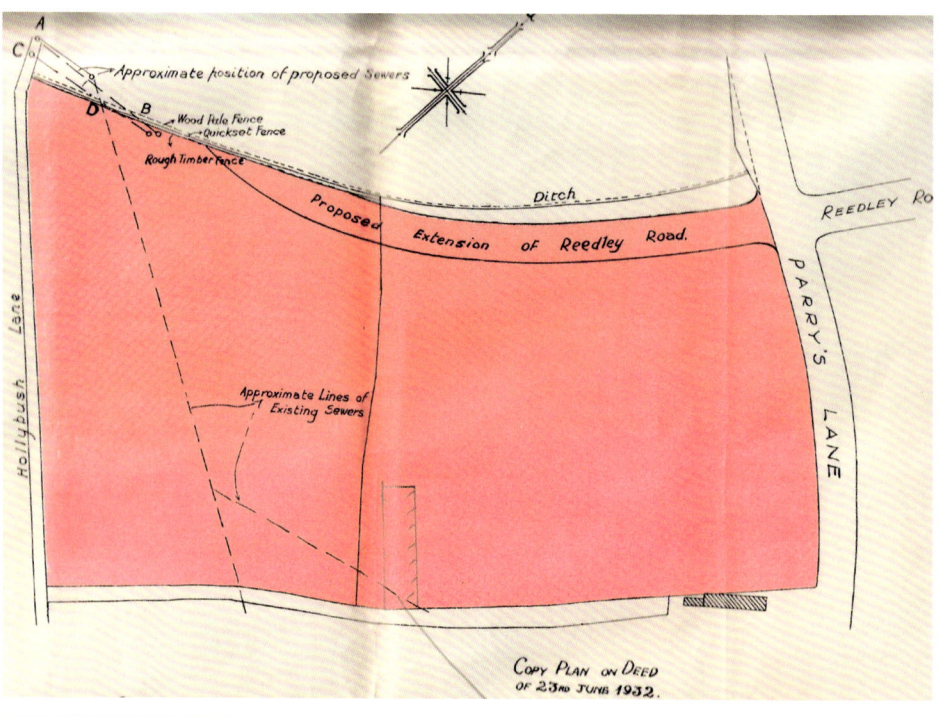

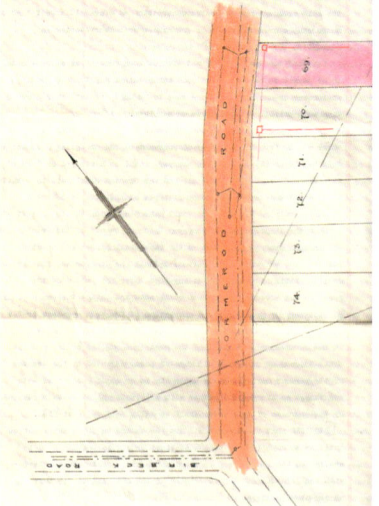

Abstract of the Title

OF

Mr. JOSEPH SMITH

to land situate in or near Parry's Lane, Stoke Bishop, in the City and County of Bristol.

Above, map showing 32 acres purchased; right, plot 69

were the 32 acres that Joseph Smith bought from Gwendoline Hannah Weston-Stevens in 1932. A later map showed part of Smith's acquisition divided into plots, with No 69 shaded pink.

He passed Plot 69 on to builder Allan Rogers, who built a house which he sold to Stanley George Ackroyd Brook of Henleaze. In 1935 Plot 69 became a house in Ormerod Road.

Within a decade Stoke Bishop had changed from being a rural enclave of Gloucestershire to becoming a suburb of Bristol, albeit a leafy one.

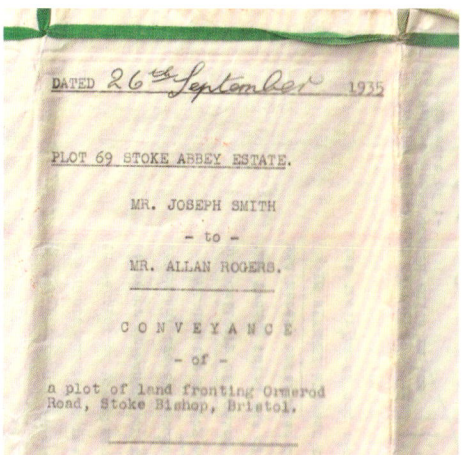

PLOT 69 STOKE ABBEY ESTATE.

MR. JOSEPH SMITH

– to –

MR. ALLAN ROGERS.

C O N V E Y A N C E

– of –

a plot of land fronting Ormerod
Road, Stoke Bishop, Bristol.

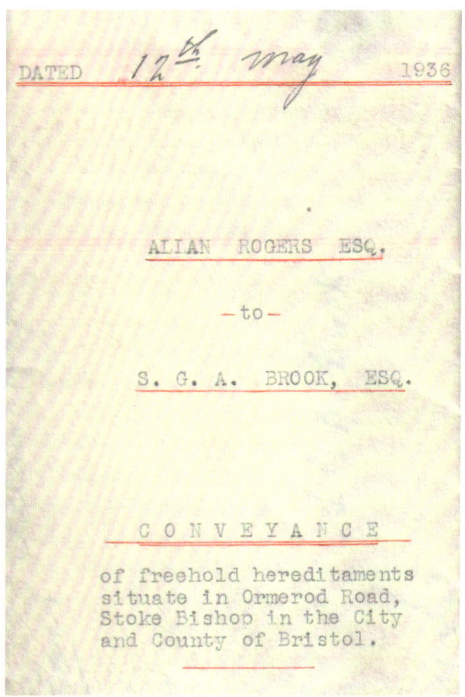

DATED 12ᵗʰ may 1936

ALIAN ROGERS ESQ.

– to –

S. G. A. BROOK, ESQ.

C O N V E Y A N C E

of freehold hereditaments
situate in Ormerod Road,
Stoke Bishop in the City
and County of Bristol.

Clockwise from above, documents
showing the transfer of Plot 69 from
developer (Smith) to builder (Rogers) to
owner (Brook) to become a house in
Ormerod Road

Chapter Seventeen

Roads

1918-1939

We have seen how the roads through Stoke Bishop caused difficulties for heavy vehicles negotiating steep gradients and sharp bends which often led to accidents.

This was brought to a head during the Great War when armaments destined for the Western Front via Avonmouth became stuck in what were little more than country lanes. But after the war changes did come about. In 1926 work began on widening and improving the two main roads through Stoke Bishop.

Stoke Hill and Druid Hill

Traffic coming down Stoke Hill met a sharp right hand bend at the Village Hall as the road wound its way past Oak Lodge, the old post office, Stoke Cottages and the Tagart Fountain before continuing up an equally twisty Butcher's Hill to Shirehampton Road. In the two decades after the war these bends were ironed

The newly completed road bypassing the old post office and Stoke Cottages. Note the fields on the left

out and a wider, faster road was created through the village. In 1926 a throughfare was constructed across land belonging to the Chetwood-Aiken family of The Glen which bypassed the old road and turned it into a country lane and ultimately a cul-de-sac. In 1934 Butcher's Hill was widened and got its new name of Druid Hill. (Presumably, with its reputation for accidents, Butcher's Hill was deemed inappropriate.) The dangerous zig-zag bend at the bottom of the hill was removed making it less steep. But accidents still happened. A double decker bus ran into a lamp-post during a snow storm, in exactly the same spot as the tractor accident of 1911!

Three years later, in 1937, improvements were made at the top of Druid Hill at the junction with

Widening the zig-zag bend at the bottom of Druid Hill

Improving the junction of Druid Hill and Shirehampton Road

Shirehampton Road, where there is now a roundabout. The Stoke Lodge wall was lowered to improve visibility and the whole area widened. The result of course of all these 'nicks and tucks' was to upgrade the old toll road to Shirehampton at the expense of the village. Crossing the road became and still is a perilous business.

Parry's Lane

Although used more frequently by heavy traffic because it had fewer bends and was less steep than Stoke Hill, Parry's Lane was also little more than a country lane and was so narrow in places that vehicles had difficulty in passing. Work began to improve it in 1925. The road was closed to all traffic and the bus route diverted along Stoke Lane. Many trees were cut down, hedgerows grubbed out, S-bends straightened and the new road doubled in width. Good quality houses at the Downs end graced one side of the new thoroughfare. It was opened in September 1926 and all would have been well had the Highways Committee of Bristol Corporation not decided once again to change the name. They thought that Parryswell or

Widening Parry's Lane

Paddyswell Road would be more appropriate for a modern highway with ancient associations. A well had indeed stood at the top of the hill (opposite the entrance to Wills Hall). An old picture shows it with a pump.

The story goes that Irish cattle drovers landed at Avonmouth and took their herds along Parry's Lane to the city, stopping for water at the well. As a result some people started calling it Paddy's Well, corrupted to Parry's Well on an 1880 OS map, but clearly the locals wanted Parry's Lane to stay as there was a howl of protest when the change of name was proposed. After a public consultation and a majority in favour of keeping the old name, the Committee relented and the new road remained Parry's Lane, despite the fact it no longer felt like a lane.

The iron pump that stood on the site of Paddy's Well

The Portway

The road that was to provide Stoke Bishop with a fast route into the city was the last to be built although it was the first to be planned. As we have seen, as far back as the 18th century, any dock built near or at the mouth of the Avon was faced with the problem of transporting goods into Bristol along inadequate roads. The railway had helped, but the original Port and Pier Railway ended in Hotwells with no terminus in the city. The Avonmouth Dock was opened in 1877 and was greatly expanded with the opening in 1908 by King Edward VII of the Royal Edward Dock.

The docks played a vital role in shipping military supplies to the Western Front, but this only highlighted the unsuitability of the roads to cope with the heavy wartime traffic. A new road into the city became imperative and in order to avoid the hills the only possible route was along the edge of the Gorge. With the cessation of hostilities a plan was launched to build a low-level road using German prisoners of war. It was then discovered that much of the route ran through a prohibited area where no Germans could be employed. The scheme was shelved only to be revived a year later in 1919 when a labour force drawn from demobilised soldiers was put to work.

The obstacles confronting the engineers were formidable, not least the narrowness of the land available along the Gorge. There was a towpath but not of sufficient width for a modern highway. The only possible route was already being used by the

The towpath along the Gorge before the Portway was built

Bridge over the Trym being built with caissons (left) sunk to support the arches (right)

Port and Pier Railway. To solve the problem an Act of Parliament was introduced to terminate the railway's operations and replace the track with a new road. Provision for a tramway was also included but this was never constructed.

Work began in May 1919. On average 800 men a day were engaged on the project. At the time there were no large earth movers available to facilitate the digging, but a narrow gauge railway laid along the length of the road did allow men and materials to be moved more easily about the site. Yet the bulk of the work was done by blood, sweat and hard manual labour.

The completed bridge with its six spans

An aerial picture showing the collapsed concrete that has slipped into the mud

Crossing the Trym at Sea Mills proved to be the most challenging part of the operation. Originally it was proposed to make the crossing in three spans, but unstable ground forced the designer to increase it to six. Caissons, hollow concrete cylindrical drums with steel shoes, were sunk into the soft subsoil. The earth that was pushed up was removed and concrete poured into the cylinders to erect the piers on which the arches rested. The core structure was constructed from masonry, which was blasted from a rocky promontory that had been blocking the route at Hotwells. This core was faced with dressed stone, topped by capstones of Corsehill stone brought from a quarry in Dumfriesshire in Scotland.

A second obstacle facing the contractors lay a few yards further up river where the road crossed the railway line at Sneyd Park Junction. This was surmounted by slinging steel-girders at an angle across the railway and resting them on masonry abutments. But not everything went to plan. Underground streams running into the Avon softened the soil and sections of concrete used to shore up the road were washed away into

The Minister of Transport cuts the ribbon to open the new road

A tranquil view of the newly built Portway

the river. Again the solution was to run the road over sunken piers.

Such was the interest in what was then called the low-level road, that Bristol Corporation secured the attendance of the Minister of Transport to open it. On Friday 2 July 1926, the Rt. Hon. Lt-Col. Wilfrid Ashley formally opened what at the time was thought to be the most expensive road ever built in the country. There were two tape-cutting ceremonies, one at Hotwells and the other at Avonmouth. Whatever we think of what was eventually called the Portway, those at the time thought of it as something to marvel at. In his speech the Minister noted, as reported by the Western Daily Press, how *the Corporation were not only anxious to do something useful, but that was also beautiful, and the citizens were lucky men and women. Not only had they made a good road but had not disdained to consider the beautiful and the aesthetic, and the road with its trees would not only be a means of locomotion, but a promenade by the side of the beautiful river*.

Early photographs and writings about the Portway underline the leisure aspects of the new road. Tennis courts were laid out at the Sea Mills entrance along the Gorge and shortly after it had opened the Western Daily Press reported: *It has already achieved wonderful popularity. Everyday, especially at weekends, local motorists swarm upon it, whilst each evening there is an almost constant stream of pedestrians upon the spacious well-made footways.* Certainly the postcards of the time show a surprising lack of traffic, with people sat on seats serenely taking in the view. How

Ships collide and run aground in fog off Sea Mills, December 1929

long this lasted we can only guess, but such scenes only return on the infrequent occasion the Portway is closed to traffic, usually because of a rock fall.

River Catastrophe

Despite the Portway and the developments at Avonmouth, the docks in the city centre continued to thrive and shipping could be seen alongside train, bus and lorry making its way upriver. But one winter's day soon after the new road was opened a remarkable calamity occurred on the river off Sea Mills.

At high-tide the river was often full. This was the case on the evening of Friday 29 December 1929 on a stretch of the river known as Sea Mills Reach, between

The Peursum slides into the Bristol City

218

Horseshoe Bend and the Trym. Laden steamers were making their way up and down river, among them, the Peursum, inbound from Savannah with a cargo of turpentine and tobacco, and the Etrib, from Smyrna, carrying dried fruit. All was going normally until a bank of fog suddenly descended and reduced visibility to zero. Mayhem followed. Ships collided with one another or ran aground. Reports vary as to the number involved but there were a least five steamers and half a dozen smaller craft. Vessels were turned around, with rudders and propellors ripped off. The Etrib lost her bridge, while the Peursum lay with her stern on the bank and her bow in the river. Alarmingly, as the tide fell, the latter slid down the mud onto another steamer, the Bristol City, which had listed so much that her crew had had to abandon her.

The fog persisted and there was a fear that when the tide returned more havoc would ensue. Fortunately it didn't and as the miasma slowly lifted a scene of extraordinary chaos revealed itself. Most of the ships were re-floated and the others towed into the docks.

In the Taunton Courier, alongside the collision story, was a piece head-lined 'Wall Street Cracks – More People Ruined Than Ever Before'. The mayhem on the Avon was nothing to what was going on in New York!

Chapter Eighteen

Shops

1932-2010

Not surprisingly Stoke Bishop was slow to develop retail outlets.

With the area being largely the preserve of big houses, there was little need for shops. The larger estates were often self-sufficient in food and what they couldn't produce themselves, they would order from the Bristol stores or further afield. Their servants grew their own vegetables and often sold the surplus, while local farms, like Green's Dairy, delivered milk and meat. But the houses of the new professional families, large though many were, were not large enough to produce enough food and the demand for produce from local suppliers grew. Ironically the village was the last to get shops. The first emerged on the edges of the parish.

Rockleaze Road

Around 1925 shops started to appear in Rockleaze Road in Sneyd Park to serve the concentration of Victorian semi-detached villas in Downleaze and Rockleaze. In

An early picture of the shops in Rockleaze Road

Kelly's Street Directory for that year, the listing for Rockleaze Road named Frank Turner as a provision merchant and two gentlemen Messrs Thomas and Sincock as postmasters and stationers, their establishment described as Rockleaze Town sub-post office. Further along the road were a police station, with the sergeant in charge one Charlie Greenslade, and a telephone exchange run by Mrs Emily Newbury. Both the latter were shortlived, with the telephone exchange being transferred to a purpose built establishment in Stoke Bishop in 1932 and the police station replaced with a police box on the triangle of grass at the end of the Avenue.

Shirehampton Road

The next shops appeared in Shirehampton Road in 1929. They were a branch of Lloyds Bank and William Rothwell's sweet shop, catering for society's financial needs and its sweet tooth. In between the two was Thomas Partington's general store. These premises stood on the junction with Bell Barn Road opposite the Mill Pill (today called the Mill House), that was being run as a shop by Thomas and Jesse Prestidge. By 1932 more shops had been built on the east side of Shirehampton Road. Among the owners were the Bristol Co-operative Society, Mrs Lily Furber, a ladies hairdresser, Leonard Roy Brown, a pork butcher, Marion Foster, a ladies outfitter, E

An omnibus stops outside the first shops in Shirehampton Road

221

Luton & Sons, bakers and confectioners, another shopkeeper, Mrs Eveline May Partington, and the Cornish Stores, a firm of grocers who were to become an established part of Shirehampton Road for many years. A fishmonger's arrived two years later and was followed by a hardware store, completing a wide range of goods on offer. Sylvia O'Driscoll remembers Shirehampton Road in the sixties (At this time Trymwood Parade had been built on the west side of the road, greatly expanding the shopping opportunities).

1938 Cornish Stores' well-stocked shop window

'The local shops were utterly amazing. The choice was fantastic. We had the Danish House with a café, a greengrocer's, a butcher's and baker's. The Co-op. Country Casuals. There was Mason's, a general store and they would deliver. Patricia's that sold toys and children's clothes. Ronto's, a dress shop. Two hairdressers. A chemist. Two hardware shops, one either side of the road.'

(Martin Sisman) *'There was an off-licence upstairs in the Mill House, with outside steps on which the old lady who run it stored her empties ready for collection by the brewery, Georges. We boys used to collect and return empties for the few pence they yielded, sometimes augmented by collecting a few from the crates on the way in.'*

Stoke Bishop

Stoke Bishop village, despite the housing developments nearby, had no proper shop until 1932. The post office continued to supply a range of produce and there were always houses offering goods for sale, particularly garden produce and confectionary. *'I remember going down to Mrs Rawlings' little sweet shop at the bottom of Stoke Hill and buying sweets with my pocket money, like sherbet and that sort of thing'* (Russell Pratten). *'She had a little shop in her front room and I remember going into this little house to buy some sweets. The children going to school - they called her Granny Rawlings'* (Daisy Rawlings).

With the demand for services growing, the new road provided the catalyst for

The first commercial development in Stoke Bishop. Garage, Telephone Exchange, houses and a parade of shops. In the distance is The Glen, soon to be demolished and a second parade of shops built on the site

change. It cut across a meadow called Court Hay, owned by the Chetwood-Aiken family and, when John Chetwood-Aiken's widow died in 1931, the family saw an opportunity to develop the plot further. Houses, the Telephone Exchange from Sneyd Park and a small parade of shops were built along the new road. These included the Stoke Bishop Pharmacy, under its proprietress, Miss L.E. Fitz-Gerald. Next door William Snelgrove ran a grocery store and at the end of the parade, in the appropriately named The Corner House, was the post office, transferred from across the road. It also embraced a newsagents and stationers.

This modest start was probably not enough to satisfy the needs of the many newly arrived families. This changed a few years later. Glen House was in a derelict state and felt to be beyond repair. In 1934 it was demolished and a much larger parade of shops built. A local advertisement read *'Now under construction, Glen Estate,* (with) *modern shops built to purchasers' requirements'.* By 1937 all the vacant premises seemed to have been filled. Essential shops included a butcher's, greengrocer's and ironmongers. There were two ladies hairdressers and two ladies outfitters. Kate's home-made cakes, a tobacconist and a fancy-goods shop were also part of the mix, as was Stoke Bishop Radio, to be replaced two years later by a dairy, an outlet for Green's Dairy. There was no pub but E.A. Mitchell Ltd, a wine and spirit merchant, satisfied demand. *'My main memory of the village was the post office where you could*

View from Butcher's Hill (Druid Hill), early 1930s. The first shops can be seen in the distance on the right and at the top left beside the old post office is the original Scout hut, later used as a boys' club

The completed village in 1938 with the new parade of shops on the site of the demolished house (The Glen)

The post office in the 1950s, still called the Corner House, with Snelgrove's grocery store next door; right, 1950s mobile veg van in Glen Drive; below, Ford Brothers in 1965 before it became Druid Stores

buy sweeties if you behaved. There was a cake shop where they would sell buns when they went stale. I would buy them for my mum and she would say thank you, but they must have been horrible.' (Christopher Smith)

I was always being sent to the butcher's to get meat or running to get ice-cream, having it wrapped up and running back... before it melted... At the grocer's they wrapped up your groceries in brown paper bags and waxed paper.' (Margaret Pinnock)

The pattern was established and, until the nineteen seventies, the food shops remained constant with the providers of other goods coming and going. Over the years there was a shoe shop, a milliner's and a dry-cleaner's, but perhaps the most significant new arrival was that of Ford Brothers in around 1950 setting up a general store similar to the Cornish Stores in Shirehampton Road. Although they were described as the purveyors of cooked meats in Kelly's Directory, they were more and set the template for the general food store of the future.

(Martin Sisman) *'Ford Brothers had a separate butcher's shop and I worked there as my holiday job after leaving school in 1959, driving their delivery van, having just that summer passed my driving test. Like all teenagers, showing-off was irresistible, and doing wheel spins and handbrake turns in the cul-de-sacs of Stoke Bishop in a Morris Minor delivery van was arguably not the best advert for the local butcher, but the speed of deliveries beat any Deliveroo of today! Most of the large Sneyd Park mansions were still in single ownership, so my deliveries were to the cook or housekeeper below stairs, preceded by the screech of brakes and flying gravel. Then back to the shop and to cranking the sausage-making machine out the back and the chore of cleaning up at the end of the day. But traditionally butchers were closed on Mondays, and early closing*

David Grierson with the post office in the background

day was on a Thursday afternoon, so peace returned then to the local roads. I do remember that in affluent Sneyd Park the quality of fillet steak was judged by the price, and no doubt the mark-up paid the wages of the 'lad'.'

(Richard Stride) *'I'd be sent down the hill to Ford's from time to time on errands for my mother. I didn't have to pay as they'd slot a card into the till and it would go on my parents' tab. Once a week their man would arrive with a very neatly packed box of groceries and bring it in through the 'back door'. Of course only formal visitors came in through the front door – tradesmen, family and close friends just walked in through the 'back door', which was actually at the side of the house, not the back.'*

Postmaster Extraordinary

In 1938 two brothers, J.W. & R.A. Grierson, took over the Corner Shop, along with the post office, and for the next 66 years the business was to remain in the Grierson family. To a small child *'Mr Grierson was there for years and years and years...'* (Margaret Pinnock).

In 1992 David Grierson took over from his parents and was a colourful figure in the village. His grandparents met each other in the Falkland Islands where his grandmother owned a boarding house in Port Stanley and his grandfather was a passing Scottish shipwright. When the conflict with Argentina broke out in 1982 customers were surprised to see the Falklands flag flying outside the post office. David knew everyone who came in the store by name and it remained a favourite destination for the children of the village. *'It was quite a narrow shop but packed full of interesting things to look at. I coveted a Britains figure of a Mountie, but couldn't afford to buy him.'* (Richard Stride). Another earlier connection with the Falklands was the wool shop run by David's aunt. It was called Malvinas, the Argentine name for the Falklands. The shop was in the lower parade roughly where the fish 'n chip shop is today.

Change

The 1973 edition of Kelly's Directory lists only one addition to the established shops in Stoke Bishop and that is a florist. Yet within two decades the complexion of shopping habits was to alter radically. Harbinger of change was the arrival of the Waitrose supermarket in Henleaze in 1972. For busy professionals its appearance made the weekly shop a reality and no longer did householders have to go from shop to shop, but could now acquire all they needed in one store. It wasn't long before Stoke Bishop was surrounded by a ring of superstores with ample parking. One by one the specialist food shops, like the butcher's in Stoke Bishop village, began closing, unable to compete with the bulk buying of the new supermarkets. Soon only the general stores survived and even their existence was a struggle.

But the greatest threat came in 1994 when a planning application was made to build a superstore on the site of The Grove, off Parry's Lane. The house had been demolished in 1937 and the grounds became the Clifton High School for Girls playing field. Now the school in partnership with a developer was proposing a 50,000 sq. ft. building with petrol station and 500 space car-park. Not for the first time the residents of Stoke Bishop protested. A well-organised campaign was launched and despite the recommendations of his own inspector, the Environment Secretary, John Gummer, refused the proposal. *'He said the superstore would be an alien and intrusive element in a residential area'* (Bristol Evening Post). The campaigners had obtained a temporary reprieve but by 2004 little remained of the core village. In that year Stoke Bishop lost its post office and its hardware store. Only the greengrocers and the chemist continued trading. But eventually they too went out of business.

Taste Buds, Stoke Bishop's first eatery

Martin Blunos; right, Lettonie with the red awning and Markwicks the butcher next door

Café Society

As Stoke Bishop moved towards the 21st century, its natural sense of affluence came to the fore. Lifestyle was the hallmark of the new incumbents, high end home interiors, hair and beauty salons and most noticeably places to eat. There had always been at least one off-licence, but in 1977 a modest delicatessen called Taste Buds started providing morning coffee and light lunches. This was followed by the arrival of Bruno's, an upmarket restaurant. It changed hands and became Semailles, before being taken over in 1988 by celebratory chef, Martin Blunos, and renamed Lettonie (French for Latvia, from where Blunos's parents had emigrated). His cooking had an east European flavour, with the blini (a Russian pancake) being his signature dish. He earned his first Michelin star in 1989 and his second in 1991. This success put Stoke Bishop momentarily on the international foodie map.

As a teenager, Matthew Sheather earned money washing up at Lettonie's. *'It was hard hot work. I was on my own in a small space at the back of the kitchen. There was no dishwasher. All the washing up was done in the sink. I had to change the water when it got greasy. It was stressful for Martin. He was always looking out to see who was in.'* Sadly the premises at Stoke Bishop proved too cramped and Martin Blunos moved to Bath and an Indian restaurant took over, the Bengal Raj, while an oriental restaurant, Star Anise, opened in the premises once occupied by Taste Buds. Easy parking and a quiet and secure location established Stoke Bishop's culinary credentials.

Garages

The owners of the big houses had the money to buy and the room to park a car,

Sneyd Park's first garage in the Avenue; below right, chauffeurs beside their cars ready for hire

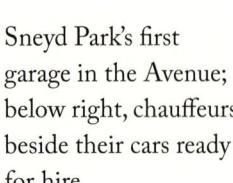

so it wasn't surprising that the first commercial garage appeared in Sneyd Park around the same time as the shops in Rockleaze Road. It was situated at the end of the Avenue and was little more than a corrugated roof supported by garden walls. The owners were H.N. Pidgeon & Sons Ltd. and while car

repair was an essential part of their work they unexpectedly grew a hire car business.

Ron Smith, a family member, has noted that while the people in the area *aspired to motor cars, a lot of them couldn't drive or wouldn't drive, so the garage provided*

The extensive premises of Sneyd Park Garage in the 1950s in Stoke Bishop village

Sea Mills Service Station on the corner of Bell Barn Road

initially chauffer driven hire cars and then went on to be a supplier of motor cars.' A remnant of the Sneyd Park garage can still be seen in the Avenue.

When the new parade was built in Stoke Bishop village, the Pidgeons moved their business to the larger site on the corner of Stoke Hill and Old Sneed Road. Ron Smith recalls that the bank said there was no need for a garage as it was a residential area. So he sold off half the land he had bought to the Post Office for a new telephone exchange and with the profit built the garage using bricks from The Grove, which had just been demolished. Sneyd Park Garage, as it continued to be called, had a car show room, a maintenance area and a petrol pump forecourt. In 1995 a large part of the premises was sold for housing and only the car repair business remained.

A motor business existed briefly in Shirehampton Road on the corner of Bell Barn Road and Sneyd Park continued to benefit from a garage that opened in Julian Road, on the site of the Bristol Tramways & Carriage Co. cab stables. Originally called Bishopston Garage, it was renamed Brookland Mobile when brothers, Graham and Ian King took it over in 1982. They remembered it as *'a great place to work. We don't count our clients as customers but as friends. We've grown old together. In the early years the general store in Sneyd Park used to bring round hot plates at lunch time'.* It is still there today as J's Autofast Repairs.

Chapter Nineteen

Sport and Recreation

In the first half of the 20th century formal sporting activities took root throughout the parish.

There had been shoots appearing in the previous century but landowners had been slow to release land for playing fields and with most of the population in service in the large houses, opportunity for organised sport was limited. But this was to change with the arrival of the professional families to the area.

Stoke Bishop Cricket Club

Cricket seems to have been the first recorded sport played in Stoke Bishop. A photograph exists showing the Rockleaze Cricket Club in 1875. A membership card of 1884 stated among its rules that players should wear *'skull caps with a small peak and the colour to be red and black.'* But its subsequent history is unclear and it seems to have disbanded by 1910.

More certain is the creation of the Stoke Bishop Cricket Club in 1889. Its first year got off to a spectacular start, as the next year in 1890 it was recorded that a mounted cricket ball was presented to one of its players. He was C. Lapham and he had taken 117 wickets in the Page Wood Competition. This extraordinary feat

The Rockleaze
Cricket Club in 1875

The Stoke Bishop Cricket Club. The vicarage can be seen top right

became the stuff of legend for the Club, which first started playing on the Downs. In 1911 it moved to land rented from the then owner of Stoke House, the wholesale grocer, W.E.Budgett. The location was adjacent to St Mary Magdalene's vicarage on Eastmead Lane, off Stoke Hill. The Revd. David Wright, the vicar, has been recorded as enjoying the cricket from his garden. When the Great War intervened

the pitch must have become neglected, because when play resumed the Club had relocated to The Grove, the home of Colonel Joseph Butler. It can be identified in the picture from the familiar wall bounding Parry's Lane. The picture also shows the players' wives and the tea hut.

In 1929 a fourth move was to be more permanent. In that year the Club signed an agreement with spinsters, Annie Julia and Mary Elizabeth Butlin, owners of Stoke Lodge, to play on the estate's cricket field. Initially the lease was for one year at a rental of £20, but the Club quickly found the beautiful ground to their liking, despite there being a large tree in the middle of the playing area, and they stayed for forty four years. The agreement allowed the Club to erect a small temporary

Players' wives, Daisy Rawlings, Vi Watkins and Mary Cox (kneeling) take a break from making tea. Note the wall of The Grove bordering Parry's Lane. The dog's name is Tarzan

The first pitch at the bottom of Stoke Lodge with the tree inside the pitch. The pavilion can be seen in the background. Eventually pavilion and pitch moved to the middle part of the field

pavilion and tea hut, to take up and *'relay the turf on a portion of the land to form a cricket pitch, but not otherwise to break up or destroy the turf on any part of the land'*. Surprisingly the Club was given the right to graze sheep or young cattle (but not rams or bulls) if it so desired, although the option was never taken up.

The location was indeed idyllic with sweeping views to Blaise and majestic trees forming the perfect backdrop to the cricket. Dave Watkins remembers happy times going to watch the game as a child. *'Every other weekend in the summer, we'd go to*

A game in progress with Cheyne Road and Woodland Grove in the distance

Stoke Lodge. Our father played in the cricket club and we as children used to go along and play our own little game on the side and wander around Stoke Lodge.' The Watkins family were something of an institution in the Club.

'My grandfather, Howard Watkins, played in the very early days, before the First World War, and he was supposed to be a very good fast bowler and his son Donald followed in his footsteps as a bowler and was captain of the cricket club in the 1960s. His sons, me and my brother Stephen, we played cricket for Stoke Bishop towards the end of its time at Stoke Lodge.' Oddly they often had to compete with another sport. *'While we were playing cricket there were archery targets set up at the bottom of the field!'*

The years immediately after the Second World War were a high point for the club. The first eleven counted among its number two brothers, Ken and Tom Graveney, who went on to play county cricket for Gloucester. Tom became a member of the England team and between 1951 and 1969 he played in 79 Test matches, scoring 4,882 runs. He was described by The Daily Telegraph as *'the greatest, as well as the most elegant and graceful, professional batsman to emerge in Britain in the years after the Second World War'*. As a young girl Heather Pelmear remembers seeing the brothers play.

Tom Graveney practising in the nets

'The stars of the show were Tom and Ken Graveney. I was very thrilled when they were chosen for the county and then for England, though sorry they were no longer available to play locally. I used to talk to their younger brother Maurice who was more my age. He did not aspire to the same heights as the older brothers. They were probably only in their early twenties but already grown-up to me.'

A New Ground

Over the years the Stoke Lodge pitch became difficult to maintain. Bristol Corporation purchased the ground in 1947 and in later years they found they had insufficient funds to keep the ground in good condition. The Bishops (as they colloquially called themselves) were forced to look around for another venue.

Conveniently they found one on the other side of Shirehampton Road, a large playing field that had been carved out of the Druid Stoke House estate.

On 22 April 1926, Fyffes, the banana importers, celebrated the opening of a new sports ground and pavilion the company had built for its employees. The occasion was reported in a typically colourful way by the Western Daily Press: *'Genial sunshine favoured the event, tempering the northerly wind, with the result that the gentler sex, in gay spring colours, lent a touch of brightness to a very happy gathering.'*

Speaking from the verandah of the new pavilion, the director of Fyffes, Hal Stockley, said *'he hoped the ground would be used by everybody – marine and shore staffs, their wives and sisters... He wished them good luck and was sure, if they played their games in the same spirit as they did their work, they had nothing to worry about.'* The ground passed into the hands of the National Smelting Company (later absorbed into Rio Tinto Zinc) and it was NSC with which the Cricket Club negotiated to use the grounds. They played there until RTZ sold the land for housing in 1996 and once more found they had to move, this time to the University of Bristol's Coombe Dingle Sports Complex, where they still play.

Mrs Hal Stockley opens the new pavilion while her husband looks on

Football

Peripheral to Stoke Bishop, but a spectacle seen every Saturday, is the forest of white goal posts that springs up across the Downs, as nearly 40 football teams battle it out for advancement over four divisions of the Downs League. The weekly event is almost unique in the history of football. Unlike other leagues there are no away matches. All teams play each other in one place on one day.

Football began to be played on the Downs in the 1880s, as the green expanse, no longer the riotous place it once was, allowed for more orderly sporting activities. These were greatly facilitated by the arrival of the tram, which enabled players to get to the Downs with ease. In 1905 the scattering of teams who were already playing each other were brought together as the core of a new Downs League. When news of its formation spread around Bristol, the League quickly expanded. Although the games provided entertainment on the edge of the parish, the connection with

Sneyd Park Football Team, 1907-8 Season

Stoke Bishop was never more than marginal. One of the founder clubs had taken its name from the locality. Sneyd Park Amateur Football Club was founded in 1897 and was among the first to join the new league. There is no evidence that the players came from Sneyd Park, but the team from the outset was one of the strongest in the League, never having dropped from the top division throughout its history. Sporting Greyhounds was formed by a Stoke Bishop resident, but drew its squad from outside, while recently a home grown Stoke Bishop team did emerge but had a short life. Over the years the League has had success in feeding players into the professional game, its most notable star being Eddie Hapgood, who went on to play for Arsenal.

Croquet

Another beneficiary of the Druid Stoke House estate was the Clifton and County Croquet Club which came to Stoke Bishop in 1939 and took up residence next door to the Fyffes sports ground. The rough field was levelled, layered and sown to create three croquet lawns. In 1953 the owner wanted to sell the land, but the Club could not raise the necessary asking price to acquire it. The President, Dr. Laurence Ormerod, was able to persuade Bristol Corporation to buy the land and to allow the Club to rent it from the Corporation. Four years later, the Club was renamed

Mallets strike before keen-eyed spectators in 1939

the Bristol Croquet Club and through a number of vicissitudes over the years, most noticeably from a declining membership, the Club fought successfully to survive and is now rated as one of the leading clubs in the country.

Anyone for Tennis?

If you were to walk through Stoke Bishop on a summer's evening in the twenties and thirties, you would doubtless hear the regular thud of ball on grass followed by cries of delight or frustration. By the end of the 19th century, tennis as a pastime had become so popular that most houses of any size had their tennis court. When houses came on the market the tennis court was always promoted as a desirable feature. Locarno on Sea Walls, Pitch and Pay, Downside, Druid's Garth and Howecroft all had *'Tennis Lawns'*. The Holmes had two. Initially the courts were grass, but hard surfaces began to make their appearance. 45 Downleaze, although

Women playing tennis on the Downs in the 1950s

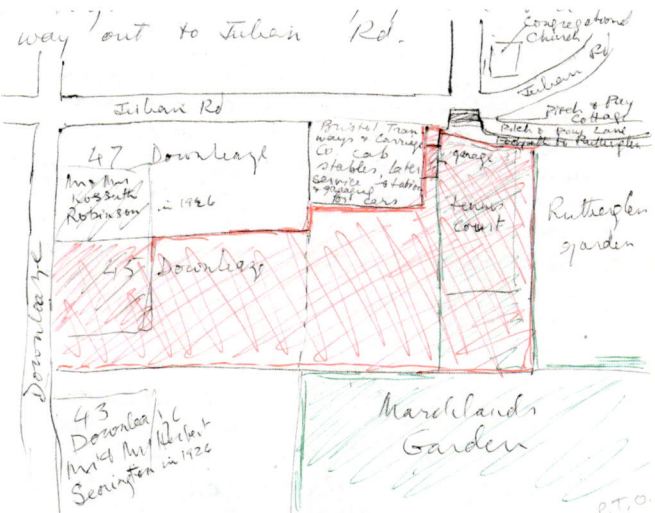

way 'out to Julian 'Rd.

Julian Rd

47 Downleaze

Mrs Mrs Kossuth Robinson in 1926

45 Downleaze

43 Downleaze Mr & Mrs Herbert Serington in 1926

Downleaze

Bristol Tram ways & Carriage Co. cab stables, later service station & garaging for cars

Congregational Church Rd
Julian
Pitch & Play Cottage
Pitch & play Lane

garage

Tennis Court

Rutherglen garden

Marchlands Garden

P.T.O.

45 Downleaze showing the tennis court. Note the adjacent stabling for the Bristol Tramways and Carriage Co., which later became a garage

it fronted Downleaze had a garden that ran behind its neigbour No 47 and came out on Julian Road. The map shows how the owners managed to squeeze in a hard tennis court.

Tennis was a social game and tennis parties quickly became popular. Margaret Goodbody was conscious of the number of tennis courts when she was a girl in the thirties. *I can remember ten, but I expect there were a lot more. Most of them were grass which someone had to mow with a hand mower and mark up before anyone could play. There were also areas on the Downs which were marked out for tennis, but there was no netting to keep the balls in, so they were not used much.'* Communal tennis courts and private clubs popped up, often on spare land between the houses. One example were the courts that lay at the back of Avon Way and Sea Mills Lane, which, like so much open land, eventually became housing. When the Portway was built, a cluster of tennis courts, surfaced with grit from the construction, was laid out in the Gorge to improve the leisure amenities of the new road. At the Village Hall badminton was introduced.

Tennis Courts in the Avon Gorge in the 1930s beside the Portway

Horse Riding

Another feature of the big houses was the extensive outbuildings they acquired, principal among them being the stables. When the Mythe in Julian Road was being advertised for sale, the prospectus described a cobbled yard and entrance to *'Stabling, including Loose Box and two Stalls with Loft Over, and Harness Room'*. Although this was 1951 and much of the stabling block would be converted to garages, the option to stable a horse was still there. Stoke Bishop was still rural enough to allow horse riding in the area, over the Downs or across Kings Weston Down and Blaise. A number of stables with accompanying paddocks survived into the fifties, including one in Eastmead Lane. Another at the end of Sea Mills Lane, tucked up against the Portway Bridge, was called in the fifties the Roman Farm Riding Stables and it was where Rosemary Havens learnt to ride. Others like Liz Tomlinson got the occasional ride. *'My mother would ask if I could have a ride and I would be led up and down Sea Mills Lane.'* Earlier during the Second World War, the Americans frequented the stables and would hire a horse to ride out onto the Downs. *'It was 3s 6d an hour but 5s for the Americans'* (Rosemary Havens). When the stables were abandoned, people sleeping rough moved in.

Rosemary Havens clears a fence near the Portway

Entertainment

The twenties was the great age of organised entertainment. Picture houses, dance halls and theatres sprang up in even the smallest towns. Stoke Bishop never had any such amenities. What amusements it had were home grown, as improved roads and transport now allowed people to seek their entertainment further afield. They were surrounded by a ring of cinemas they could visit, the Orpheus in Henleaze, the Carlton in Westbury-on-Trym, the Savoy in Shirehampton, or they could travel into the city.

The Village Hall was Stoke Bishop's only venue and in the years after the Great War it still clung to its slightly stuffy image of wanting to improve those who crossed its threshold. But if it was to attract more people, it would have to change. Women over the age of 30 now had the vote and started to use the Hall in their

The Stoke Bishop Players perform J.B. Priestly's play Dangerous Corner

own right. During the summer of 1921, dances were held for the first time. Such was their success they were eventually put on every Saturday night with a live quartet providing the music. Electric lights were installed and the hall extended to accommodate a new stage. The appeal to raise money to pay for these improvements failed to reach its target and the hall fell into debt. But the dances remained popular. Daisy Rawlings, who was living in Clifton at the time, remembers coming over to Stoke Bishop, where Bert her future husband was living, and joining in the 'merry revels' at the Village Hall. The expensively acquired stage was eventually put to good use in the 1950s when the Stoke Bishop Players theatre group was formed and performed such classic dramas as Chekhov's Uncle Vanya and J.B. Priestly's Dangerous Corner.

A curious postscript to the entertainment scene was the establishment of a private club in Riverside House in Sea Mills Lane. It opened in 1926, a joint venture between the landlords and Georges Brewery. Little is known about the type of club it was, but most likely it was a private gentleman's club which allowed alcohol. One can only speculate where its members came from. Was it from the big houses? Did they arrive by train? What is known is that the club only lasted two years. In 1928 it was closed down by the police as a result of complaints from the neighbours about noise.

Chapter Twenty

New Uses for Old Houses

The nation's big houses were not well served by the Great War.

Many had been requisitioned by the military (although this seemed not to have happened in Stoke Bishop), the owners lost sons on the battlefield and after the war the estates faced crippling death duties and soaring costs for the repair and maintenance of buildings which could date from the 17th century. Added to this was the difficulty of recruiting staff to run what was in effect a small village and owners began to consider selling their properties. When Pitch and Pay came on the market in 1938, the prospectus showed the extent of what a private owner could face. It was a three storey building standing in five acres of ground. The lower floor included two halls, a lounge, drawing room, dining room and library. There was a school room and large kitchen, with butler's pantry, china pantry, servants' hall, scullery, larder, dairy, coal house and cellars. On the first floor were two en-suite bedrooms and five single bedrooms or dressing rooms. The attic upstairs contained four maids' bedrooms and a boxroom. All this, before even considering the extensive outbuildings and gardens. Little wonder that down-sizing became a

Maintaining Pitch and Pay was a daunting task for its owners after the Great War

242

preferred option. By the time the Second World War broke out, few of the large houses were in private hands.

Stoke House

Grief hung like a pall over the Nott family after the death of the three Nott brothers on the Western Front and their father back home. It must have seeped into every corner of the house and although the mother and several of the daughters continued to live there, one can easily imagine their constant pain. In 1926, they finally sold the house. It became a school, which proved to be one of the favoured uses for the old houses.

Canynge House was a boarding school for girls which occupied Stoke House for six years. It made good use of the ample space available to it, turning the ballroom with its sprung floor into a dance room and converting the elegant early 19th century Orangery into a swimming pool. The latter, when it later became a chapel, was covered over to create a store room, but the pool's painted blue walls are still visible. Mrs Seligman, who remembered the school, said *'it was very cold in winter as the heating was inadequate'*. A planning application to improve the buildings was put to Bristol Corporation in 1931, but it was probably turned down as a year later Canynge House had moved on.

The next occupant was Clifton Theological College, established to train men for the ordained Anglican ministry. Interestingly it kept the swimming pool, which its successor, Trinity College, did not! In 1971 it merged with two other institutions, Tyndale Hall, a Bible missionary society and Dalton House, a women's training college, to create Trinity College, which opened its doors for the first time on 1 January 1972. Over the years the College has become one of the leading theological

The girls of Canynge House enjoy a swim in the pool in the Orangery on a summer's day

colleges in the country with an international reputation. Its students come from all over the world with St Mary Magdalene, the parish church, being a beneficiary. Trainee ordinands are sent on placements there or simply come to worship. Over the years Trinity staff have preached at St Mary Magdalene giving the congregation the fruits of their learning. Several of Trinity's principals have gone on to become bishops and two, George Carey and Rowan Williams, to become Archbishops of Canterbury.

Old Sneed Park (Nazareth House)

As we have seen, after the death of Sir George White, Old Sneed Park fell into disrepair, drained as it was of staff and afflicted by the taxes on wealth. In 1923 the family put house and estate up for sale. The buyers were a group of nuns from Cheltenham, known as the Sisters of Nazareth, who converted the house into an orphanage. The Sisters were part of a Catholic organisation which traced its origins to the work of Victoire Larmenier, a young novice from Rennes in France, who in 1851 was sent to England to establish houses for the poor. Soon Nazareth Houses, as they were called, were appearing all around the country. The sisters who owned the one in Cheltenham (which still exists as a care home) were seeking to expand and seven moved first to Westbury-on-Trym, to Cote Bank on Westbury Road. When, in 1929, Falcondale Road was built across the estate, they were forced to

Old Sneed Park when it was Nazareth House, showing the grey stoned dormitory building that was added

leave and moved to Stoke Bishop, buying Old Sneed Park and the adjacent Little Sneyd farmhouse. At first only 70 boys were taken in, but by the early thirties the number had risen to 100 and eventually girls were boarded.

In 1932, all but 32 of the original 130 acres purchased were sold for housing and the orphanage became officially known as Nazareth House. Soon the Sisters in their distinctive black and blue habits became a familiar sight around Stoke Bishop, although not always a friendly one if you were a small boy caught scrumping apples.

A class of orphan boys at Nazareth House

Geoff Cutter remembered a nun, who saw him picking apples, start taking her belt off as he ran away.

The quality of life experienced by the children brought up in Nazareth House varied widely. In 1954 the Bristol Evening Post published a positive report.

'Here, amid delightful country surroundings, the children are housed and educated until they reach the age of 14, when jobs are found for them.' It went on to describe the kindergarten. 'Over 50 babies under five years occupy the spacious nursery. It is bright and spotless with cots and cradles as well as a playroom well stacked with toys given by kind friends... The Sisters devote their life's work to the care of these little ones, trying as far as it is possible to make it up to them for what they are losing in not being members of a real family.'

In 1965, the City of Bristol Young Farmers' Club arranged with the nuns to take 20 children to the seaside for the afternoon. The organiser described the occasion. *'We collected the children after lunch and drove them, two or three to a car, to Berrow Sands. Most were aged between five and 10, although a few were younger than this. I don't think any had seen the sea before as so many of the children made a dash for the water fully clothed. We gave them a picnic lunch, drinks, ice creams, made sand castles and played games.'* The outing was so successful, it was repeated over the next three years.

In November 1970 the Sisters decided to close the Bristol home and put it up for sale. The children were moved to other Nazareth homes or found places in alternative Bristol homes. The Bristol Evening Post reported: *'all the nuns took with them was their altar, church benches and a stained glass window from the front entrance'*. Alas they probably also took with them another legacy, which they must have hoped would remain their secret. Thirty years later reports began to emerge that showed that not all had been well at Nazareth House. Tales of neglect and ill treatment were published in the press and although no official investigation was carried out into the allegations of what went on at Sneyd Park, censure has been visited on Nazareth houses elsewhere. Said one employee: *'Nobody could hold up their hands and say that over that period of time no mistakes were made but I never actually saw any abuse going on. Discipline was strict and much firmer then. It would be wrong to suggest every nun and every helper was guilty of abuse because that simply wasn't the case.'*

Soon after the Sisters of Nazareth left, Old Sneed Park was to suffer a final ignominious catastrophe.

Bishop's Knoll

With the death of Robert Bush in 1939 and the moving away to Lyme Regis of his widow, Marjery, Bishop's Knoll ceased to be a private house. During the Second World War, it was taken over by the Bristol Aircraft Company after Filton had been badly bombed and used to house its apprentice school. After the War, in a fitting acquisition, the Bristol Royal Infirmary opened a hostel and training school for preliminary nurses. The unit was formally opened by Princess Margaret in March 1949.

A pattern was beginning to emerge of bringing young people to remote Stoke Bishop away from the bright lights of the city with the inevitable consequence of them becoming frustrated. The trainee nurses seemed to have made the most of

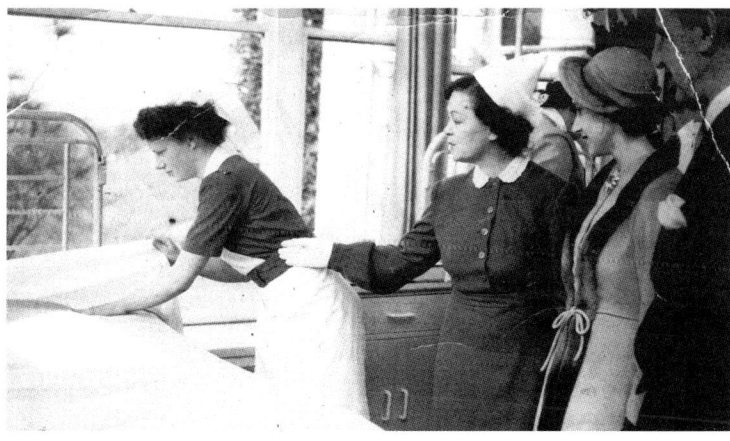

Princess Margaret is shown a training ward

A victorious return from hockey

their exile by running sporting events and creating their own entertainment. But a window was always left open for anyone coming in after curfew from a trip to the city. Jeanette Austin remembered experiencing a strange happening.

> 'One night I was woken up by something. At first I thought it was one of the girls letting themselves into our room. The room was in darkness but at the end of my bed I could make out the figure of a man. I could see that he was wearing a wide brimmed hat with corks hanging from it and a big heavy cape around his shoulders... I remembered that Bishop's Knoll had been used as a hospital for Australian soldiers injured during the First World War. This sent a shiver down my spine...'

Glenda Lindsay who lived in the flats built on the site of Bishop's Knoll had an equally disturbing experience.

> 'My husband and I had never smoked. Nobody as far as I know smokes in the whole of this staircase. I have in the evenings in my bedroom smelt smoke. Soldiers were living here and they definitely smoked. Make what you will of that!'

In the 1960s the training programme for nurses was reorganised and relocated. The nursing school left Bishop's Knoll and the empty house, ghosts and all, faced an uncertain future.

Schools and More Schools
During the first half of the 20th century Stoke Bishop must have echoed to the

excited chatter of schoolchildren either at play or out and about in crocodiles. We have already seen Stoke House become a school. It was joined during this period by at least five others, which together with Stoke Bishop School, three orphanages and a growing University presence, made Stoke Bishop, for a time, the educational rival to Clifton. In fact one or two of the schools relocated across the Downs from Clifton. They found larger premises with spacious grounds for physical education and access to the Downs for games. They were almost all preparatory schools taking pupils up to 13 plus and preparing them for entry to public schools.

Braidlea

One of the largest was Braidlea, founded in the late 19th century in a house on the corner of Downleaze and Julian Road. Its owner, E.H.V. Elliot, in 1905, moved it to where he now lived. Curiously this was the Well House, William Baker's old house in Ivywell Road, but which had been renamed Braidlea in 1889. When Elliot moved into the house in 1905 he kept the name and gave it to the school. In 1936 Braidlea merged with Avondale, a Clifton school, located in College Road.

The combined numbers were now too big for Braidlea House and new premises were found at Clevelands on the corner of Goodeve Road and Sea Walls Road. The school, which became known as Braidlea-Avondale, remained there until its closure in 1973.

An advert for the school gives a flavour of what life was like. The headmaster at the time was W.C. Heatherington from St John's College, Oxford. He would be looking after 30 to 40 boys some of whom would be boarders, with a staff of two masters and two mistresses. *'Boys,'* it said, *'are prepared for the Public Schools and Royal Navy.'* To this end the school advertised a *'boxing instructor'*. But it wasn't without good facilities. *'All the classrooms have central heating and gas fires... A cinema is installed as an aid to the study of geography and general*

The original site of Braidlea School in Downleaze

PT in the garden after Braidlea had moved to Goodeve Road

knowledge.' Safeguarding was taken care of. *'The domestic arrangements are in the hands of the headmaster's wife and the boarders are looked after entirely by her and the headmaster.'*

'The time I spent at Braidlea was the happiest of all my schooldays. It was set in a beautiful large Victorian house in Goodeve Road which had a lovely lawn surrounded by wide hedges and two Cedar trees. All this area was our playground. Here was a warm atmosphere and

Braidlea's Great War Memorial Shield

very little corporal punishment. It was the home of the headmaster, Mr Hetherington, who lived there with his wife and five children.' Tony Everett (a pupil at Braidlea from 1941 to 1944)

The school song promoted its ethos:

> *'School days, busy days,*
> *Learning how to live.*
> *Answering call,*
> *Taking all*
> *Braidlea has to give.*
> *Eye on the ball*
> *And your bat straight*
> *And you can't go wrong.'*

Another reminder of the school can be found in St Mary Magdalene. On a wall inside the church hangs a large brass shield in honour of the boys from Braidlea who fell during the Great War.

St Goar

St Goar was a preparatory school that had moved around a lot before coming to the Mythe (off Pitch and Pay Lane) in 1952. Its odd name came from the Patron Saint of a little Rhineland village, St Goar sur Rhine. Its prospectus does not explain why it was given that name, but it was a school with a strong religious character. It was founded in 1887 in Clifton, moved to Westbury-on-Trym, then to Westbury Park before coming to Sneyd Park. As with Braidlea it prepared boys for *'all the English Public Schools'* and had *'special terms available for the sons of Ministers and Clergy'*.

XIV

Another large preparatory school occupied Druid Stoke House in 1952. This was XIV, a school that had also originated in Clifton. It was founded in 1898. A postcard dated 1905, in the Bristol Archives, describes it as occupying 12/14 Apsley Road and calling it W. O. Penbor Private School. It was later renamed the XIV School, using the Roman numerals for 14. The writer (possibly a teacher) assured the parents that *'your little son is very well, very good and very plucky'*. In 1970 C.K. Stevenson, described as *'the owner, benefactor and Headmaster'*, died. He had clearly been the lynch-pin of the School during its time at Druid Stoke House. The School wrote on his death: *'It was not generally known to what extent the School benefited from his personal contribution but this became quickly apparent to the group of people faced with the self-imposed task of running the School after Mr Stevenson's death.'* One of those individuals was the Chairman of the Governors, the Venerable Leslie Williams, the Archdeacon of Bristol, formerly vicar of St Mary Magdalene. Clearly the task ahead proved too much and within a decade the school, like so many of its compatriots, had closed. A project to build a hall, gymnasium and extra

Postcard written to parents of a boy at 12/14 Apsley Road (XIV) in 1905

100 yards finish (under 10s) with RM Wadlow (XIV) coming first

classrooms never materialised. When the school lay empty two derelict Nissan huts sat forlornly in the playground. Yet once there were so many prep schools that they regularly played against one another in sporting activities. In 1927 the Western Daily Press reported on the *'Preparatory Schools Sports'*, held on the Downs, opposite the Sea Walls, which included Braidlea, XIV and Avondale (which was later to merge with Braidlea). *'The weather conditions being ideal a number of parents and friends watched the events.'*

Girls Schools

Girls schools were equally prolific. We have seen Canynge House for girls occupy Stoke House. In 1947 Drinagh overlooking the Gorge on Knoll Hill became Colwyn School for Girls. Its principal was Mrs P.J. Wynell. It had day and boarding facilities and advertised small classes aimed to give individual attention to slow learners. Another girls school, founded around 1928 took up residence in 1950 in Hazelwood House. Known as Hampton House School for Girls, it took in boarders and its principal then was Miss Grace Cook.

Smaller private houses were used for schools. There was a girls school in Old Sneed Road, run by a Miss Taylor *'who'* says Felicity Smith, a former pupil, *'ruled with a rod of iron'*.

In the late thirties No 12 Little Stoke Road housed Little Stoke School for Girls (5-12) and small Boys. The principal was Miss Beryl V. French, who gave as her address Ubley in the Chew Valley. The school was described as belonging to the Parents' National Educational Union (PNEU), an organisation devoted in the first instance to home or governess education, but which later included schools.

Its child centred philosophy was based on the teachings of 19th century educationalist, Charlotte Mason, who argued that children were born as individual human beings and should be respected as such in the way they were taught. Among the activities offered were a percussion band and out-door nature study. A garden was also a noted feature. Whether Beryl French had any teaching help is unclear but, in the entry in the 1939 wartime Register, she had living with her in the house two elderly single sisters, who were described in the catchall phrase of the time as having 'unpaid domestic duties' (This description was also applied to any married woman who had no job).

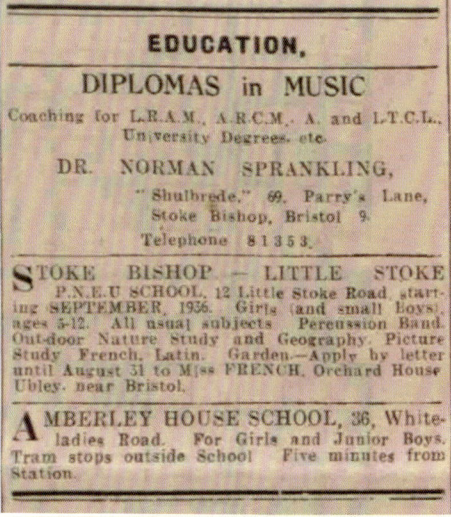

A 1936 advertisement in the Western Daily Press announcing the opening of Little Stoke School

The house with its two downstairs rooms and four upper rooms seems too cramped to be a school, but it clearly existed and survived until the outbreak of war.

More Orphanages

As well as Nazareth House, there were two other orphanages in Sneyd Park. Dr Barnado's took over The Towers around 1949. A striking Victorian House on the corner of Hazelwood Road and Goodeve Road, it had been the home of the Robinson family, who owned the wholesale stationery, paper bag and packaging company. Renamed Elizabeth Bishop House, it cared for young children and had two resident superintendents and two matrons, Miss C. Coulton and Miss C. Padwick. When it closed in August 1970 the children were moved to Myton Gables, a home in Warwick.

At the time the Barnado's policy was moving away from large homes to smaller family-like accommodation with house parents, a blue-print that was to be reflected in the Müller Home that was set up in Severnleigh on Stoke Hill. The Müller Orphan Homes bought the house in 1952 at the time when the main Müller Orphanage on Ashley Down was closing down. Government policy was to encourage smaller foster homes to be created in place of large institutional children's homes. The Müller policy placed eight to ten children in 'scattered homes'

The Towers, later Elizabeth Bishop House, was demolished in 1970

around the city with *'house parents'* to which they could relate.

Severnleigh was one of these *'scattered homes'*. David and Irene Farley were house parents during the seventies and eighties. They had daily help, but running Severnleigh as a family house was a massive undertaking. Gyl Evans met the Farleys and made the following notes. *'In the early years washing and drying laundry was initially by hand and it was only with great difficulty and good fortune that they managed to get a slightly damaged front loading washing machine. Ironing was done in the evening with the children watching TV so Irene could keep an eye on what they were watching and any arguments! ...The children went to five different schools and David was the one sorting out the dinner monies. The children found they could use cash to buy other things, like cigarettes and vouchers, and so they might come home literally starving. To stop this David had to visit each school, each week, with dinner money.'* Care policy changed even further and in 1986 the Müller Orphan Homes sold Severnleigh to Benson Brothers, a firm of local building contractors, who converted the house into seven flats.

Severnleigh today converted into flats

Towerleaze

Of all the conversions, perhaps the strangest was that of Towerleaze which sat on the rise overlooking the Gorge on Knoll Hill. It was one of the first of William Baker's big house builds and until 1934 had been a private house. In that year it opened as a Health Hydro, under the directorship of Tom Elliot, and over the years built up an international reputation for natural therapies. In its prospectus it stated that *'in the last thirty years there has been a greatly increased demand for more natural methods of treatment, as opposed to treatment by drugs'*. Among the treatments offered were osteopathic and chiropractic manipulation, electrotherapy, hydrotherapy, sunbathing and fasting. Guests were subject to a strict regime in relaxing and beautiful surroundings *'overlooking the River Avon and the Bristol Channel with the Welsh Hills in the distance'*. A brochure stated: *'Dress is informal and little luggage need be brought.'* It was *'a rule of the house that from lunch time until 3pm silence shall prevail'*. Treatments were in the morning and *'patients, with health permits, may go out in the afternoons and evenings without restriction.'* And there lay the problem, as Joy Harrison, who worked at Towerleaze as a nurse, observed.

The Towerleaze Hydro's director, Tom Elliot

'Part of the hydrotherapy treatment was colonic irrigation, which was very necessary when people are fasting. They were very naughty sometimes. They would go to Clifton to the shops and have something nice to eat. Because they were having colonic irrigation and there was an observation point in the apparatus, we knew they had been cheating.'

Over the years a number of celebrities passed through the doors of Towerleaze, including Thora Hird, Pete Murray, Stanley Matthews and, when she was in Hello Dolly at the Hippodrome, Dora Bryan. Had a murder happened at the hydro, help would have been close at hand, as the other unusual occupant in the area was the South West Forensic Science Laboratory, which had taken over Oakfield, a massive Italianate house on Hazelwood Road!

The nurses and staff of the Towerleaze Hydro, with the director, Tom Elliot and his wife, seated in the centre middle row. Joy Harrison stands behind Mrs Elliot

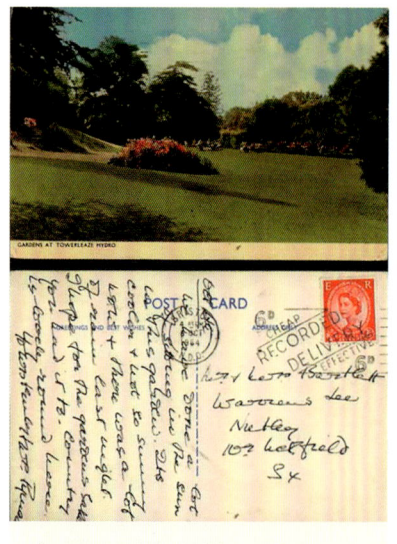

A postcard from Towerleaze

Cars parked outside the Towerleaze Hydro

Chapter Twenty-one

Downside and the University of Bristol

1911 onwards

Perhaps the biggest change of private house to public institution was the transformation of the Downside estate into a huge university campus and the bringing of hundreds of young people out to a semi-rural environment away from the city lights.

When William Edwards George died in 1922, no single heir had been appointed to succeed to Downside and its estate. Henry Herbert Wills, of the tobacco family and of Barley Wood in Wrington, was quick off the mark to buy the house and the southern part of the estate when the George family put it on the market. He gave Downside and 26 acres to the embryonic University of Bristol with a view to building a residential college for men on the site.

In the early years of the University's existence, finding enough accommodation

Downside in its heyday

256

for its students proved difficult. In 1909 Clifton Hill House had been established for women, but the men were scattered around the city in a variety of unsuitable houses. The Wills family had been the principal driving force behind the foundation of the University and it was they who were to provide the first purpose built hall of residence.

Sadly Henry Herbert died shortly after the purchase but his wishes were carried out by his brother, Sir George Wills, who wrote that their chief object was *'to help solve the problem of hostels in place of lodgings and to foster the growth of a spirit of corporate life amongst undergraduates. It is my wish, if the Council approves, to take immediate steps to give effect to this project of ours as a memorial to my brother'*. The architect chosen was the celebrated Bristol designer, Sir George Oatley, whose work included the new Wills building at the top of Park Street and the nearby Saint Monica Home of Rest. The Hall was constructed as a quadrangle with the house earmarked for the warden forming part of one side. It was clearly inspired by Oxford and Cambridge colleges and is the only one of its kind in the University.

The new hall was opened on 14 December 1929 by Winston Churchill, who was the current Chancellor. At a lunch that included barley soup, poached halibut, grilled lamb cutlets and madeira pudding, Churchill *'declared there to be no finer hostel than Wills Hall among the universities of the British Empire'*. The 150 undergraduates gave him a rapturous applause and carried him aloft into the quadrangle.

Sir George Oatley's Wills Hall. Downside is at the top left of the quadrangle

Oatley also designed the Hall's Dame Monica Wills Memorial Chapel in a grand Romanesque style. It was hoped that it would fulfil Dame Monica's *'earnest wish that the Chapel should be used to make those residing better and more loyal members of the religious bodies to which they may severally belong'*. This was fine for their spiritual well-being, but less so for their social life and the young men of Wills Hall quickly found themselves migrating back to the city.

University Chancellor, Winston Churchill, at the opening of Wills Hall

Churchill Hall

Over the years more waves of undergraduates found their way over the Downs to settle on Stoke Bishop's green fields and bit by bit the acres that H.H. Wills had purchased were being eaten up by buildings of variable quality. First to arrive were the male occupants of Churchill Hall in 1956. The Hall was also due to be opened by Winston Churchill, but frailty and illness prevented him coming and he never visited the Hall.

Life at the start was very elitist. Like Oxford colleges, there were regular formal dinners, a served breakfast, with kidneys on the menu, and every day the students' rooms were cleaned. Over the years this regime relaxed, but Churchill was one of the last of the halls to maintain its all-male status. It went mixed in 1978, with Wills Hall following in 1985.

Badock Hall

Tumbling down the hillside, its buildings looking more like a large urban housing estate than a university hall of residence, Badock Hall (named after Sir Stanley

This 1935 picture shows *'the young gentlemen of Wills Hall taking tea with the young ladies of Manor Hall'*, a female student residence in Lower Clifton Hill (Cabot Tower can be seen in the background)

258

Churchill Hall, left, and Badock Hall

Hugh Badock, a former pro-chancellor) represented the largest influx of students at the time. Whereas Churchill initially catered for just over one hundred students, Badock had room for four hundred when it opened in 1964. From the outset it was mixed. Jackie Aslan came to Badock in 1973 and recalls what it was like.

> *'All newcomers pronounced the name as if it rhymed with haddock. We were all disappointed not to be living in Clifton, which we regarded as the heart of student utopia, but soon adapted because of the tremendous community spirit of the Halls. My first impressions were what an ugly building. I was lucky to have a single room. Boys were on the bottom two floors and the girls on the top two. There was one fairly basic bathroom on each floor and a kitchen. We ate in hall. The only self-catering occasion was Saturday supper, being the catering staff's evening off. Each student received two slices of bread, a pat of butter and an egg to boil. Most of us weren't aware of our neighbours. I never gave a moment's thought to other people living here. None of us did. We were all in our ivory tower and as far we were concerned Bristol stopped just north of the Downs. There was nothing beyond that, only fields.'*

After their first year, remembers Jackie, all students wanted to get back into Clifton. *'Being here was a bit like a boarding school, jolly good fun in the first year, but you can't repeat it.'*

Downside Survives

A familiar sight during the last decades has been the gigantic cranes towering over the ever decreasing open space of the old Downside estate as more and more student accommodation was built. Halls such as Hiatt-Baker, named after the eminent biologist Hiatt Cowles Baker, now offered 700 places in a mix of catered and self-catered accommodation. The whole campus was renamed – somewhat euphemistically – the North Residential Village and became home to two and a half thousand students. Today it has a shop, a café and most

New halls being built in the North Residential Village

importantly a bus hub. In term time a regular bus service runs from the heart of the campus into the city. Fears though that the estate could vanish under a sea of concrete have been largely unfounded. The fine Gothic house still sits on its eminence with uninterrupted views of the distant hills and is skirted by its original garden terraces and tennis courts. Spread out below is a wild flower meadow that echoes the farmland from the days of the Georges.

The Holmes

In 1939 another house was purchased by the University for student accommodation. This was the Holmes, which turned out to have had a long connection with the University. It was built in 1879 by William Edwards George as a dower house for his wife, on a plot of land purchased by the Georges at the time of the Stoke House estate sale in 1869. It stood on the edge of the new road that was to become Stoke Park Road. It was however never used for the purpose for which it was built and William leased the property to a number of tenants who in one way or another had a connection with the University.

In 1884 William Mills Baker took on the lease. The Bakers were a family of drapers who had come to Bristol to make their fortune. They created the firm of Baker and Baker, which traded in both the retail and wholesale parts of the drapery business. They had three large stores in Wine Street, Bridge Street and Mary-le-Port. William Mills showed himself to be a strong supporter of the new University College which was forerunner of the University of Bristol. His son, Hiatt Cowles

Baker, became a distinguished botanist and he laid out the gardens of the Holmes for his father. He chose a naturalistic ornamental style with a large collection of unusual plants and trees.

The next occupant was Alfred Capper Pass, who owned a Bristol smelting company. He leased the house from 1892 and he too was a supporter of University College. The house reverted to the Baker family around 1900 when Herbert Middleton Baker (a nephew of William Mills Baker and cousin of Hiatt Baker) arrived with his family. He bought the freehold in 1921.

His wife was an ardent gardener and spent many hours working with her head gardener, Mr Cully, planning and designing new features. Pamela, one of her daughters remembered their efforts with affection. *'Cully loved to tell us how he carried the two lovely blue conifers down one in each hand and planted them in what was just a field... He and my mother selected many of the larger rocks in the garden from the slopes at the top of Cheddar Gorge and had them transported to Stoke Bishop'* (not something that would be sanctioned today). It was a family home and must have been a lively place as Herbert Baker added a croquet lawn to the two existing tennis courts and bought the field opposite the front gate.

> *'It was of course bought to protect (the view from) the house. I learned to ride my pony there. I remember my mother's distress when standing at the front gate we could see a single recently-built house in the far distance! .... The lane below the gate* (Stoke Park Road) *was rough and we used to pick blackberries there in the autumn and toboggan on tea trays in the winter. There were no houses of course beyond Claverton* (next door)'

The grand roof line of the Holmes seen from the rear

The Bakers outside the Holmes

Another retainer was the butler Henry Cainey, a redoubtable man who had earned the Military Medal for bravery in the Great War. He had the job of overseeing the cleaning and polishing of the old furniture, the porcelain and silver the Bakers collected, as well as managing the large dinner parties and summer hay parties which they gave. When Herbert Baker died in 1943 and the Holmes was sold to the University, Mr Cainey became the chief steward of Churchill Hall. He served there until his retirement in 1982, four days short of his 85th birthday.

The University intended to take possession of the Holmes, soon after its purchase in 1939, but sadly events overtook it.

Chapter Twenty-two

World War Two

1939-1945

Almost as soon as the Prime Minister, Neville Chamberlain, had announced that *'this country is at war with Germany'*, the air-raid siren located on the roof of the Village Hall sounded across the parish.

It was, as it turned out, a false alarm and the next few months, in a period that has been called the phoney war, saw no enemy action, but the suspense of not knowing what might happen told on people's nerves and they quickly found their life was changing.

In the first instance the enforced black-out proved to be the biggest challenge in that material was expensive. This was bearable for ordinary houses, and people often improvised anyway, but for large buildings it could prove too costly. This was the case at St Mary Magdalene with the pattern of services revised accordingly. Evening Prayer during winter months was held at 3.30 in the afternoon and 8am Communion was put forward to 8.45am. Heather Pelmear remembers the first weeks of the war.

> *'The wardens had to make sure that no home was showing any light. There was very little light from the street lamps as the glass was darkened. House windows were covered with a transparent film to prevent the glass from shattering and there were water buckets and sand buckets at each house. Gas masks were issued and were carried with us everywhere for the first year. The threat was mustard gas. Posts were sited at regular intervals to give warning of gas. They had a flat square top which was painted with a special paint which would change colour if gas was present - this luckily never happened and I think towards the end of the war we ceased to carry our gas masks.'*

The Village Hall was scheduled as a casualty centre and was used by the Red Cross and the Air Raid Wardens for instruction and practical exercises.

People began to notice newcomers to the area as houses were requisitioned for war duties and personnel billeted in people's homes. Woodville at the end of the Avenue became home to the RAF, Sneyd Park House, on the corner of Goodeve Road and Knoll Hill, became a Territorial Army Centre and Bishop's Knoll was called up again and housed the Bristol Aircraft Company's apprentice school after Filton had been badly bombed. But the most colourful new residents were members of the BBC's Variety Department and the BBC's Symphony Orchestra evacuated to Bristol at the start of the war.

BBC's 1940s entrance in Whiteladies Road

As a producer at the time noted: *'The BBC is a good organizer, but moving hundreds of people and their families to different parts of the country gave the accommodation and catering officers headaches.'*

Mr Goodbody of Downleaze remembered when the house started to fill with music. *'On the day war broke out, the BBC billeting officer came round requiring us to say how many spare beds we had. It chanced that my mother had two spare beds and my brother and his wife, who had the top floor flat, also had two spare beds. So, by the evening my mother found herself housing Jack Mackintosh, a very celebrated trumpeter with the BBC Symphony Orchestra... Across the road in Downleaze a number of members of the BBC Salon Orchestra were billeted. The famous oboist, Leon Goossens, was I think billeted on the Matthews family (and discovered to his surprise that they had never heard of him!)... The violinist, David Wise played his violin in the Downleaze drawing room with my mother who was an excellent pianist accompanying.'* It must have been a wrench when the orchestra was eventually moved to Bedford in September 1941.

Another task that taxed householders was providing a place of safety in the event of bombing. Basements were prepared and equipped and shelters built in the gardens, whether home-made or the Government issue Anderson Shelter, the latter consisting of green corrugated curving metal sheets bolted together at the top and sunk into the

264

ground. Vera Horseman was at Stoke Bishop School when war broke out.

> 'When we went to school at the end of the summer holidays we were sent
> home for a further fortnight so that the shelters could be built. At the end of
> the fortnight they still weren't finished, so we practised what we had to do
> in an air raid – sit down under our desk as quick as we can.' Eventually
> the shelters were finished. They were situated away from the school on
> Hollybush Lane. 'We practised getting to the shelters as quickly as possible,
> without running. Our gas masks were always hanging on the back of our
> desks and were supposed to be the first thing we grabbed. Instructions were
> given that if the siren went either on the way to or from the school, we were to
> go to the nearest house and ask if we could stay there until the all-clear.'

Blitz

It was during August 1940 that the first bombers were seen over Stoke Bishop, their
target, the docks at Avonmouth and the aircraft factories at Filton. On 1 September
the Western Daily Press reported that *'at Stoke Bishop six bombs caused damage to*

Bomb damage in Kewstoke Road. The van belongs to the Post Office whose men
were repairing phone lines

several homes'. A fire broke out in St Mary Magdalene, but was quickly extinguished. On 25 September the Luftwaffe made a surprise daylight raid on Filton, killing 92 workers and seriously damaging the production of the Bristol Beaufighter. *'We had to rush to the shelters one morning when Filton was bombed. I think it was the same morning an unexploded bomb fell in Little Stoke Road'* (Vera Horseman).

It wasn't long after that Bristol itself became the target. On the night of 24 November, waves of German bombers tore the heart out of the city centre. Sixty fires were started, 207 people were killed, with many old buildings, still built of wood, reduced to ashes. It was the first of nine such heavy raids, most of which lasted all night. Heather Pelmear, who lived in Woodland Grove, remembers that night. *'The devastation to the centre of Bristol was immense. We could see the sky lit with the fires burning, though we were down in the valley over the Downs away from the centre.'*

Although Stoke Bishop was never a deliberate target, its proximity to Avonmouth and the River Avon meant that it was in danger. The German pilots used the river and any moonlight that reflected off it as a navigational aid to direct them to the docks. Chimneys were built along the river in the hope of disguising it by blanketing it in smoke, although it was doubtful how effective this was. *'One of the sounds that has really stayed with me is of the engines of the German bombers, a distinctive throb which our planes did not make. It is a sound that still sends shivers down my spine'* (Heather Pelmear). Often it was on the return that the bombs fell with the German crews jettisoning any payload they still had.

A record of the bombs that fell on Stoke Bishop shows that most landed without exploding, but on the night of Monday 2 December 1940 a number of houses were damaged either by direct hits or exploding close by, among them Stoke House and houses in Druid Stoke Avenue, Kewstoke Road and Church Avenue. The latter's collateral damage blew out the clerestory windows and those of the south aisle of St Mary Magdalene. When the stained glass figures were replaced, the glaziers inserted clear glass around them considerably lightening the church. On another occasion a whole batch of bombs fell two by two in Old Sneed Park, faithfully mirroring the twin bomb racks of a Heinkel III aircraft.

As the planes flew over, the population below sat the night out in their shelters, reasonably safe from all but a direct hit. But the nights were long as Heather Pelmear remembers:

'The nights in the shelter were kept light hearted by our neighbours, Jack and Bobbie Weaver. We had a paraffin heater down there and roasted chestnuts.

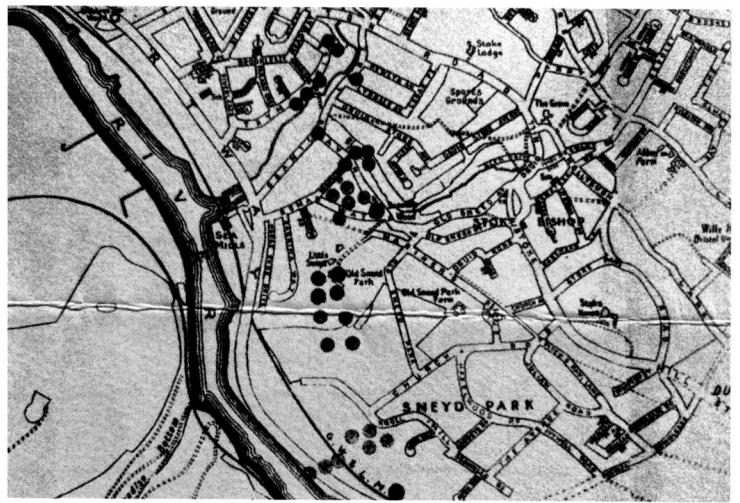

Map showing parallel pattern of bombs dropped in Druid Woods, off Roman Way and across Old Sneed Park

When the raids were very frequent, almost nightly, they used to put potatoes in the ashes of their fire before they went to bed and then bring them to the shelter later if there was a raid.' But there were times to play. *'The closest bombs dropped to us were about four hundred yards away, beside the path we took to go to the Shirehampton Road shops. There were two craters close together, perfectly circular and about twelve foot in diameter. They had steep sides with only a small flat area at the bottom. Before many days the local youngsters were exploring them and found that they could cycle around the slopes, keeping near the top. They soon wore a track around the circumference and liked to see how fast they could go, leaning out at an angle towards the middle.'*

School Bombed

Incendiary bombs caused much damage and fire-watchers were placed on points around the parish to raise the alarm before fires got out of hand. Students from Stoke House (Clifton Theological College) clambered up ladders and over duckboards to reach the roof of St Mary Magdalene, posting themselves on a nightly vigil. The church escaped serious damage, but the school was not so lucky. On the night of 2 December 1940, June Feather's father was on fire duty on the roof of Woodlands, on Church Road near the junction of Stoke Hill.

'He came home in the morning and he said you can go to school but I think it has been bombed. It looks like it's been bombed. So we went to school very excited of course as we were only youngsters. We found the school was just a

shell. There was the headmistress Miss Webb. She was crying. She was very upset, which we didn't altogether understand as we knew we weren't going to school that day. I was a little bit put out when I saw the apron I had made for my younger sister in the infants hanging out of the window in tatters.'

'I came round the corner past the shelter to go to school and all that was left was a smoking ruin and so there was nothing for it but to go back home again' (Vera Horseman).

The only part of the building left unscathed was the headmaster's house, which was the original Stoke Bishop school building gifted by John Battersby-Harford. Also bombed was No 1 Stoke Cottages, home of the caretaker and his wife. Their daughter, Margaret Evans, spoke of how the family had to move to Cardiff where her grandparents lived.

Miss Webb vowed that, though they had lost their school, the education of her pupils would not suffer. The children found themselves scattered around the parish, but their learning went on. Dorothy Duddridge, a later headmistress, recalled *'there followed a time of wandering. The children shared part-time instruction with Westbury Park School and this was supplemented by home visiting on the part of the teachers'*. Vera Horseman takes up the story. *'Miss Webb used to come round to various houses where five or six of us gathered and we had school at home.'*

Classes were also held in a new hut placed in the playground. The headmaster's house once more became a schoolroom. But none of this proved adequate, especially later in the war when children were returning after being evacuated. In April 1944 the school appealed to the Village Hall. The Ministry of Food was also wanting the hall to issue new ration

RAF aerial view of the school, showing the burnt out class rooms (right) and surviving headmaster's house (left). The new hut is the dark oblong in the playground

books. Canon Worters, the vicar of St Mary Magdalene, protested and said the children should come first. He lost the argument and the School had to wait until the ministry had finished its programme.

Casualties

Casualties on the home front in Stoke Bishop were few, although tragically a bomb hit a house in Reedley Road killing Arthur Steed, his wife Doris and their two children Sheila (10) and Agnes (7). Arthur was a platoon commander in the Home Guard. A funeral service was held on Thursday 4 June 1941 at St Mary Magdalene for a member of the Auxilary Fire Service. He was W.A. Rowe of Druid Hill and was the chief superintendent engineer of Fyffes. The report in the Western Daily Press said he *'was killed as a result of enemy action while on duty at his station'*. It doesn't mention where that station was but it was most likely to have been in Avonmouth. Not all the Germans got home. A pilot in difficulties had to bail out and parachuted into the fields near Great Brockeridge and was captured by workers wielding pitchforks.

GIs in Stoke Bishop

26 January 1942 saw the first American soldiers steam into Belfast to an enthusiastic welcome. The attack on Pearl Harbor had happened the previous December and had brought America into the war. Now seeing American troops, although small in number – they were just over 4,000 – gave the hope to the country that it was no longer alone in its fight against Germany.

Two GIs pose with their host family in Red House Lane. The house is still there

Very soon American camps had popped up all over Britain. The nearest to Stoke Bishop was at Kings Weston. Huts were erected on what is today Shirehampton Golf Course and stretched the full length of Shirehampton Road. Mess huts were put up on Stoke Lodge (one is still there) to feed Americans billeted in private houses. There were appeals for donations of home comforts such as gramophones, games, books, playing

GI camps

Kings Weston Camp on today's golf course and running along Shirehampton Road

1950s photo of American Hut in Stoke Lodge...

...still there today and used by Bristol City Council for storage

cards to make these huts more welcoming. The church also provided succour. Church House, St Mary Magdalene's annexe in Julian Road, became a '*services canteen*', dispensing hot and cold drinks and hot meals to the troops. Under the capable management of the churchwarden's wife, Mrs Brocklehurst, 60 volunteers kept the canteen open every day in the lunch hour and between 7.30pm and 9.30pm in the evening.

The children had vivid memories of their new visitors. '*I can remember at the bottom of the road* (in the village) *American forces playing baseball which I had never seen and also they gave us chewing gum and tinned fruit which we'd never seen. And the girls were given nylons. They were introducing us to new ways of life*' (Geoff Cutter). '*I watched the GIs on a route march in Sea Mills Lane. The sergeant was on a bicycle – they were all over the place... They were a crazy bunch – they used to tear around in their jeeps... But they were good to the kids – kids having nothing. They used to put film shows on for them up in their assembly hall* (at Kings Weston camp)' (Keith Horley).

But it was early in 1944 that the American presence was to have the greatest impact on Stoke Bishop. People began to notice a greater activity than usual. It was in the air that a major push was imminent. No one knew where or when, but could the long awaited invasion of Europe be about to happen? It was a question on everybody's mind.

On 5 April a transport ship docked in Liverpool carrying men from the 304th Port Company. They were part of the 519th Port Battalion, whose task it was to load and unload ships. Known as longshore soldiers, their arrival confirmed that something was afoot. They boarded a train for Bristol and would have been assigned to Kings Weston camp had there been room for them, instead the men were billeted around Sea Mills and Stoke Bishop and the officers took up residence in requisitioned Pitch and Pay.

American officers outside Pitch and Pay

Life for a billeted GI was a curious one. There was natural apprehension on both sides. The Americans thought the English would be reserved and distant, the English that the Americans would be raucous and uncouth.

That may have been the case elsewhere in Bristol but in Stoke Bishop both were pleasantly surprised,

The Black
Swan in Stoke
Lane. Better
known as the
Dirty Duck,
it would have
been familiar to
the GIs

even though most hosts hadn't volunteered to take in a soldier. Before the Americans arrived, a policeman had gone round the houses to check whether there was a spare room. If there was, the owner was ordered to release it.

For the GIs in Stoke Bishop their experience for the most part was a pleasant one. It seems they treated their hosts with respect. At the start they were told, probably with some threat if they disobeyed, that their billet was for board only and they were not to eat their host's food. All meals were issued in the mess huts on Stoke Lodge. But for one GI his host would have none of it and insisted he ate with the family. He was brought tea and crumpets every morning and to his surprise was given eggs and tomatoes, which he noted were a rarity even in the mess hut. By 1944 the Dig for Victory campaign had reaped dividends and most households supplemented their rations with homegrown vegetables and eggs from the chickens they kept.

Those billeted in Stoke Bishop soon found it was an easy walk to the Black Swan in Stoke Lane, which they learnt from the locals to call the Dirty Duck. But English beer proved an acquired taste as one GI wrote: *'It's funny you go into these places and they have these long handles for the beer. The beer was warm!'* The 519th Port Battalion was all white and so any high spirits would not, as happened in other parts of Bristol, acquire unpleasant racial overtones. Nevertheless the American authorities had patrols out at night to pick up any drunks before the local police got to them.

The key to the success of the approaching D-Day was secrecy. Everyone suspected something, no one knew exactly what. The men of the 304th Port Company hoped

The Landings on the D-Day beaches in Normandy for which the longshoremen of 304th Port Company had prepared

to see action and not be left behind at the ports of embarkation. Their wish was to be with their colleagues on the beaches. It would be dangerous but vital work. Once the initial wave of soldiers had hit the beachheads and dug in, they had to be supplied. The longshoremen's task was to unload cargoes into DUKWs,

General Omar Bradley

amphibious barges, and get them to shore. They were aware that these operations would be under fire. But they did not know that their fate was in the hands of a group of men who poured over charts in a big house less than a mile away.

The Holmes Goes To War

As we noted in the previous chapter, the University bought the Holmes in 1943 as student accommodation. Before it had a chance of developing the building, it was requisitioned by the American army as the

The leaded lights in the entrance hall of the Holmes, which caught General Bradley's eye

headquarters of General Omar Bradley, commander of the US First Army and one of the principal planners of the Normandy landings. He was popular with the troops and was known as the GIs' General. While most of the detailed work was done at Clifton College, Bradley treated the Holmes as his private residence and would entertain important visitors like Churchill to discuss policy. Because of the high stakes involved, security was tight, as Mr Cainey, the butler, found out one day to his great discomfort. He had gone over from his house to check the boiler at the Holmes and found himself facing a sentry with a fixed bayonet. He was unceremoniously frogmarched to the boiler and escorted from the premises by two military policemen. After this he decided to steer clear of the Holmes until the Americans had left.

In his autobiography Bradley refers to the Holmes twice. *'V Corps had requisitioned a residence for me beyond the Bristol Downs, a billet spacious enough to house my key staff officers and aides. An English country home with ballroom, greenhouses, stables. The house, we were told, had been tentatively earmarked as a home for wayward girls. When the first American army trucks rolled into its drive, the neighbours were said to have shrugged with resignation, if not relief.'* Apparently, the Salvation Army had made an offer for the house, hence the reference to wayward girls! Knowing what was ahead of them, Bradley and his officers lived well. It seems they had the *'best chef in the army'* who treated them to steak for breakfast each morning.

The other reference was more poignant. *'It was 7.15 when I went down to breakfast at my quarters in Bristol on the morning of June 3rd. We had loitered late over dinner the night before, our last evening together in England. Today we were to board Admiral Kite's flagship for the invasion. D-Day had been set for June 5th, and the warm summer sun that poured through the leaded glass windows of the Holmes cheered us with the promise of good weather.'*

The suddenness of the Americans' departure took everyone by surprise. Later in the war the Western Daily Press described it thus: *'There was sorrow when the call came in the middle of the night and all the Americans in the neighbourhood lined up on Stoke Hill to be picked up and taken away for the D-Day adventure.'* The 304th Port Company left Stoke Bishop on 31 May. The promised good weather did not

materialise. D-Day was postponed until 6 June. But the 519th Port Battalion did get to France and saw action on Utah Beach.

Stokeleigh's Secret

In the spring of 2020, a fascinating reminder of the Americans' presence in Stoke Bishop came to light at Stokeleigh on Stoke Hill. Now a care home, one of the rooms was being redecorated by Dave Parton, who was in charge of maintenance. As he scraped away layers of woodchip paper, he came face to face with a woman's

Dave Parton uncovers the Stokeleigh murals. Below a detail from the bar scene showing a cowboy with his arm around a glamorous woman

breasts. Further investigation revealed murals that were very American in style.

One depicted a Mexican bar. A glamorous woman stood beside it with long blonde hair, heavily made up, wearing a seductively slouched red hat. In attendance were two rough cowboy-like characters, much the worse for wear, one slumped at the bar with his arm around the woman, the other holding a bottle of rye whiskey. It had been dramatically painted and is a colourful reminder of men far from home. Dave told St Mary's Messenger: *'I shall be covering them carefully with plaster board. That will ensure they will survive for the future.'*

Chapter Twenty-three

Post War and Beyond

Tuesday 8 May 1945 marked the end of the war in Europe.

Like the rest of the country, Stoke Bishop celebrated VE Day with a mix of joy and sadness. People poured out onto the streets, hugging and cheering each other and forming impromptu congas. A large street party was held in Glen Drive. Mugs were issued with *'Glen Drive Victory Celebration 1945'* written on them. Alan Aburrow was just old enough to remember it. *'I was the youngest attendee at the VE Day Street Party that was held in Glen Drive on 12 May.'* Among the highlights were the races run along the road.

Prefabs
Long before the war ended, the government was acutely conscious that lack of materials and construction workers was creating a critical housing shortage and that it needed to act once hostilities were concluded. The solution was the building of thousands of prefabricated bungalows. Aircraft factories, like Filton, were drafted

Peter Day and William Allen race in VE Day celebrations in Glen Drive in 1945

Postwar prefabricated houses in Hadrian Close

in to help produce the frames and individual sections that could easily be loaded onto lorries and erected on site. German and Italian prisoners of war were put to work clearing waste ground, digging drainage channels and laying the concrete bases, on which they often scribbled their names. It was reckoned that a prefab could be put up in 40 hours. It had a life expectancy of 10 years.

Scarcity of sites was a problem. Every part of Bristol was scoured for suitable places and Stoke Bishop would not find itself exempt. It had never had any form of council housing in the parish before and the possible arrival of prefabs must have caused some eyebrows to be raised. Two sites were earmarked. Hadrian Close beside the Avon was built over the Roman settlement of Abona, but as the new bungalows would be gone in ten years that was not a problem. Alas the 21st century arrived and half the bungalows still stood and Abona remained underneath.

The second site lay within the Victorian Italianate gardens of Sneyd Park House on Goodeve Road. The house was built in 1880 for James Derham of Derham Brothers, boot and shoe manufacturers, who had a factory in Barton Street. Several owners followed and the house was finally sold in 1942. It must have been empty when the prefabs went in. The colossal green house or palm house that stood adjacent to the kitchen garden had gone, but the walls of the kitchen garden were still there, as were the Byzantine gazebo and arcade that graced the northern edge of the property. The new prefabs, known as Sanctuary Gardens, sat amid the remains of the garden with, in some cases, welcome fruit trees.

The irony of the prefab was that it could cost more than a two bedroom house. It was equipped with an array of modern conveniences that included fitted wardrobes, a gas boiler and gas fridge, airing cupboard and pull-down kitchen table. Most had two bedrooms, with bathroom and toilet, a living room and kitchen, and sizeable garden. But the speed of its erection was all important to a government desperate to house the young couples that had married during the war.

Helen Lewis remembers visiting her Grandma, Mary Lewis, in Sanctuary Gardens. *'The kitchen was a good size and afforded a table for three* (for Mary, her husband Cecil and son Trevor). *The kitchen had linoleum and the sink had wonderful rubber extensions to the taps. The coal fire had a sturdy glass window and an opalescent brown metal surround. There was a gas poker to help start the fire.'* But, despite the modern heating, Helen found the prefab cold. *'The windows dripped with condensation. Bubbles made wriggly lines down the pane and we watched the drips and raced them.'*

What was designed to last for only ten years proved to be more durable than could have been foreseen. Location and community spirit and the chance to purchase their home created a love affair between resident and prefab. Only through council pressure were the prefabs in Sanctuary Gardens sold off in 2010 and replaced by upmarket private housing. One in private hands has survived, while those remaining in Hadrian's Close are still inhabited over seventy years after they were first erected.

Other council houses were built, mainly in the north around Druid Stoke Avenue and Cedar Park. Liz Tomlinson was born in one of a cluster of council houses in Druid Stoke Avenue, whose tenants were carefully vetted. *'When Dad applied for the house, it was necessary for him to go in for an interview'.* Her father worked for Horne Brothers, in men's retailing, clearly a respectable enough profession. *A customer*

A carefully composed 1949 photo of children playing in Sanctuary Gardens. Note the prefabs behind

came in and tipped him the wink about the new council houses in Stoke Bishop. It must have been a shock to the home owners when they were told they were going to have a lot of council houses built around them.'

Stoke Bishop had always been a place to which people escaped and this isolation all too easily gave it a reputation for snobbery in the outside world. One woman's experience: *'I was in the BRI and soon learnt to keep my mouth shut. When asked by those in the ward with me where I lived, I naively said Stoke Bishop,*

A solitary prefab survives in Sanctuary Gardens

to which came the reply, 'Oh she's from Stoke Bishop'.' Another woman remembers going to a school outside Stoke Bishop and getting the same reaction: *'It was quite uncomfortable when they said, 'Oh she's from Stoke Bishop!' It was quite a shock to realise I was a very lucky girl.'*

A Child of the Fifties

But growing up as a child in Stoke Bishop in the fifties was a carefree time. There were plenty of places to play. It still felt very rural.

> *'Glen Drive ended abruptly with a five bar gate.'*

> *'We would often venture further afield to explore Rabbit Wood* (the University fields).'

> *'There was a well there, which we were forbidden to go anywhere near, so we spent a lot of time playing in the well and roaming those woods.'*

> *'The stream was brilliant to play in because you could get sticklebacks and newts and we had little fishing nets to scoop them up with. My memory of the water was that it was really clear.'*

> *'I'd go down the track* (now a road called Hollymead) *to Eastmead Lane, then a muddy track with a long derelict building* (Howecroft Court) *that was great fun for playing in.'*

'Spring tides supplied a bit of fun on the banks of Sea Mills Harbour and a favourite dare was to free-wheel on our bikes down and under the railway bridge and see if we could get through without getting our feet wet.'

'I used to go with my mother to feed the pigs (in Church Road). *They were very happy friendly pigs. We used to call them the piggeries.'*

'You went out in the morning and you came back when you felt like it.'

'I remembered climbing trees, going off for half a day. No one worried about it.'

'We'd go out to play and my father would call us in for tea by standing outside the front door and blowing his bugle. He was never very good at it, but the noise carried a long way.'

A New School

In the immediate post war period Stoke Bishop School struggled on in its bombed out state. To the first hut in the playground a second was added and placed on the school garden to provide more classrooms. An expansion of the existing site was urgently needed not just to accommodate displaced pupils but to deal with an increase demand for places resulting from the post war 'baby boom'. In 1951 nine new schools from across Bristol were opened collectively by the Minister of Education, the Rt. Hon. George Tomlinson, at Southmead Secondary School on Friday 13 April. One of those schools was Stoke Bishop Voluntary Primary School

An architect's model of the new Stoke Bishop School

James Beattie
Michie's Not
Angles But
Angels mural
that sat in the
entrance hall of
Stoke Bishop
School

or, as it was to be known colloquially, Cedar Park.

The school was designed to take 200 pupils. The official opening brochure described the site of three and a quarter acres as *'an attractive one in an elevated position with views toward the Severn'*. It stood on land that was once part of the Druid Stoke House estate. It looked and felt very modern. Its construction was in the words of its first head, Dorothy Duddridge, *'of load bearing brick walls with pre-stressed, pre-cast concrete roofs covered with asphalt'*. It was prepared for the modern age with each classroom being equipped with a radio point.

The entrance hall was dominated by an imposing mural. Its subject was ambitious, nothing less than the arrival of Christianity in Britain. Entitled Not Angles But Angels, it depicted St Augustine meeting the Anglo-Saxons whom he described as angels on account of their blond locks. It was designed and executed by artist James Beattie Michie, who had been employed as an architect by the Commonwealth War Graves Commission, tidying up and designing many cemeteries and who taught architecture at the West of England School of Architecture in Bristol.

Big though this school seemed, it immediately proved not big enough. In the words of Dorothy Duddridge, *'the Old School – as the Village School now became known – had to be used as an annexe'*. In charge of the classroom in the village was Miss Trump. To a small child the new school seemed very imposing with long corridors, plenty of space and a huge playground, which was in contrast with the Old School, *'a wooden hut with brambles and thickets around it'* (Margaret Pinnock).

'The old school had no on-site facilities for providing school dinners. Therefore, every lunchtime, pupils would walk (two-by-two, crocodile fashion) in all weathers up Hollybush Lane to Stoke Lodge to eat their cooked lunch in an old Nissen hut which had been used by troops billeted in the area during the war. There were no choices of what to eat – you ate what you were given. From memory, the subsidised school lunches cost six pence per day' (Alan Aburrow).

Under pressure the Ministry of Education consented to two new classrooms.

With the passing of the 1944 Education Act, the school had a new relationship with its long-term partner, the church. Dorothy Duddridge wrote that *'the school became Controlled, which meant the compulsory introduction of managers not belonging to the church. Despite this, the close contact between church and school has always been maintained and the school has remained first and foremost a Church School'*. Today its official title is Stoke Bishop Church of England Primary School.

Youth activities

Out of school, young people had a number of opportunities for coming together. When Stoke Bishop School finally evacuated its bombed building in the village, it left its huts which were then occupied by various youth groups, which included the Scouts, a Youth Club and Crusaders, a young people's Christian organisation. There was also a youth group run by St Mary Magdalene in its annexe in 11 Julian Road, known as Church House. Here Bible study was mixed with table tennis, darts and Saturday night discos.

Saturday night disco in St Mary Magdalene Church House in 11 Julian Road in 1962

The Scouts

In the 1930s the Scouts used a small hut behind the old post office. The post office had been bought by the Village Hall and turned into a Men's Club. But the hut was too small for the Scouts' needs and they decamped to an old schoolroom which had been added to the collection of temporary classrooms around the bombed Stoke Bishop School. The wooden hut lay to the west of the school, close to its garden, and sat on boggy ground. An extension was added in the 1960s. This new section, probably ex-military, came from Avonmouth and gave the complex its distinctive U shape. Where the school hut had avoided the silted up fish pond, the extension went right across it, promising difficulties for the future.

The other hut, which sat in the school playground, was also used by the uniformed organisations. Shirley Cross remembered running Guides from there. *'We had a fashion show in the hut put on by Jones Department Store and I remember the coat hangers they supplied were sold off to augment our funds.'* The Guides shared the hut with

the Crusaders, who provided spiritual guidance and exciting activities for their young charges. *'They took us to Ashton Court where we played pirates in the woods'* (Jonathan Sheather)

By the late 1990s, the School House was renovated and became a private residence. Only the Scout hut remained and this, it became clear, would soon no longer be fit for purpose. By the turn of the century it was beyond repair and likely to collapse as it had no proper foundations. Part of it sat on breeze blocks on boggy ground. The Scout leaders finally bit

The derelict extension of the Scout hut sits precariously on breeze blocks with the original school classroom beyond

the bullet and decided the only solution was a new hut. But what had given the Anglo-Saxons and later generations sustenance was now a huge obstacle to any development of the site.

It was feared that, because any new building would in part have to straddle the pond, deep and expensive foundations or caissons would be required. On examination, the ground proved to be sufficiently stable to allow standard, and cheaper foundations, to be employed.

But there was another obstacle. Since the school had been bombed, there was the

An architect's model of the new Scout hut

possibility of unexploded bombs buried in the soft ground. Fortunately none were found during the exploratory excavations. All was now clear for the new hut to be built once the money had been raised. It is planned that this new building will not be just used by the uniformed groups, but will become a new community resource.

Chapter Twenty-four

A Decade of Destruction

1970-1981

'I remember very clearly when Nazareth House was burnt down. We understand children broke in one night and set it on fire and it was particularly sad waking up next morning and seeing a smouldering ruin which had previously been such an attractive part of living in Stoke Bishop.'

Michael Brooks' sentiments echoed the feelings of many who saw the destruction wrought by the fire and who asked the question whether this venerable old house, that had stood proudly on its eminence since the 18th century, would rise from the ashes.

As we have seen, the Sisters of Nazareth left in 1970 and Old Sneed Park estate was put on the market. The sale document indicated thirty two and a half acres of freehold land, part of which had *'residential development potential'*. But it also stressed that *'part of Nazareth House is likely to be regarded as being of architectural*

The burnt out roof of the dormitory block of Nazareth House; right, firemen tackle the blaze using a hydraulic lift

interest'. Any developer was required to build new housing around the old house, although the recently erected dormitory block could be and was being demolished when the fire broke out on the night of 22 August 1972. It apparently started in the roof and quickly swept through the upper part of the building. The damage from the fire made it uneconomic to save the old building and it was demolished along with the rest of the complex. The origin of the fire has never been established, although rumour has it that children had broken in to the empty building and set light to it. But one has to ask how they managed to get into the roof?

But whatever the cause, levelling it and replacing it with a stark block of flats was perhaps the most spectacular example of the huge change that was to overtake Stoke Bishop and in particular Sneyd Park in the late sixties and early seventies. The Victorian houses that were built as a result of the Martin Act had in the perception of the day come to the end of their life. In post war Britain they were too big for single occupancy and often proved to be unsuitable for institutional use. People continued to want to settle in Stoke Bishop but didn't want the burden of a large house and grounds. The answer was simple – demolish the houses and replace them with flats. So began the wholesale demolition of houses that had given character to Sneyd Park. The planners insisted that the mass of the new blocks should not exceed that of the building being taken down, either in height or width. But the square, angular construction of many of them gave a brutalist feel that sat uneasily with the surroundings. They were only softened by the landscaping and the retention of the mature trees from the original house, as in the case of Woodside, on the junction of Church Road and Hazelwood Road.

First to be demolished was Hazelwood House in 1957 when the girls' school moved out. It was replaced by monolithic Hazelwood Court. The Mythe followed in 1970 and within a few years the area lost Howecroft, The Towers, Towerleaze, Drinagh, Oakfield, Clevelands, Pitch and Pay, Woodside, Locarno and Sea Walls. Of the spectacular houses that crested the lip of the Gorge, only The Oak, Cooks Folly, Avon Grove and Tower Hirst remained.

Perhaps the saddest loss was Bishop's Knoll. Michael Brooks, who was working with the estate agents Chappell & Matthews at the time, attended the sale in 1972: *'I remember very clearly coming to the auction sale and sitting in the magnificent ballroom, with its domed ceiling, listening to the auctioneer selling the house. It was heartbreaking knowing it was going to be demolished.'* But it wasn't until 1981 that flats were built on the footprint of the old house, after considerable wrangling over the design. A firm of Bath architects drew up plans that were approved by the Fine Arts Commission that included Sir Hugh Casson and were given the green light by Bristol City Council.

The ballroom at Bishop's Knoll in its Victorian splendour

But the final building contractors rejected them as being too costly and submitted plans of their own. In an area of great sensitivity the resultant structures were discreet but undistinguished. They afford, as do most flats in Sneyd Park, spectacular views, but at what loss. One resident, looking back, understands this: *'I feel today it would never have been allowed to be demolished. It was a beautiful house with lovely large rooms. The ballroom had a ceiling modelled on one from Buckingham Palace'* (Glenda Lindsay).

Another graphic example was the proposed development a little further up the Gorge at Sea Walls. The house, which took its name from the vertiginous cliffs, had been demolished and a massive block of flats had been designed to cascade down the hillside towards the Gorge. *'Impressively futuristic or characterless and ugly?'* asked the Bristol Evening Post. Such was the outcry the height was reduced, but the flats went ahead.

Seawalls Flats

Enough is Enough!

The creeping destruction of Sneyd Park's Victorian heritage raised growing

Houses that have been Lost

The Mythe, Julian Road

Towerleaze, Knoll Hill

Pitch and Pay, Pitch and Pay Lane

Oakfield, Julian Road

Locarno, Seawalls Road

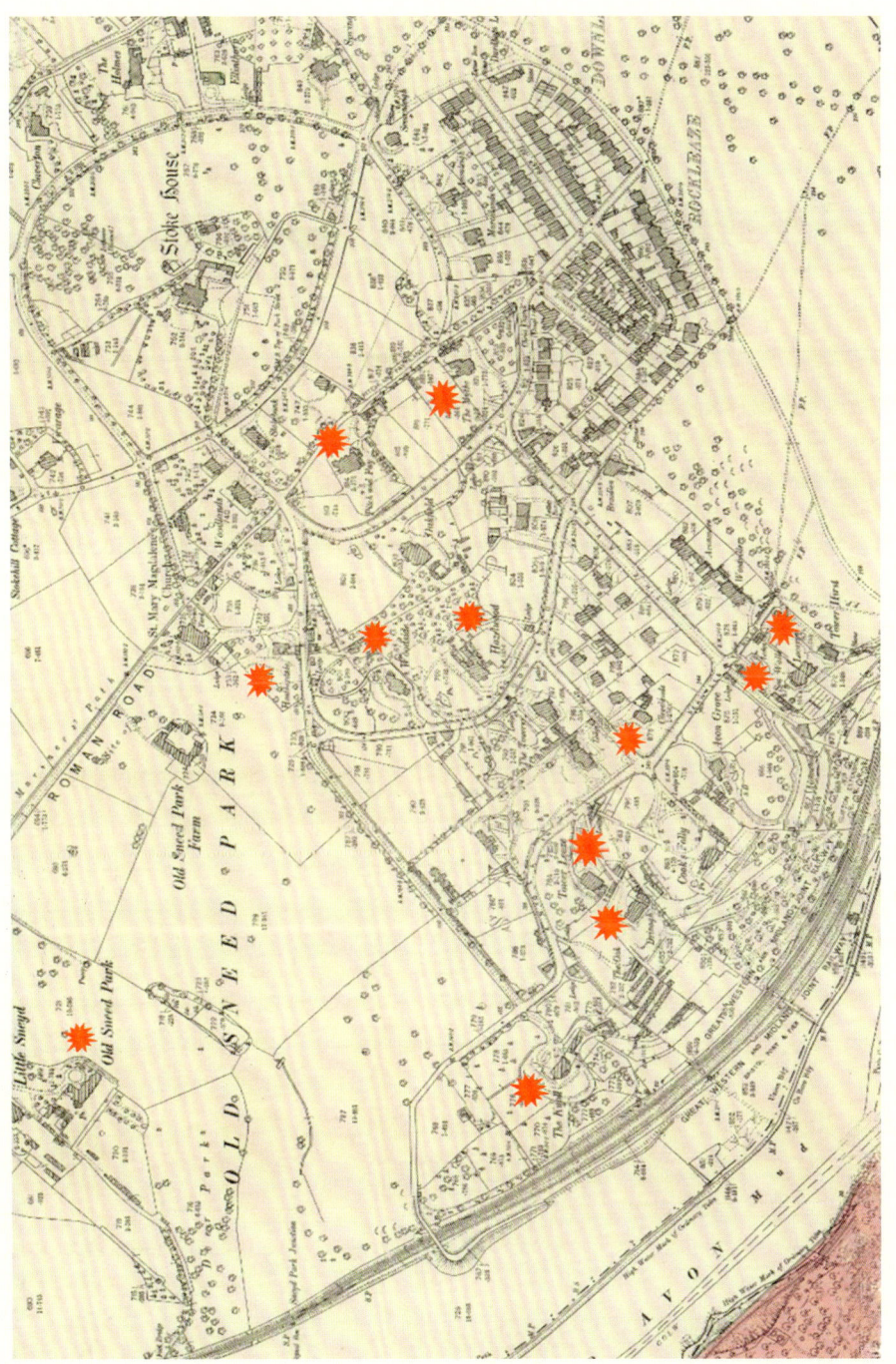

Houses demolished in Sneyd Park, 1950–1980

concerns among the area's residents. In 1969, those concerns were turned into action. On 11 August of that year, the Sneyd Park Residents' Association came into being with the express purpose of limiting flat development. Aubrey Matthews, a member, has described the early years: *'The whole character of the area was being completely destroyed and we decided we must do something and we had a very hard job in the first two years. The council just did not want to listen to us.'* The catalyst was the mysterious fire at Nazareth House. *'Shortly after that our voices started to be heard and we started to increase membership. The more members we had the more they listened.'* Every new planning application was minutely scrutinised and commented on where necessary.

Demolition slowed down, but in-filling became a new scourge. More and more land was sold off to squeeze in an unsuitable new-build. The Association launched a campaign to secure conservation status for the area. Their efforts bore fruit when, in February 1981, the Sneyd Park and Downs Conservation Area was established. A year later, Old Sneed Park, now renamed Glenavon Park, found itself being threatened by unsuitable development and was hastily brought into the scheme. At the same time a non-statutory planning policy was jointly agreed by the Association and the City Council Planning Department introducing restrictions on in-filling. It was laid down that no more than six properties could be built per acre and that there should be sufficient provision for car parking. A victory had been achieved, but as the Association well understood, constant vigilance was needed.

The Survivors

As the houses fell victim to the bulldozers, they left behind their trappings of wealth. Chief among these are the great boundary walls that gave the owners security. These magnificent structures in large part have survived but now guard blocks of flats. Equally imposing are the huge trees the Victorians planted. Cedars of Lebanon, Wellingtonias and Cypresses have all grown to maturity but their survival has depended on tree protection orders and the watchfulness of residents.

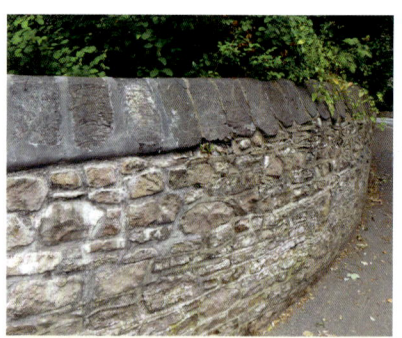

A surviving wall on Stoke Hill

One irony is that while the houses of the wealthy are no more, the lodges and gatehouses that were inhabited by their servants still survive. There are over 20 such buildings in Sneyd Park making it one of the densest concentration of lodges in the country. Old Sneed Park, being the largest estate, had three entrances and hence three lodges, all of which have survived. One is at the top of Mariner's Drive opposite the church. Another is the lodge to Little Sneyd farmhouse, adjacent to Old Sneed Park, renamed St Christopher's Lodge when it was part of Nazareth House. The third is at the bottom of Mariner's Drive, sporting its distinctive thatch. The latter was built in 1807 and bears a resemblance to the cottages created by John Nash at Blaise Hamlet in 1811. The date is about right but there is alas no evidence that Nash had any involvement. Until recently the thatch was constructed of Norfolk reed pegged in with hazel spars sourced from Frome. Such is its durability, the thatch, which now comes from Turkey, has a life expectancy of 30 to 40 years.

What of the houses that did survive? After the remaining private owners and the schools moved out, the surviving houses were turned into flats, examples being Woodlands, Sneyd Park House, the Grange and Cook's Folly, or they became care homes. We have already encountered Stoke Leigh on Stoke Hill and Druid Stoke House, but when in 1984 the University sold Claverton, Waltham House and Down House (site of the second Ostrich), they all became residential or nursing homes (although Claverton is now converted to flats).

Pitch and Pay Park

Pitch and Pay estate had, like Old Sneed Park, been nibbled at over the years. In the 1850s it had been divided and the Mythe built on the southern part. This was demolished for housing. The ancient farmhouse was sold and demolished in 1962 and on its three acres or more of land there rose an experimental development of

The thatched lodge at the bottom of Mariner's Drive, once an entrance to Old Sneed Park, dating from 1807; right, re-thatching roof with Turkish reed

44 modernist homes, in a mix of detached and terraced housing. Numbers 1-14 were the first to be built, with the rest following two years later. The houses all had three or four bedrooms to attract young professional families, who were drawn to a community environment. To its critics the new estate smacked of a communist enclave in the middle of Sneyd Park. As one resident put it *'everything inside the house is mine, everything outside the house is theirs'*.

Pitch & Pay Park was created for Span Developments by a firm of Bath architects, adhering to the principles laid down by the young architects, Geoffrey Townsend and Eric Lyons, who had founded Span in the 1950s. The Span ethos was to build affordable *'homes in a garden'*. The firm operated mainly in the London area. The Bristol development was only the second in the provinces. Eric Lyons was adept at expressing his philosophy in pithy sentences. *'The test of good housing is not whether it can be built easily, but whether it can be lived in easily.'* And again. *'No house is an island – you can't pretend there isn't one next door.'*

To keep the cost low the houses had a modular design and were partly prefabricated off site. The aim was to create high density accommodation within a landscaped environment and as far as possible to make it car free. The latter was not achieved at Pitch and Pay, but careful attention was paid to landscaping with new planting and the retention of many of the old farmhouse's original trees. Bernard Lane, who has lived on the estate since close to its inception, pointed out how the estate is connected by a network of footpaths. *'The idea was that people should talk to each other as they walked around the estate.'*

Another characteristic of Span estates was the concept of a legally constituted Residents Association, membership of which was a condition of sale, and which included covenants that placed mutual obligations on the house owners to maintain

Pitch and Pay Park

the properties and grounds. It was designed to enhance the feeling of community, but for the individualistic Briton, whose home was his castle and who, within reason, felt he could do what he liked with it, this was often hard to come to terms with.

The estate at the time of its creation won several architectural awards for its forward looking modernism. Today it no longer feels modernist, but it sits comfortably within its leafy and sinuous rural paths, affecting a sense of well-being and charm. But perhaps the Span developers had the last laugh. The estate was divided into two parts and there was no road that linked the two. A taxi driver coming in the wrong entrance was and is faced with a frustrating detour to get to the other side!

Surviving estate wall and green spaces in Pitch and Pay Park

Security

Over the course of this history, I have written little about crimes committed – footpads on the Downs, the rare murder, petty theft and the suffragette violence – but from the seventies onwards crime waves that plagued the rest of the country spilled over into Stoke Bishop. A gangland murder in Tunstall Close, two cannabis farms raided in Sneyd Park hit the headlines, but by far the most widespread offences in affluent Stoke Bishop were burglary and car theft. It became commonplace to hear the clatter of helicopter blades overhead as the police helicopter sought to pin down malefactors. In May 1992, the Evening Post ran an editorial on *'Curbing the Car Thieves Menace'* and quoted the police statistic that 1,300 cars had been stolen in north west Bristol so far that year. *'A senior Avon police officer said yesterday that police saw stolen cars being driven dangerously two or three times a night.'*

A stretched Somerset and Avon Police Force could only intermittently put a community policeman on the beat in Stoke Bishop, which left houseowners creating their own protection. This usually took the form of burglar alarms, security cameras and electronic gates, but in 1993 the Sneyd Park Residents Association went one stage further. They brought in a private security firm to patrol the neighbourhood. It was novel enough to catch the attention of the national press. While in its five years of operation it was claimed to have reduced household and car crime, it also attracted

A surveillance camera captures an intruder

negative comments and accusations of vigilantism. It folded when the man who ran it was revealed to have had a criminal background.

Greater awareness of the dangers of crime and the use of more sophisticated surveillance lowered the crime levels, but there was now growing concern over the erosion of green spaces and a determination to do something about it.

Chapter Twenty-five

The Fight for Green Spaces

1970 onwards

Generation after generation moved to Stoke Bishop seeking to enjoy the country air and channel breezes, but by 1970 such pleasures were more elusive.

By the end of the century it was estimated that housing would have taken over every inch of green space. Two sports grounds, RTZ and Clifton High School's playing field at the Grove, were already lost to new housing estates and what was left of the open spaces at Old Sneed Park were being threatened with development, while the future of the Stoke Lodge parkland was looking uncertain. The situation was bleak, but amid the thorn bushes that sprang up along the Gorge came the first shoots of hope.

The Gardens of Bishop's Knoll

In 1985, when the Bishop's Knoll developers came back with revised and less attractive plans for flats on the site of the old house, they were obliged to offer something in return. What they bequeathed were the extensive gardens that tumbled down the hill on which Bishop's Knoll perched. They entrusted their upkeep to the Woodland Trust, which over the years has done much to make the gardens accessible. Glenda Lindsay remembered exploring them in their jungle-like state. *'Further along it was obviously a terraced garden and*

The garden terraces of Bishop's Knoll are hidden by a tangle of creeper

296

The skeletal wrought iron pergola that once supported fruit trees and climbing plants

we fought our way along to what were remnants of a stone summerhouse, very dilapidated and broken down. We climbed over broken stones and could see there was a gap in the far wall. My five year old granddaughter said, "Granny look, this is the way to the Secret Garden!" What they had uncovered were the spectacular remains of elaborate brick terracing that allowed the Victorian gardeners to grow fruit and vegetables on the steep slopes. Bishop's Knoll sought to be self-sufficient in food production and so every inch of difficult terrain was brought into cultivation. Amid the rubble and brambles the ingenuity of the Victorians can be glimpsed. Part of the site has been restored and allows the visitor a vertiginous ascent through a very fine wrought iron pergola and up a giddy-inducing staircase of narrow brick steps. To the north of the gardens the owners had planted an extensive woodland with a number of unusual specimen trees, to which the Woodland Trust has added native trees of its own.

Old Sneed Park Nature Reserve

The northern boundary of Bishop's Knoll Nature Reserve came into contact with the south western edge of Old Sneed Park that had so far escaped the developers. Plans had been submitted for the development of the whole estate, but the City Council refused permission for the lower valley to be developed. In a 1979 report for the Department of the Environment Property Services Agency, S. Taylor wrote: *'The rest of the grounds, which extend to Bramble Drive and the railway line have begun to look like a wasteland with a lot of secondary growth and small bushes growing. The contractor's roads and temporary buildings and general aftermath of construction work is evident.'* At that time hope of extending the development was very much alive. There were plans to *'build detached houses dotted around the grounds, which are wooded in parts and include a lake'.* When these plans came to nothing, the developers lost interest and ceded the land to Bristol City Council, along with the wild man who allegedly lived in the woods.

Safe for the moment, but a neglected piece of land doesn't stay neglected forever and Ron Stagg who lived in Glenavon Park knew this. He contacted his local councillor, who suggested the Sneyd Park Residents Association be called in to help, but they were too busy with in-fills. So a small group took matters into their own hands. They bravely stepped out to arouse enough interest in establishing a working group that would, in partnership with Bristol City Council, seek to restore the derelict land. It was 1995 when a new organisation was officially formed, called Friends of Old Sneed Park Nature Reserve. The task ahead of them was a formidable one and fell loosely into two parts – fund raising and working parties. But it caught the imagination of the neighbourhood and over the next few years the dedicated work force through sweat, toil and camaraderie gradually saw their efforts bear fruit and wildlife begin to return.

The biggest part of the restoration involved dredging the lake. The water was drained, and the silt tested and found to be free of toxic chemicals. Diggers removed the mud and deposited it in nearby hollows. The dam was repaired and the lake refilled.

It wasn't long before the reserve began to delight visitors as they wandered among the wild flower meadows, spotted the southern marsh orchid, relaxed beside the lake with its family of ducks and debated whether what they were looking at was a comma butterfly. Herons were spied, but most excitingly deer came back to what had been a medieval deer park. Paths linked the two reserves and there was now only one piece of land still to be fitted into the rural jigsaw.

Working party in the Reserve making hay

Gateway to the Gorge

As cars on the Portway approached one of the finest landscapes in the country they passed on their left a derelict and gated stretch of land. This was where rubble from the Blitz was dumped, but after the war it had been turned into playing fields. For 30 years, until 2000, it had been the sports ground of the Bristol & West Building Society. Thereafter it had lain fallow for fourteen years while a number of inappropriate schemes for developing it were put forward, mostly involving high density sporting activities such as five-a-side football that promised light polluting all weather pitches. There was outrage that one of the most iconic entrances to any city could be so marred.

In 2015 the Avon Wildlife Trust acquired with the help of donors the 12 acre site thus completing a large nature reserve at the foot of the Gorge, a wildlife corridor for hedgehogs, badgers and slow worms. The land would be turned into a mix of wildflower meadow and woodland. But it was also to have two unusual sculptures. One was an installation of a pair of whales, constructed of wicker and steel, emerging from the green grass. They had originally been part of an environmental exhibition in Millennium Square where they soared out of a sea composed of thousands of blue plastic bottles. Ironically their move brought them close to the old 18th century dock at Sea Mills where blubber had been boiled down on the quay.

Another, later creation was an eco-inspired sculpture of a woman's head created from wooden poles and offering shelter in its crevices to insects, birds and possibly bats. The figure was commissioned by Peter White, a local resident, as a memorial to

Wicker and steel whales; right, head of Ruth White

his mother Ruth White, née Paddock. Peter and Timothy Bennett gave generously towards the purchase of the sports ground and the new space has been named Bennett's Patch and White's Paddock in recognition of this.

Stoke Lodge Parkland

Giving the public access to the beautiful expanse of Stoke Lodge parkland proved to be more intractable. We left the story in the nineteen twenties with the house and grounds still being in private ownership. In 1923 the Fry family moved to Howecroft and sold Stoke Lodge to three unmarried sisters, Annie, Mary and Emily Butlin. They were active in the city and engaged in charitable work. The Western Daily Press reported on 24 June 1924 that *'by the kindness of Miss Butlin the garden party for schoolboys, arranged by the Bristol branch of the National Laymen's Missionary movement, was held on Saturday last at Stoke Lodge... Exhibits illustrating the mode of life and religion of the peoples of China, India, Tibet, Labrador and the South Seas were shown'.* As we have seen, Stoke Bishop Cricket Club came to play on Stoke Lodge in 1929 and their games were much enjoyed by the Butlin sisters watching from the belvedere in the gardens of the house. A precedent for sport had been set.

Annie Butlin died on 28 July 1940, her sister Elizabeth on 7 May 1946. Emily, the surviving sister, decided to put the house and grounds on the market. Among the effects auctioned was a Rolls Royce Drophead Foursome Coupé. The purchaser of the estate was Bristol City Council. The Western Daily Press wrote: *'Stoke Lodge Estate, an estate of about 22 acres, which represents the biggest single area in Stoke Bishop not yet covered by houses, has been purchased by Bristol City Council for over £25,000... It is to be hoped that the lovely cedars and other trees can be retained in the Education Committee's proposals.'* Over the years these proposals, which have included temporary housing and a new school, veered dangerously close to destroying that hope. Finally it was agreed that the land should be laid out as playing fields.

The parkland became a space for all. Rugby, cricket and football were played on formal pitches while scouts organisations and churches held garden fetes and sports days. In the early seventies St Mary Magdalene mounted its annual Summer Day beneath the great cedar tree. Highlight among the sporting events was the tug of war between the vicar's team and that of the churchwardens. Roy Henderson, a notoriously competitive vicar, always made sure that he had recruited the strongest members of his flock well in advance. He always won!

Through local efforts, a play park was established in 2014, which provided a much needed safe place for young children to run around. With its popular zip

The Revd. Roy Henderson marks out the tug-of-war pitch during St Mary
Magdalene's Summer Day; right, the popular children's play park

wire and elaborate climbing frames, it gave considerable scope for imaginative play.
Parents were encouraged not to lift their child onto a frame but to let them climb
at their own level. The play park was rarely unoccupied. Elsewhere two schools,
Fairfield until 2000, and then Cotham used the pitches for their school sports. In
this lay the seeds of future conflict.

The Cedars and Other Trees

One of the joys for visitors coming to Stoke Lodge was the chance to gaze upon the
collection of magnificent cedars of Lebanon. They had been planted in the 1840s
and were in recent years reaching full maturity. Sadly one by one they began to die
and had to be felled. The last to be cut did not suffer the ignominious end of the
others, but was transformed into a captivating tree sculpture, created by wood artist
Andy O'Neil, celebrating the diverse wild life of the parkland. Two cedars survive.

Many youngsters climbed the trees in Stoke Lodge and one young teenager has
lasting memories of heaving herself up into its sweeping branches, where as she
recalled, she enjoyed her first date. One of the oldest surviving trees is the Lucombe
oak, which was planted like the cedars around 1840. Standing close to the children's
playground, it was named Bristol's Tree of the Year in 2019. It gets its name from
William Lucombe, an Exeter nurseryman, who in the 1760s noticed an oak sapling
that was a non-deciduous cross between a Turkey and a Cork oak. It was popular
in parklands of the day because it can live for over 200 years.

Clockwise from top left: the Lucombe oak; cedar of Lebanon; Andy O'Neil carves his animal artwork from the felled cedar; the stunning result

Community Versus School

In August 2011, Cotham School signed a 125-year lease with Bristol City Council to use the field as its sports ground. Earlier in the year, a group of residents had submitted an application to register the parkland as a Town and Village Green, which if successful would ensure permanent open access for the public. Cotham deemed this incompatible with their plans to erect a security fence around the entire perimeter of the playing fields that would allow only a narrow corridor for the public to use. To resolve the dispute, a Public Inquiry was held.

In October 2016 the Inspector gave his report, concluding, '*I recommend that the land be* <u>not</u> *registered as a town or village green because, in the twenty year period, use by local people has not been* <u>as of right</u>. *Otherwise my recommendation would have been that the land be registered. I do not think any of the other reasons argued for by the objectors should lead to the rejection of the application.*' The Inspector's argument

rested on two signs that had been erected by the defunct Avon County Council warning *'members of the public not to trespass on this playing field'*. In addition to the two signs and a third the Council later put up, the parkland could be accessed at multiple points where there was no official sign.

On 12 December 2016 the Council's Public Rights of Way and Greens Committee met to consider whether the signs, which had been present for some of the 20-year period referred to by the Inspector, were sufficient to deny registration of Stoke Lodge green space as a TVG. With votes evenly balanced it was the chairman's casting vote that led to the rejection of the Inspector's recommendation and the decision to proceed with the TVG registration. Cotham applied to the High Court for a judicial review of

From top, erecting the fence; police attend as the fence is put up; residents gather to protest against the fence

the Committee's decision. The judge directed the Committee to review its decision and after considerable debate the original decision was overturned.

Cotham was now encouraged to proceed with erecting the fence and when the contractors moved onto the field they were met with a group of passive protestors in sufficient numbers to cause alarm. The School, fearing a violent disturbance, called the police and asked them to come in riot vans and the protesters watched with dismay as the eight foot fence shut out their beloved parkland. The fence was necessary the School argued to keep out intruders while the field was in use. But it became a hated presence especially when the narrow path around its outer perimeter became a mud churned track in the winter.

As the months went by, the affair began to descend into farce with items on the financial cost to the School appearing in Private Eye and a covert camera found installed in a metal junction box to *'deter vandals'*. Two new TVG applications were submitted that in turn provoked a second legal process. This once more got embroiled in issues over signage with the Inspector once again recommending the TVGs do not go ahead. The Public Rights of Way and Greens Committee meeting on Wednesday, 28 June 2023 decided otherwise and, with a majority of six to one, decided that Stoke Lodge should be registered as a Town and Village Green. The land was duly registered on 22 August 2023, although legal battles continue.

The Botanic Garden

The primeval dell showing maturity

Another of Stoke Bishop's surviving green spaces, the four acres of ornamental gardens at the Holmes in Stoke Park Road, were to have a change of use. In 2005 the University of Bristol Botanic Garden moved across the river from Bracken Hill and relocated to the Holmes. The site was chosen as being of a similar size to Bracken Hill and close to the University campus. The Botanic Garden, from its inception in 1883, had moved four times, and it was hoped this would be the last. *'The move,'* said Garden Director, Professor Stephan Hiscock, *'gave us the opportunity to design the new garden in a new way, different from traditional botanic gardens. Ours was the first university botanic garden to be created in the United Kingdom in nearly 40 years.'* For Nicholas Wray, the Curator, it had the perfect

Nicholas Wray, the Curator, welcomes local people to a preview of the garden

conditions for creating something new. *'The mature trees, old walls and house all provide shelter.'* With advice from Kew Gardens and design input from the Eden Project, a startling amount of varied planting was ingeniously woven into what was a relatively small area. Judith Sheather, writing in St Mary's Messenger, took the reader on an early tour of the new garden. *'From the entrance, the path will lead around a new large pool for rare native, aquatic and wetland planting. A rocky outcrop will be home for threatened local plants, the Bristol Onion and Spiked Speedwell. The former sunken rock garden becomes an evolutionary dell to plot the chronological development of land plants from algae and moss to ferns, conifers and magnolias. The warm ridge above and the area sheltered by the Hollybush Lane wall is ideal for the Mediterranean Climate Collection.'* Herbal medicine featured largely in curating the garden, with the introduction of Chinese and European medicinal features. Behind the walls of the kitchen garden, now alas a car park, rose state of the art glasshouses, housing plants from temperate to tropical zones. Stars of the show were the giant waterlilies. One, the Victoria Amazonica, delighted Victorian visitors to Kew when a small child was placed standing on its strong leaves. That won't happen at the Holmes but the leaves still amaze.

At the time of its opening the director of Kew, Sir Peter Crane wrote: *'This important investment by the University will not only enhance teaching and research but will also enrich the City of Bristol and its citizens.'* Beyond these formal words is an asset that is part educational, part inspirational and part entertainment. From a casual visit ending in a cup of coffee at the café to a jazz concert on a summer's evening, from lectures in the study centre to richly displayed art exhibitions, the Botanic Garden has carried into the twenty-first century the tradition of Victorian gardening, so much part of Stoke Bishop gardens, where the enjoyment of beautiful planting is combined with the desire to educate and learn.

Chapter Twenty-six

Into the Twenty-first Century

The dilemma of anyone writing a history about their locality is how and when to end it.

By its very nature local history is ongoing and the last years, nay decades, can only be observed in a subjective way, the rigours of historical analysis being difficult to apply. This chapter then is less of a history and more of a snapshot of the last few years.

After the building turmoil of the seventies, a quieter scene prevailed as Stoke Bishop moved towards the next century. There was less large scale development and a sizeable tract of countryside had been preserved for people to enjoy. Owners looked at their own houses and explored ways they could enlarge them on their existing footprint. Some knocked their home down and started again, but most sought to gain extra rooms by going up into the loft or creating a modest extension. A time traveller from the thirties would still recognise the Stoke Bishop they had left, with construction work still as prevalent today as it was then. They would feel at

A typical sight of the new millennium

home negotiating what would appear to them to be one large building site, with every other house swathed in scaffolding and vans parked and lorries off-loading their materials.

As the count-down towards the Millennium approached, everyone held their breath and hoped the doomsayers' dire predictions would not materialise. Computers

The architect's photograph of the re-ordered St Mary Magdalene church, 2011

had taken over people's lives and that they would soon crash in meltdown was not something anyone wanted to contemplate. It was therefore with a huge collective sigh of relief that midnight 2000 passed seamlessly and everybody could carry on as normal. For St Mary Magdalene this meant progressing with its dream to provide a church building for the 21st century.

The church offered the largest indoor space in Stoke Bishop but it was inflexible, so plans were put in place to re-order the interior of the church and rebuild the seventies church hall. The plans were ambitious and when it was heard they came with a price tag of four million pounds, there was a sharp intake of breath. The church hall scheme was put on hold, but the re-ordering of the church went ahead. The architect, Kelvin Sampson, sought to strip the building back to the simple lines of John Norton's original design, but with one radical change, the replacement of the pews with chairs. This caused consternation among those who saw the pews as intrinsically part of the much loved Victorian church. The floor boards were ripped out, under-floor heating inserted and a floor of grey tiles laid over the whole.

Scaffolding filled the nave, to allow access to the most remote parts, including the frescoes just below the chancel roof. When David Ritchie, the vicar, climbed up to

A meeting of the Stoke Bishop Local History Group in a brighter Village Hall

the highest level to see them he felt he was *'among the angels'*. Entering the newly re-ordered church for the first time was a breathtaking experience for many. It felt bigger, more spacious, more cathedral-like, and, for the most part, it won over the doubters.

The Village Hall, too, was enjoying a make-over, with an upgraded kitchen and better audio/visual facilities. Between them, Church and Village Hall could now cater for most demands of the community, whether it be weddings, hosting classical concerts and opera, badminton, exhibitions, neighbourhood meetings, dog training and pilates. Both served as polling stations during elections.

In Shirehampton Road and the village, the turnover of shops carried on apace. Individual food outlets all but disappeared, with the greengrocers and the chemist in the village being the last to close. But then the Co-op, in both Shirehampton Road and the village, stepped in to provide a one-shop service. In the

Neil Patel amid the burgeoning shelves of Welcome

Shirehampton Road shops

village it was called Welcome and was run by Neil Patel who created an emporium that was little short of miraculous. The store was greengrocer, grocer, baker, butcher, stationer, newsagent and garden centre all rolled into one in a space that required great ingenuity to stock everything that was on offer. And then most recently Neil has brought back the post office to the delight of residents.

Restaurants and take-aways continued to come and go. Both centres had a fish and chip shop, an Indian restaurant and restaurants that have spread out onto the forecourt. When lit up at night they create a lively atmosphere. Other needs were catered for, whether one was a cyclist or required financial advice, but perhaps the other most prolific group of shops were those devoted to health and beauty, offering grooming from hair to toe and promoting inner wellbeing. The longest serving shopkeeper in this cluster has been Salvatore Parrinello, a barber who has kept men's hair in trim since 1994. Not surprisingly he finds his clientele err on the

Salvatore Parrinello in his barber's shop

310

conservative side. His most popular cut remains *'short, back and sides'*.

An intriguing feature of millennium Stoke Bishop has been its frequent use as a film location, the result of Bristol becoming a popular film centre. Casualty has found its way into the parish on a number of occasions, once when it took over the vicarage. Martin Clunes was seen in Kewstoke Road when two of the houses there stood in for London in the second series of Manhunt. On another occasion an explosion and fire rocked a house in Stoke Park Road. No damage was done to the house. The special effects team had constructed a false front which they blew

Martin Clunes on location in Kewstoke Road

up. But the most celebrated scene must be the wedding of Dr Watson in Sherlock which took place before the distinctive blue door of St Mary Magdalene church. Benedict Cumberbatch and Martin Freeman were in attendance.

The defining moment of this snapshot came in December 2019 when a deadly coronavirus was first identified in the Chinese City of Wuhan. Called Covid-19, it spread around the world with alarming speed, reaching Italy on the 30 January 2020 and the UK a day later. On the 16 March the Prime Minister, Boris Johnson, announced that *'now is the time for everyone to stop non-essential contact and travel'*. Ten days later lockdown became law, forcing people to stay at home and avoid all social contact.

The pandemic would transform people's lives. They clapped for the NHS and kept their social distance. Yet, amid all the horror, the grief and the heartbreak, one positive thing came out of that terrible time. People started to appreciate their

Supporting the NHS in chalk

surroundings. The rules allowed daily exercise of one hour, as long as no contact was made. In their solitary walks residents discovered footpaths and green spaces they had not walked before and heard birdsong with a clarity that was free of background traffic. They were unwittingly experiencing Stoke Bishop's *'sublime landscape'* that their 18th century forebears delighted in 300 years ago.

A customer waits to enter Welcome's socially distanced premises

An empty Stoke Hill during Covid

Bibliography

Selected Archives and Books Consulted

Abbreviations: **SBLHG** (Stoke Bishop Local History Group)
BGAS (Bristol and Gloucestershire Archaeological Society)

Archives

Stoke Bishop Local History Group Archive
The first port of call for anyone studying the history of Stoke Bishop. Begun by Penny Jetzer, this has grown over years into a sizeable collection of documents and photographs

Bristol Archives
An eclectic repository of Bristol related documents and photographs. The catalogue and some material online

Know Your Place
An essential resource for understanding Bristol's development. It is an online collection of maps from 1840 that can be overlaid to compare changes in a locality. I found it invaluable in seeing how Stoke Bishop developed. It can be accessed through the Bristol City Council website

British Newspaper Archive
Newspapers are a window on the world of their time and an essential resource for the local historian. A subscription service

The History of Parliament Online
Biographies of members of Parliament and other documents useful for finding out about the many MPs resident in Stoke Bishop

Internet Archive
A valuable online repository of out-of-print books

Bristol and Gloucestershire Archaeological Society
Founded in 1876 the BGAS has a wealth of research material, most of which is online

ALHA Avon Local History & Archaeology
Books & Newsletters on a variety of local subjects

Bristol Historical Association
This has a fine collection of local history pamphlets, eighty of which are online

St Mary's Messenger
A wealth of local stories

Books

Five books which are essential reading for anyone researching Stoke Bishop history:

A Pictorial History of Stoke Bishop – Penny Jetzer, Diana Bourne, Elizabeth Floyd, Monica Carp 1998 | A pioneering work, now out of print, but available to consult through the SBLHG

North Bristol Through Time – Anthony Beeson 2014 | Amberley Publishing

A New History of Gloucestershire – Samuel Rudder 1779

Memoirs Historical and Topographical of Bristol and its Neighbourhood – Samuel Seyer 1821-23

The Annals of Bristol – John Latimer 1893

Introduction

SBLHG Archives (also see photo credits)

Chapter 1: From the Stone Age to the Romans

Prehistoric Bristol (The Prehistory of the Lower Bristol Avon) by L.V.Grinsell 1969 | Bristol Branch of the Historical Association

Evaluation Work at the Druid Stoke megalithic monument, Stoke Bishop, Bristol 1983 by G.H.Smith BGAS

Two Cemeteries from Bristol's Northern Suburbs ed Martin Watts | 2006 BGAS

Romans in the Bristol Area – Branigan 1969 | Bristol Branch of the Historical Association

Sea Mills, The Roman Town of Abonae by Julian Bennett | Excavations at Nazareth House 1972 City of Bristol Museum & Art Gallery Monograph No 3

Transactions of the Bristol Gloucestershire Archaeological Society (all online) contain various reports by Tratman, Boon and others

Chapter 2: From the Anglo-Saxons to the Middle Ages

The Bristol Region in the Sub-Roman and Early Anglo-Saxon Periods by David Higgins | Bristol Branch of the Historical Association 2006

Two Cemeteries from Bristol's Northern Suburbs – ed Martin Watts | 2006 Cotswold Archaeology & Bristol and Gloucestershire Archaeological Report No 4

The Anglo-Saxons by Marc Morris | Penguin Books 2022

The Anglo-Saxon Charters of Stoke Bishop: A Study of the Boundaries of Bisceopes Stoc by David Higgins | Transactions of the BGAS Volume 120, 2002

Record of Domesday Holdings (Hull University Online)

An Analysis of the Domesday Survey of Gloucestershire by Charles S Taylor | BGAS 1889

Chapter 3: The Sadleir Legacy Part 1 1544-1691

A Memoir of the Life and Times of the Right Honourable Sir Ralph Sadleir by Major F Sadleir Stoney | Longmans Green & Co 1877

The County Houses of Gloucestershire Vol 2 (1660-1830) by N Kingsley | Phillimore 1992

Bristol & Clifton Old & New by John Taylor (1877 reprinted 2023)

Bristol: A People's History by Peter Aughton | Carnegie Publishing 2000

The History of the Society of Merchant Venturers of the City of Bristol by John Latimer | J W Arrowsmith 1903

Chapter 4: The Sadleir Legacy Part 2 1700-1800

The Transactions of the BGAS volume 129 (2011), pp 155-196: Some Local Placenames in Medieval and Early Modern Bristol by Richard Coates with the collaboration of Jennifer Scherr (Pitch and Pay)

The Keep Military Museum, Dorchester (William Munro)

Stoke Bishop and Stoke House by Bryan Little | Pamphlet 1988

Archives of Trinity College

Chapter 5: A New Dock 1712

Sea Mills Dock – a paper by James Russell for Bristol & Avon Archaeological Society 2010

A Historic Survey of the Lower Trym Valley by Peter Harris 1994

Mariner's Mirror Vol 25 (1939) pp 349-350

Bristol Privateers and Ships of War by J.W. Damer Powell | J W Arrowsmith 1930

Chapter 6: A Farming Revolution 1700-1801

Clifton and Westbury Probate Inventories 1609-1761 - edited by John S Moore ALHA 1981

A Picturesque Guide to Bath, Bristol Hotwells by Mess. Ibbetson, Laporter and J Hassell | London 1793

Chapter 7: Land Sale Part 1 1800-1840

Stoke Lodge – What a History by Helen Powell | We Love Stoke Lodge website

The George Papers – courtesy of Ry George

Bristol & Co by Helen Reid | Redcliffe Press 1987

Guinness's Brewery in the Irish Economy 1759-1876 by P Lynch and J Vaizey Cambridge University Press 1960

Chapter 8: Land Sale Part 2 1853-1869

Sneyd Park by Michael Morgan | Published by the author 1977

Sneyd Park: A Local Study and Guided Walk | The Sneyd Park Residents Association 2001

The Archives of Trinity College

Battersby Harford Papers | Bristol Archives

Chapter 9: A New Church 1860

Memorials of Stoke Bishop by David Wright | John Wright & Co, Bristol 1897

Autumn Violets and other Recollections of the late Daivd Wright | John Wright & Co, Bristol 1897

A History of St Mary Magdalene, Stoke Bishop by Ronald Warne | Privately published 1959

St Mary Magdalene, The Story of Stoke Bishop Church by Roy Henderson & Keith Sheather | St Mary Magdalene PCC 1999

Chapter Ten First School and Village Hall: The Early Years

History of Stoke Bishop Hall by Penny Jetzer | Stoke Bishop Community Association 1985

Chapter 11: Pubs, Inns and Taverns

SBLHG Archives/Author's own papers

Bristol Times & Mirror Nov 3 1916 | Letter from Rev H.J. Wilkins, vicar of Westbury-on-Trym, confirming there were two Ostrich pubs

Gloucestershire & Avon Life, Feb 1982 | Article on pubs in Stoke Bishop

Clifton and Durdham Downs: A Place of Public Resort and Recreation by Gerry Nichols | Bristol Branch of the Historical Association 2006

Chapter 12: Stamps, Steam and Jubilee: Queen Victoria's Last Years

Lines to Avonmouth by Mike Vincent | Littlehampton Book Services 1979

Bristol Suburban by Mike Oakley | Redcliffe Books 1990

The Clifton Extension Railway by Michael Farr | Article in Railway World May 1965

Dr Goodeve and Cook's Folly by Michael Whitfield | ALHA Books 2010

Chapter 13: Change and Protest: The Edwardian Years

The Bristol Suffragettes by Lucienne Boyce | Silverwood Books 2013

Chapter 14: The Great War 1914-1918

Leaving Home To Fight by Liz Tomlinson & Jenny Weeks | SBLHG 2018

Trinity College Archives

Soldiers of Gloucestershire Museum | Nott brothers letters

Voices of Stoke Bishop | A play by Keith Sheather 2014

Bristol's Australian Pioneer by Chris Stephens | Bristol Books 2016

Chapter 15: Twilight of the Farms 1918-1939

SBLHG Archives

Green Family Genealogy compiled by John Moore

Chapter 16: A Postwar Housing Boom 1918-1939

Sir George White of Bristol by Charles Harvey & Jon Press | Bristol Branch of the Historical Association 1989

Stride Papers – courtesy of Richard Stride

George Papers – courtesy of Ry George

The Henleaze Book by Veronica Bowerman | Redcliffe Press 1991

Michael Brooks Collection | 1930s housing

Ormerod Road Papers – courtesy of Albert & Pauline Pearson

Chapter 17: Roads 1918-1939

SBLHG Archives

Chapter 18: Shops 1932 – 2010

SBLHG Archives

Chapter 19: Sport and Recreation

SBLHG Archives

Stoke Bishop Centenary Brochure by Terry Hutton John Watkins Bob Hammond & Dave Watkins | Stoke Bishop Cricket Club Archive 2022

Chapter 20: New Uses for Old Houses

SBLHG Archives

Trinity College Archives

Severnleigh House: A History by Gyl Evans | Privately published 2011

Chapter 21: Downside and the University 1911 onwards
George Papers – courtesy of Ry George
Trinity College Papers
A History of Wills Hall by M.J.Crossley Evans & A.Sulstan | University of Bristol Press1994

Chapter 22: World War Two 1939-1945
Riding Through The Storm (My Early Life & Memories of Wartime Bristol) by Heather Mary Pelmear | An unpublished memoir
Longshore Soldiers by Andrew J Brozyna | Apidae Press 2010
Short History of the Holmes and its link to D-Day by David Ewart | Churchill Hall 1977

Chapter 23: Post War and Beyond
SBLHG Archives

Chapter 24: A Decade of Destruction 1970-1981
SBLHG Archives
Sneyd Park Residents Association: How It Started by Ian Beattie | Sneyd Park Residents Association files 2016

Chapter 25: The Fight for Green Spaces 1970 onwards
Old Sneed Park Nature Reserve by Eileen Stonebridge | Friends of Old Sneed Park 2020
We Love Stoke Lodge website
University of Bristol Botanic Garden website

Chapter 26: Into the Twenty-first Century
SBLHG Archives

Picture Credits

Photographs and illustrations not credited are either from the photographic collection of the author or taken from non-copyright books

Abbreviations: SBLHG (Stoke Bishop Local History Group)
BA (Bristol Archives)

Chapter 1

1	Cromlech newspaper cutting *(British Newspaper Archive)*
2	Cromlech in field *(SBLHG)*
3	Cromlech: Skinner sketch (British Library *(@ The British Library Board Ms_33655_98 33655 0001)*
8	Abona quayside painting *(Christine Molan)*
9	Abona bakery painting *(Christine Molan)*
10	George Boon *(BA)*
10	Tratman's wall *(BA)*

Chapter 2

14	Saxon Village drawing *(David Higgins)*
17	Map Victorian fish pond *(SBLHG)*
17	Fish pond in 1930s *(SBLHG)*
20	Saxon boundaries drawing *(David Higgins)*
26	Domesday Oak *(SBLHG)*

Chapter 3

29	Letters Patent Edward VI *(BA)*
30	Sir Ralph Sadleir *(Royal Collection Trust)*
38	Kip engraving Stoke House *(Trinity College)*
39	Cann chair *(Burrell Collection, Glasgow)*
40	Sneed Park 18th century drawing *(Ian Beattie)*
41	Kip engraving Sneed Park *(Ian Beattie/Gloucestershire Archives)*

Chapter 4

44	Samuel Jackson view of Gorge and Cook's Folly *(Bristol Museum & Art Gallery)*

Acknowledgements

Many people have contributed to this book, too many to feature everyone in this brief paragraph. But I am eternally grateful to all who gave me documents and photographs, and shared their memories of growing up in Stoke Bishop. They have been threaded through the book to enrich its tapestry. I particularly want to thank the committee of the Stoke Bishop Local History Group for entrusting me with this project. Thanks goes to Elizabeth Floyd for her enduring support and appreciation of what I have written, to Liz Tomlinson whose skill at searching the newspaper archives has given me stories to include that I would never have known about and last, but not least, to Jenny Weeks whose continuing faith in the project has never wavered. Her extensive knowledge of the area, her wide source of contacts and her determination to pursue every last detail has allowed this book to be as accurate as we could possibly make it. We are lucky to have as our production designer, Andrew Buchanan, whose talent has produced an elegant and professional product. I thank him for his patience in accommodating endless, frustrating changes, often occasioned by new information coming in at the last minute. I am grateful to all those who have read the manuscript and corrected my grammar, typing mistakes and facts, and especially to my wife, Judith, who not only proof read the text, but often queried my logic and made valuable alternative suggestions. Throughout, she has been my support and confidante and I thank her for her selfless patience. Lastly I want to thank Gill Cleverdon for giving me access to her late husband John's extensive collection of local history books. It was a real treasure trove and saved me many hours of fruitless searching elsewhere.

Thanks

Alan Aburrow
Dr Clive Archer
Jackie Aslan
The Revd. Jema Ball
Ian Beattie
Sue Brown, *Librarian, Trinity College*
Diana Bourne
Gail Boyle FMA FSA, *Senior Curator (Archaeology & World Cultures) Bristol Museum & Art Gallery*
Michael Brooks
Ron Cross
Gill Cleverdon
Rebecca Clevett
Gyl Evans
Dr Jamie Davies
Tony Everett
Steve Fowler
Sandie Foxhall-Smith
Ry George
Magda Goss
Ali Harris
Christopher Harries
Vivien Haresnape
Rosemary Havens
Sue Holliman
Daniel Holloway
Keith Horley
Julia Irish
Heather and Tony Jackson
Mike Kain
Dr C S Knighton, *Principal Assistant Keeper of Archives, Clifton College*

Bernard Lane
Glenda Lindsay
David Mander
Elliot Metcalfe, *Director, The Keep Military Museum, Dorchester*
June Miller
John Moore
Flora Nash
Sylvia O'Driscoll
Richard Outhwaite
Salvatore Parrinello
Albert Pearson
Rupert Peploe
Margaret Pinnock
Jo Pople
Helen Powell
Jonathan Sheather
Matthew Sheather
Martin Sisman
Christopher Smith
Felicity Smith
Joanne Smith, *Registrar, Ironbridge Gorge Museum*
Mary Somerville
Andrew Stone
Dr Richard Stone
Richard Stride
Dave Watkins
Dan & Andrea Watts
Peter Weeks
Sir George White
Nicky Woodfield

Index

X,Y,Z